The Business Side

of

School Success:

What Superintendents and Other

School Leaders Need to Know

The Business Side

of

School Success:

What Superintendents and Other School Leaders Need to Know

Brian L. Benzel, Ph.D.

Kenneth E. Hoover, Ph.D.

James Parla, Ed.D.

Copyright © 2022 by BHP Authors, LLC
Copyrights protect creativity, diverse voices, freedom of speech, and promote a vibrant culture. Thank you for buying an authorized version of our book and complying with copyright laws by not reproducing, scanning, or distributing any part of it without permission. Brief quotes may be used with attribution of the authors.

Cover art from iStock.com
Back cover photo from iStock.com

ISBN 13-979-8-8171-4334-8

Praise for The Business Side of School Success...

A great resource for both the aspiring superintendent and superintendents at all stages of their careers. I wish I'd had this book when I was a superintendent.
Dr. Cindy Stevenson, retired superintendent, Colorado

These experienced authors explain complex, varied topics in a non-tradition, easy to understand framework.
Dr. James Rickabaugh, retired superintendent, Wisconsin

The authors have provided critically important information that should be available to every chief executive officer of a school system. It frames the information around scenarios faced by CEOs but is written without the jargon so common in the daily work of school business officials.
Joseph Dragone, Deputy Superintendent (retired), New York

These experienced school leaders provide valuable information about school finance and operations that I've not seen in any other publications, especially those focused on preparing future superintendents. Understanding these topics is important to superintendent success. I recommend it to colleagues.
Dr. Glenys Hill Rada, Director, Washington State University Superintendent Program and Associate Professor, former superintendent (WA)

Benzel, Hoover, and Parla have successful experiences in the strategic positions of school leadership. Now they have collaborated in pulling together their expertise to create a valuable collection of thoughtful and articulate guidance for managing a school district's financial resources. The book is an excellent source of expert advice and wisdom for aspiring and current school administrators.
Dr. Jack McKay, former superintendent (WA), Full Professor and Emeritus at the University of Nebraska-Omaha, and Executive Director, Horace Mann League

A thorough examination of the key issues superintendents must address to lay the foundation for student success.
Dr. Larry Nyland, Superintendent (retired), Seattle Public Schools and leadership consultant

This book provides essential information about school finance that should be available to all school leaders.
Dr. Alan Sebel, Associate Professor, Graduate School of Education School Leadership Program, Touro University, New York.

These authors make a strong case for every leadership team to know and understand the importance of finance and support services to effectively leading the teaching and learning work of schools. This read will be useful for the executive leadership team to read and discuss together. The case studies and follow-up questions provide an excellent guide for this process.
Stephen Nielsen, Deputy Superintendent (retired), Seattle Public Schools and consultant to school leaders

As long-time school district practitioners, Benzel, Hoover, and Parla bring a wealth of knowledge about how to support the day-to-day operations of school districts. Operations like budgets, transportation, and human resources all play critical roles in achieving the goals of an education system. The result is a guide for leaders on what to look for, questions to ask, and some actionable lessons. The book is packed with specific examples. Read it and then keep it as a resource and guide.
Dr. Simone Sangster, Bellingham (WA) School District, Associate Superintendent for Finance

Dedication

We collectively dedicate this work to the many associates and colleagues with whom we've worked over the years.

We are indebted to mentors whose counsel, experience and common sense added immeasurably to our professional efforts and the writing of this book.

And finally, we extend to our family members, especially Cynthia, Kim, and Larisa, our deep appreciation for the tolerance, love, and support they have provided to each of us.

Brian L. Benzel, Ph.D.
Kenneth E. Hoover, Ph.D.
James Parla, Ed.D.

July 2022

Wise Counsel

In finance, everything that is agreeable is unsound, and everything that is sound is disagreeable.

Winston Churchill

Budgeting only has one rule: do not go over the budget.

Leslie Tayne

Beware of little expenses. A small leak will sink a great ship.

Benjamin Franklin

Now is no time to think of what you do not have. Think of what you can do with what there is.

<u>Old Man and the Sea</u>
Ernest Hemingway

Levies are for learning; bonds are for buildings

Spokane Public (WA) Schools

Table of Contents

Dedication...	i
Table of Contents...	v
Why We Wrote This Book....................................	vii
Chapter 1: The Mission is Student Learning................	1
Section I: The Core Business Functions.................	**7**
Chapter 2: The Business Office and Its Leadership Role.................................	8
Chapter 3: Budget Development Supports the Mission....	31
Chapter 4: Revenue: An Integral Component of the Budget..	50
Chapter 5: Property Taxes: What You Need to Know......	66
Chapter 6: Accounting and Monitoring Fiscal Status........	78
Chapter 7: Program Monitoring, Fund Balance, and Reserve Funds..	87
Chapter 8: Assessing School District Financial Health......	101
Chapter 9: Co-Curricular Activities............................	113
Chapter 10: Audits and Related Issues........................	122
Section II: School Support Services and Organization...	**135**
Chapter 11: School and Community Partnerships: Maintaining the Public Trust......................	136
Chapter 12: Human Resources Leadership....................	147
Chapter 13: Legal Counsel..	161
Chapter 14: Enterprise Risk Management: What to Insure..	168

Chapter 15: School District Operations........................... 178

 A. Maintenance and Custodial Services................. 180
 B. Pupil Transportation..................................... 192
 C. Food Service... 203
 D. Information Technology................................ 209
 E. Safety and Security 217
 F. Ancillary Services 221

Chapter 16: Capital Projects and Bonds......................... 226

Section III: Summarizing the Focus........................... 240

Chapter 17: Strategic Issues.. 241

Chapter 18: So, What's Next?...................................... 248

Appendix A: Cash Flow Analysis Example...................... 254

Appendix B: Key Ratios Based on Balance Sheet Items...... 257

Glossary of Terms.. 259

Acknowledgements.. 288

References... 290

Index.. 293

About the Authors... 302

Why We Wrote This Book

Our combined experiences as superintendents, school business officials, and leaders of overall operations led us to work together to provide this examination of the essential elements of school finance and support services. Our conviction is that finance and operations must work in service to effective, successful educational practices that support all students.

This book is intended to assist both current and prospective superintendent candidates explore the range of financial and operational issues that contain opportunity and risk for leaders. Regardless of school district size, knowledge of finance and operations is essential to superintendent success. Because the superintendent is supported by the chief business officer and other specialized staff, the people filling those roles or aspiring to them will also be well served by this book.

We each have a passion for improving student achievement. And we know that accomplishing that important mission requires sound financial and operational leadership. While strong leadership for teaching and learning is essential, we're focusing on the non-instructional side of the school district because those services support students, teachers and others seeking to accomplish the district's primary teaching and learning mission. They provide the foundation for successful teaching and student learning.

Some well trained and prepared leaders have travelled the path into the superintendent's role only to fail, sometimes dramatically, because they overlooked some detail that later emerged as an egregious error. We seek to help current and future leaders from making such errors and have successful careers.

School systems are dynamic and continually responding to new issues. Certainly, the coronavirus pandemic touched the operational and financial nerve center of school systems in unique ways. These complex systems will continue to evolve as both new and long-standing external factors influence school operations.

We hope the reader of this book will find insights that support their efforts to improve functions, activities, and ideas as these changes evolve. This book is dedicated to helping superintendents avoid pitfalls and finding ways to leverage resources and services toward improving educational services and improving student outcomes.

Our focus is to give the reader access to our collective experience in a trifecta of roles as superintendent, chief operating officer (COO), and chief financial officer (CFO). We also rely on the collective experience of those who worked with us, mentored us, and advised us. We hope this book is useful for the aspiring superintendent, one taking on a new superintendent assignment, honing the skills of a veteran superintendent, or possibly when moving to another state where the rules are different. Additionally, we believe the CFO or chief operating officer roles will benefit from seeing what superintendents need to know about finance and operations while leading school districts.

The value of doing research on a topic, hinges on the quality of the data used for the analysis. We sincerely hope you find reliable, accurate data for your research needs. Have confidence in a "trust but confirm" approach to demonstrate a careful use of data and metrics. Ask a colleague, check with professionals you respect, and seek to verify the data you are using.

When examining a potential application to a new or to your first superintendent assignment, these tips for research are intended to support your efforts. We suggest researching a prospective district thoroughly. If you haven't done so already, some ideas for conducting your research include:

- What evidence shows the tone of school board relations? What can you do to improve how the school board operates? Dynamics between the individual board members and the superintendent will not go away with a new superintendent. Have a plan for how you will address the issues you identify.
- Use the website for your state's education agency to obtain the latest funding data, enrollment reports, financial history, and funding drivers. Are they moving up or down? What may be causing this change?
- Many states have a district report card focused on student learning that contains other valuable information. Use these charts and trends to determine if the district is getting better, holding constant, or getting worse. What information concerns you? What may be concerning to the average citizen or parent?
- Obtain copies of the latest audit reports at the website for the state auditor (or contact the auditor hired by the district). Most district publish these reports on their website. Use these reports or conversations to clarify questions, learn the timing for the next audit, and identify the upcoming issues it will likely review.
- Find the latest copy of the district's Comprehensive Annual Financial Statement. Look at several years if possible. The district's current budget and any explanation of its focus will provide insight. Ask questions about any trends or issues you discover.
- Review copies of the district's booklets, brochures, newsletters, and reports and note any challenges facing the district.
- Look at hiring information from Human Resources. Does the district have trouble recruiting? Does it have issues hiring certain employees?
- Read the current collective bargaining contracts. What is the status of collective bargaining? Who represents the district and what is their reputation and experience?
- Has the district experienced labor disruption in the last ten years? Why did it occur? How was it resolved?

- Check social media. Read the local newspaper. What issues about the district are being talked about? What concerns do citizens have?
- Sign-up for and read School Business Affairs, a publication of the Association of School Business Officials International (www.asbointl.org). It has valuable information that will keep your district competitive.
- What type of capital needs is the district facing? What is being done about them?
- How is technology supported and used? Is a plan in place to keep technology current?
- How does the district take care of maintenance? Do they have a backlog? What can the professional association for maintenance officials tell you about the district?
- Examine the foodservice report. Note the trendline in meals served. Is this trendline going up or down?
- Do district staff belong to and actively participate in state or national associations or organizations?

If you are already superintendent, you may want to dig deeper into these areas for your district to determine what others may be seeing and to identify areas of strategic investment.

This book addresses the primary finance and operational issues superintendents must manage. We've provided generalizable concepts that will give direction and that may require local or regional knowledge. States vary in the degree to which districts may be obligated to provide services or support to parochial or private schools, charter schools, or use public dollars for education vouchers. Such issues will emerge in the context of topics we address. While we hope the values contained in this volume will help you find answers, we strongly advise that knowledge and expertise about the local context will be required to address the unique elements of your district.

We've used our experiences to raise issues that we know you will be required to address at some point in your tenure. We urge you to seek knowledge about these issues in consultation with your school board, your leadership team, parents, other citizens, and professional colleagues. Use the state education agency, auditor and professional association websites to explore and gather information about the school district and the complex issues its addressing.

We respect and value the complexity of the various roles examined in this book. We know the challenges are many and solutions to them may seem vexing, illusive, or perhaps non-existent. We encourage you to pursue them anyway.

We wish you success in sustaining a clear and strong focus on students and their positive achievements.

Brian, Ken, and James

July 2022

Chapter 1

The Mission is Student Learning

This chapter will help leaders learn to…
 Articulate a clear focus on student achievement.
 Use fiscal tools to enrich and support the teaching and learning mission of the school system.
 Apply a process of continuous improvement.

Case Study

Joan is hired to be the new superintendent in April. From the beginning, she understands that this leadership role is going to be a challenge. Her new school district is swamped by many issues: declining enrollment, demographic changes in the community, economic stagnation in the region, and labor discord. None of the issues she faces has an easy solution and most of the solutions require collaboration with other entities like state and local government. How best can she bring the district's mission into focus?

Joan's first step will be to engage each of the school board members who had just hired her in one-on-one interviews. Her goal will be to gain a deeper knowledge of their interests and community history. She feels fortunate that she is able to arrange a transition time into the new community with a consulting contract because her soon-to-be predecessor is cooperative and open to helping her learn as much as possible before her July 1 starting date. He is clearly committed to helping her be successful and that gives her a great advantage.

Throughout her interviews with the board, stakeholders and the community, Joan's deep devotion to students and their success in school and in life distinguished her candidacy. That she made student achievement her central focus is the primary reason the board hired her. Now, she has to test their true commitment beyond the boilerplate words used in the selection process.

Joan's board member interviews revealed not only the strengths of the board members but also how they were connected in the community. It was clear that she will have their individual and collective backing to advance an aggressive educational improvement agenda. These conversations affirmed Joan's decision to make the students and their achievement the central feature of efforts to re-build community trust and support for the school system.

Now, she has to enlist the support of her colleagues. She starts by seeking a meeting with the district's school principals, central office instructional leaders, and teacher union leaders. How will they respond to her unwavering mission?

If you were the superintendent...

Would you follow the course of action Joan is taking or do something different? What?

How would you expect school board members to support you? How are you enlisting their support?

What questions should you ask as you interview your new staff? Should they be consistent?

What additional information will you need and where might it be found?

Would you share your results of these interviews with the school board and the community? Why or why not?

The Business Side of School Success

Leadership Matters

Fiscal and operational issues abound, but each of them needs to be addressed with a clear focus on the central teaching and learning mission of the school district. For that reason, we begin this book with this examination of the teaching and learning mission of the school district. Of course, that mission must be developed with stakeholder involvement and support. But a compelling, shared mission must be developed and used to drive all the resources and operational decisions of the school district.

The case study describes issues facing many school systems. Joan recognizes that the conditions of schooling and the circumstances of the community allow too many people to feel victimized. She knew that resource issues needed to be energized with a clear purpose. Joan's decision to focus on students and improving their achievement is the key motivating focus for her leadership, but she also realizes her success will come through working successfully with other adults.

To address this condition, Joan determined that how she conducted her leadership was essential to re-building trust. Her devotion to a mission focused on all students succeeding to develop and learn what they needed to know and be able to do began with her priorities. She knows that her focus will guide and support the work of others.

Resource allocation through budgeting and setting spending priorities would be a central feature of her leadership toolkit. To clearly communicate her focus on students and their learning, Joan initiated a thorough assessment of the district's current instructional program and how it was funded. She asked what was being done so she could clearly understand what the current reality was for students, their instruction, and the results obtained from current practices. She asked:

> What needs to be continued?
> What needs to be stopped?
> What should we be doing that we are not now doing?

The leadership questions outlined above were asked of teachers, principals, central office administrators. She'd asked school board members these questions, too, and engaged parents and other community members in dialogue around the same questions.

Teachers, principals and other program administrators may initially be leery of giving candid input to a new superintendent. And they may be even more suspicious of a veteran superintendent and leadership team. Faithfully and carefully asking these questions requires an unabashed devotion to listening and a willingness to assess responses and develop them into action plans.

Trust is essential to the leadership process. Knowing the district's past practices and the stories that may inhibit trust will help design ways to assess values, priorities, and action plans. Look for the stories and look for evidence in the form of practices, data, and actions.

How do we know if students are achieving?

Finding data to show what the school district's work has been accomplishing may not be easy. Start by asking key administrators what they know about the status of students and their achievement:

- Are students successfully making transitions from elementary to middle school and from middle school to high school?
- What is the trend for the high school graduation rate over the past five years? Are schools and the staff focused on improving the graduation rate?
- Are students making the grade in high school courses (e.g., number of failing grades)?
- What are the levels of proficiency for students beginning in grade 3 and beyond?
- Do the high schools have too many remediation courses in their curriculum?
- Compare the same cohort of students and their growth over time; what does this comparison reveal about student performance?

The Business Side of School Success

Finding answers to these questions reveals the degree of data sophistication in the district and the skills that exist among administrators and other instructional leaders. Whatever the current capability, use available data sources to describe student achievement in terms of student performance. Commit to continuously asking questions. Take further actions and adjust plans in response to this cycle for updating and extending data.

Linking work designed to improve teaching with assessments of student progress and success may start slowly. Jim Collins (2001, 2019) uses the image of a flywheel to slowly begin the effort. When applied to the organization, each revolution of the planning cycle accelerates the momentum and moves toward the desired outcomes for students as noted in Figure 1. Leadership focus on the district's student development mission and values is central to sustaining this process.

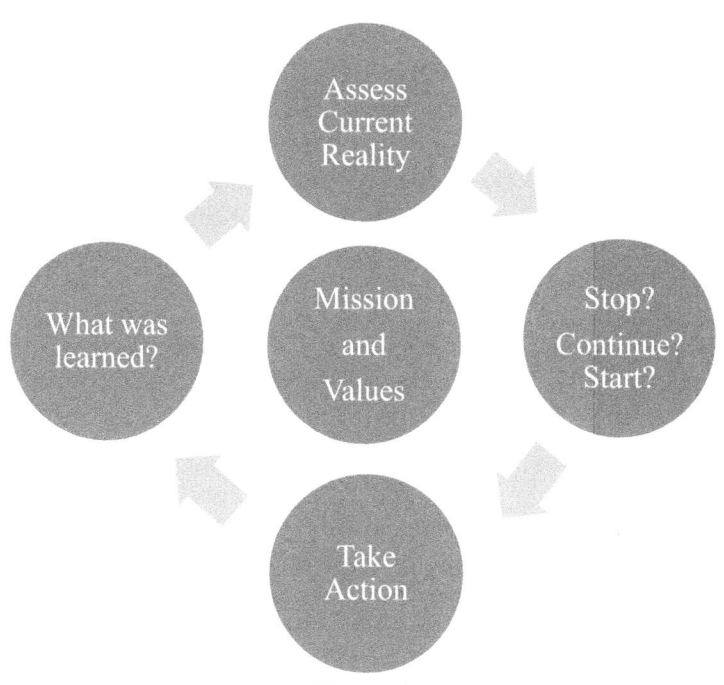

Figure 1
Adapted from PEMCO Mutual Insurance Company, Seattle, WA

Building action plans using data and feedback about barriers or identified needs helps generate hope among educators and the community. This process will accelerate as people see specific evidence that their inputs have been addressed in the plans. More importantly, resource allocations should underwrite the necessary support for people to accomplish the desired plans.

Is the district putting its resources into student learning?

When budget development begins, make sure that this ongoing cycle of questioning is central to fiscal priorities. Use the budget development process (see Chapter 3—Budget Development Supports the Mission) to reinforce the leadership priorities and enhance the energy and commitment to improvement. When teachers, support staff and parents see that district's statements of belief are evident in the school district's behavior, trust will build, and the pace of the flywheel will be energized.

Conclusion

Losing sight of the primary focus and mission of the school system is sometimes the result of being overly focused on funding and resource allocation decisions or other pressure-creating operational demands. Superintendent leadership is vital to sustaining the mission for all students and their learning success. Be clear about the district's mission and build a fundamental expectation among every member of the leadership team that keeps an intense focus on that mission.

Section I

The Core Business Functions

Chapter 2: The Business Office and Its Leadership Role

Chapter 3: Budget Development Supports the Mission

Chapter 4: Revenue: An Integral Component of the Budget

Chapter 5: Property Taxes: What You Need to Know

Chapter 6: Accounting and Monitoring Fiscal Status

Chapter 7: Program Monitoring, Fund Balance, and Reserve Funds

Chapter 8: Assessing School District Financial Health

Chapter 9: Co-Curricular Activities

Chapter 10: Audits and Controls

Chapter 2

The Business Office and Its Leadership Role

This chapter will help leaders learn to...

Understand the role of the business office and how it aligns with the mission of schools to assure that all students learn.

Examine core business functions and how they can be organized to support efficient school operations and assure compliance with financial standards.

Incorporate the various functions of the business office into the mission of the school system.

Identify the essential values and skills needed for business office leadership and functions.

Embrace continuous improvement and transparency to build understanding and confidence in the fiscal management of the school system.

Case Study

Pedro is preparing for his fifth year as superintendent for the South School District. He established solid credibility with the school board and the community. Importantly, he has a reputation within the district as a student-centered superintendent acting upon his strong interest in improving student outcomes. Growing evidence of student performance is demonstrating progress, but he understands more work is necessary.

This spring, Michael, the district's Chief Financial Officer announced his plan to retire after a long career managing the district's financial affairs. Kimberly, the district's director of human resources is relatively new; Pedro hired her two years ago.

Since Pedro's arrival, he's pretty much left in place the organizational reporting relationships that had evolved prior to his arrival. But now, he is faced with thinking about whether the organizational structure and reporting relationships should change and if so, how. This design decision will affect his CFO recruitment plans since no obvious internal candidate exists to take over for Michael.

Because Michael always resisted adding the payroll office to his span of administrative control, it is embedded with the Human Resources office. Increasingly, fiscal issues related to salary schedules and benefits are changing and putting budget pressures on the district. Negotiations with teachers and the classified employee groups are going well but tightening economic conditions in the state and region indicate that negotiations would become more contentious and complex and would rely on a strong fiscal leader for guidance.

Pedro wants to address the economic needs of the district's staff, but he worries that the years of goodwill Michael created will be hard to sustain. Kimberly shows promise, though, and is respected by the union leadership and the school board. She clearly can handle more responsibility as the point person for the upcoming bargaining work. Other support services positions have competent leaders, but none showed promise for broader duties.

If you were the superintendent…

What choices should Pedro be making to design the most responsive, effective reporting relationships for South School District?

What skills should he be looking for in a new CFO?

What additional information will Pedro need and where might it be found?

What questions should Pedro ask of himself and district leaders before the search begins?

Education is one of the largest enterprises in almost every community. Leading student achievement efforts takes people and people require resources. Integrating the student achievement mission with sound fiscal and operational management requires superintendent confidence in a strong fiscal leadership team and organizing it to support that learning mission.

Meador (2020) and the authors' personal experiences affirm that fiscal management is one of the significant elements of the successful superintendent's tenure. This chapter will focus on various components of the business office and provide guidance for superintendents who design and lead the people who support the district's fiscal affairs.

Role of the Chief Financial Officer or Chief Business Official

The chief financial officer (CFO) or chief business official (CBO) typically reports directly to the superintendent of schools and is responsible for coordinating all the district's fiscal affairs. In larger districts, this position may report to a chief operating officer (COO) along with the chief human resources officer and facility management, transportation, nutrition services and other director level positions providing support services. Even in this circumstance, the superintendent and the CFO will frequently interact.

Effective superintendents must demonstrate sufficient knowledge and awareness of business practices. This knowledge builds confidence with others in the district, the school board, and the community. The purpose of this chapter, therefore, affirms the need for a strong, positive working relationship between the superintendent and the CFO.

The business office provides a key support service function that requires knowledge about all aspects of the school district's programs and services. The CFO who is supportive, curious, and exhibits strong relationships with other managers is vital for school district (and superintendent) success. Forecasting and monitoring school district revenue sources must be paired with properly recording and monitoring expenditures according to the budget plan.

The CFO brings all these functions together to assure the superintendent and school board that sufficient funds are available each month to cover the payroll, benefits, and purchasing payments. The CFO must manage cash availability in the short run and make short term investments of funds if working capital is not immediately needed in each month. Such investments are usually limited by state law to low-risk investment instruments such as United States Treasury Bills or certificates of deposit from local financial institutions.

The CFO leads and supervises the various people performing the functions listed in this chapter. This leadership effort must be centered on alignment of the business office functions in support of the district's teaching and learning mission. Efforts to coordinate, assure proper training and knowledge of the constantly changing rules and regulations, and inspiring collaborative efforts among colleagues requires well-tuned human relationship skills, technical knowledge, and a sustained focus on student achievement.

What role is served by the business office?

The business office is led by the CFO who assembles the team responsible for planning a budget, monitoring the use of that budget and reporting monthly, and annual accounting for how funds were expended. This office is the primary resource for reporting fiscal status and performance to all stakeholders, but especially the superintendent and the school board.

Linking the leadership and the functions of the business office to the educational mission and programs that support student learning is essential for a properly functioning business office. Because every sector of the school district requires fiscal resources to operate, the business office staff must interact with and have some understanding of every phase of school district operations. Typically, this linkage is best made through a collaborative, trusting relationship between the superintendent and the chief financial officer. For a more complete examination of this relationship, see Benzel and Hoover (2021).

Adding further urgency to this relationship, "all too often…a school district's financial woes lead to the departure of its superintendent." (Parla, J. (2020, p. 19). If the superintendent's woes are of a financial nature, the CFO may also be exiting within a short time of the superintendent.

Ethically, legally, and professionally, the serious nature of fiscal leadership requires school board members, superintendents, and other school administrators to apply wise management and organization to the business office. The prudent and thoughtful linkage of resources to the purposes of students and their learning demand open, fair and clear representations of where funds are allocated and how they are used by those entrusted with those allocations.

For these reasons, a properly organized, effectively managed business office that interacts positively with all aspects of the system is vital to school district operations and student success.

What functions should be included in the business office?

Other chapters will outline the functions within some of the elements of the district that are often organized within the business office and led by the CFO (see Chapter 15—School District Operations for a discussion of transportation, food service, maintenance and operations, technology, school safety, and other issues and Chapter 16—Capital Projects and Bonds for a discussion of capital project management).

This section provides a brief overview of the typical business affairs areas that support all district functions and provides links to the separate, more comprehensive examination of the duties within business functions such as:

- budget development and monitoring.
- accounting.
- payroll and employee benefits.
- accounts payable.

- accounts receivable.
- purchasing.
- banking and cash management.
- insurance and risk management.
- fiscal reporting and audits.

How the department is organized may also reflect the skill set of the people involved. For example, budget development is more global and less detailed than accounting actions once the budget is activated and being used by managers. Budgets might round allocations to the nearest hundreds or perhaps thousands, whereas accounting must be accurate to the penny. Some people work well with both viewpoints and others have more difficulty with the shift in perspective that is required between the two activities. Design the organizational structure to amplify and best use the skill sets of the people in the business office.

Budget Development

Creating the budget is a complex, interactive process that requires the engagement of the school board, the superintendent, all executives and sometimes staff and citizens. Ownership of the process by the district's leadership team is vital. Still, the details of the budget require merging engagement in the process with sound technical expertise of the chief financial officer (CFO).

Chapter 3—Budget Development Supports the Mission provides a thorough examination of this process.

Accounting

School districts are required to account for all fiscal activity in accordance with Generally Accepted Accounting Principles (GAAP) which are set by the General Accounting Standards Board (GASB). GASB (www.gasb.org) was created in 1984 to serve as the:

> …independent, non-political organization…to promote clear, consistent, transparent, and comparable financial reporting for state and local governments….

(https://www.investopedia.com/terms/g/government-accounting-standards-board-gasb.asp)

The GASB standards are recognized as authoritative by state and local governments, state Boards of Accountancy, and the American Institute of CPAs (AICPA).

This foundational obligation underlies the framework for required reporting about school district financial activities to local, state and federal entities. These entities require the judicious application of accounting standards to assure equity and fairness and enhance the use of accounting data for comparative endeavors.

School districts typically use several distinct funds to track various aspects of the district's operations. Specialized funds are typically developed for specific purposes. See Chapter 6—Accounting and Monitoring Fiscal Status for an explanation of accounting standards and how they are used to monitor the district's fiscal status.

Whether a school district is small or large, it is subject to these accounting standards and principles. Consequently, it is essential that the business office employ at least one individual with sufficient accounting skills to navigate the numerous requirements that apply to the school district's financial reporting and management. If employing a person with accounting skills is not possible, rely upon the regional school support agency to provide school finance consulting support for financial reporting and assisting with district compliance requirements.

The accounting team is responsible to prepare a monthly financial status report for use by the leadership, the school board, and for public reporting. This report might be called the Budget Status Report or the Treasurer's Report. A more complete discussion of this reporting structure is contained in Chapter 6—Accounting and Monitoring Fiscal Status.

Revenue and expenditure accounts are separate ledgers within the General Ledger. They are derived from the school board adopted budget and form a management tool for monthly status reports and tracking both expenditures and revenue progress. States, or districts, may call this vital tool by different names, but the key concept is that month-by-month management of the annual budget be conducted to sustain trust and create understanding about the fiscal condition of the school district in dynamic times. Examining the monthly trend performance over several years adds to the comparative analysis of the current year.

Revenue: Most state school revenue formulae are driven in some way by the student enrollment count, so a subset of revenue monitoring is tied to student enrollment or attendance. It is essential that the business office track counting students in a manner consistent with state and/or federal funding guidelines.

The monthly revenue receipts are booked into the revenue ledger using account codes linked to the source of funds. Local property taxes, other local revenue sources for fees, student meals or payments are tracked by their designated revenue account. Federal and state allocations may be paid at specific times each month while others require schools to spend the local money first and apply for reimbursement. This latter approach requires sufficient working funds, often called the cash or fund balance, so the district doesn't experience short term deficits that may require borrowing.

Chapter 4—Revenue: An Integral Component of the Budget provides a thorough discussion of typical district revenue sources.

Expenditures: The expenditure status report is complementary to the revenue status report and emerges from the precise, specific accounting that is required for every expenditure the district makes. Typically, a computer-based software system is used to both develop the budget and then monitor allocations by program, sub-program (if needed), activity (e.g., teaching, maintenance, etc.,), object of expenditure (e.g., salaries, benefits, supplies), and the location of the responsible budget manager. Some states may also require that the source of funds be linked to the expenditure code.

Expenditures can be classified in many ways depending on the structure of revenue in each state. The basic requirements for the chart of accounts are often established statewide for all school districts. This effort enhances district and state level comparisons and policy analysis. Even in this situation, the business office may expand the code to allow more detailed reporting segregation. The chart of accounts is also used to build the budget and monitor monthly expenses (see Chapter 6—Accounting and Monitoring Fiscal Status).

Other General Ledger Accounts: Numerous other general ledger accounts will summarize and track fixed assets, outstanding debt and obligations, payables due from the prior fiscal year and the fund balance (both reserved and unreserved) of the system. Each system will develop general ledger accounts consistent with state law, administrative requirements, and GAAP.

Reporting the results: While state law likely requires regular reporting of the district's financial condition by its governing board, it is also sound practice to monitor and share a regular presentation of the budget compared to actuals through a monthly revenue and expense report. The chief business officer or the superintendent typically makes this public report to the school board.

The comparison of revenue and expenditures by month will demonstrate deviation for expected allocations, comparisons to the prior year or two and should contain a discussion of specific conditions that may explain the variations. Given the importance of student enrollment counts as the basis for significant amounts of revenue, it is helpful to demonstrate the month-by-month enrollment pattern in the monthly budget report to the school board.

Importantly, the monthly report is a potential early warning tool for changes in revenue that may require operational changes in variable expenses. This regular base-touch is vital to avoid confusion due to the changing dates, functions, and various funding sources. Unrecognized, this confusion undermines trust and confidence in the district and its leadership.

Other requirements and benefits for this monthly report are discussed in Chapter 6—Accounting and Monitoring Fiscal Status.

Regular public reporting about the district's financial status is essential. Such reporting requires ongoing education to school administrators, employees, the school board, and the public. This topic is addressed more fully in Chapter 11—School and Community Partnerships: Maintaining the Public Trust.

Payroll and Employee Benefits

School systems rely on people to serve students, a commitment that results in 80 to 85 percent of the total budget being allocated to employee salary and benefits. The superintendent relies upon the CFO to coordinate the linkages between Human Resources and payroll functions to know that staffing is aligned with plans. Leadership decisions seeking to adapt to changing conditions must be carefully reviewed. The superintendent must have confidence that overall allocations are maintained or adjusted when necessary.

Teachers and instructional support staff (e.g., counselors, librarians, specialists, etc.,) comprise the largest proportion of the district's employment, but each school is surrounded by additional functions that support the direct instruction and services for students. Many districts employ bus drivers and technical people to support the safe operation of school buses that transport students to and from school each day and provide special support for a variety of student activities (e.g., field trips, music events, athletic events, etc.,). Facility maintenance is another technical area that requires specifically experienced and trained people who repair and maintain electrical, heating and air conditioning systems and school structures (e.g., roofing, landscape, etc.,). Office personnel, food service workers, technology staff, and a variety of support functions are essential for protecting the health and safety of students and staff in compliance with local, state and federal laws and regulations.

This complex array of people services requires careful coordination between the human resources department and the business office. District office functions coordinate and support each school with human resources, instructional planning and operational coordination.

Payroll and benefit management functions are often included in the business office, but the close relationship of these functions to human resources may result in these functions reporting to the human resources officer. The authors generally prefer the placement of payroll and benefits management within the business office to enhance collaboration between the business office and the human resources office.

Such separation of functions also introduces internal controls designed to prevent errors and fraud. Best practices require a clear separation between the hiring function and the payment of the people hired. Smaller districts may not be able to accomplish this duty separation due to limited staff but should consult their auditors to develop procedures to mitigate risks.

The mechanics and process for how, when, and how much people are paid are often established through a negotiation process with employee groups. Each state's school employment laws add further specialized requirements to the process. Consequently, these diverse payroll duties add complexity that requires the payroll staff to interact with every element of the school system. See Chapter 12—Human Resources Leadership for more information on this process.

Whether paid on an annual contract (as is the case for most teachers and school administrators) or by hourly payment schedules (as is the case for most support staff), the payroll official gathers the data and computes the eligible payment for each respective pay period. Some staff may be paid monthly, usually the last working day of the month, while others are paid on alternating Fridays. Multiple pay periods for different groups of employees adds complexity and workload to the payroll function.

Benefits: Payroll office personnel are required to be knowledgeable about federal and state employment laws that affect mandatory benefit deductions from each employee's earnings. Different state and federal agencies issue guidance on how to apply these required deductions. Also, the rates of payments may change periodically, usually at the beginning of a calendar year or when the new fiscal year starts.

The Business Side of School Success

Federal payroll taxes and benefits: Federal and state law mandates certain taxes that fund benefits for employees. Primary among these mandatory deductions is the federal Social Security and Medicare tax using the Federal Insurance Contributions Act (FICA). These funds are withheld from individual's earnings at each pay period. Importantly, each employee's contribution is matched with an employer paid contribution and both are submitted to Internal Revenue Service with a detailed report using each employee's social security number (SSN).

For an up-to-date review of requirements check with the Internal Revenue Service website at www.irs.gov.

Retirement systems: Most states cover eligible employees with a retirement plan. Each state or jurisdiction sets the eligibility requirements for the plan. The payroll office must follow these requirements in deducting the employee's share of the plan. As with Social Security, most states require an employer match. Both are submitted to the state agency designated for management of the retirement system. These funds are placed into a state retirement fund that is typically invested by a state retirement fund investment board and used to fund a defined benefit once the employee becomes vested and retires. In some states, the employee contribution is held separately from the district's contribution. This defined contribution approach allows each employee to use a personalized investment strategy and provides portability for staff moving to another eligible employer.

The state usually provides material to share with employees about how the retirement plan operates. This information describes the obligations of employers and employees and outlines the operational characteristics of the plan.

Other mandatory benefit deductions: State law usually require additional payroll taxes paid by both employees and employers. Unemployment Compensation funds may be managed at the state level and funded by a combined employee and employer tax paid through the payroll system. Either a private insurance requirement or a state operated program likely requires an employee safety program to provide funding for individuals who experience workplace injuries are also funded through separate payroll taxes. The costs and tax level for these systems may vary based on district experience. Consequently, the business office leadership must monitor the extent of employee coverage being funded to contain costs and avoid adverse budget impacts. A fair, appropriate operation of this system will serve employees and the district, but it must be managed.

Health benefits: Medical and dental insurance programs are often offered to eligible employees based on the employment agreement or contract. Many states set these benefits at the state level, but the service provider for this coverage may be selected locally through negotiations with local employee organizations or unions. Districts may cover all or a portion of this benefit cost.

Sick leave: Tracking each employee's eligibility for and accumulated balance of earned sick leave is another requirement that has fiscal consequences. Most states limit how the leave can be used and how many days can be accumulated. Collective bargaining also influences how this benefit is administered and applied in each district. Setting proper tracking for granting leave, monitoring its use and keeping track of balances requires time and attention.

The fiscal implications of this benefit require the district to carefully track how much leave is carried forward for use in the future. This record is important to employees because accumulated sick leave may be eligible to be transferred to another school district if they change employers.

Some states allow annual conversion of unused leave to a cash payment or the retention of days that may be cashed out upon retirement. Tracking the usage of this option has annual budget implications and may be a sound reason for reserving a portion of fund balance.

Other benefits: Short-or-long term disability, supplemental retirement funds, life insurance, or an extension of medical benefits may exist based on local district determinations, usually obtained through negotiations with the employee group or union. Sometimes, an allowance for uniforms, tools, or technology may be allowed and employee donations to charitable organizations may be permitted. Each deduction or addition requires knowledge on the part of the payroll office and its staff.

This overview of the payroll function demonstrates the inherent complexity in what may seem to be logical accommodations to employee requests. These decisions influence workload and staffing requirements that significantly influence budgets and finance. For this reason, we suggest the payroll function is best located in the department headed by the Chief Financial Officer (CFO).

Purchasing and bidding

The business office is responsible for monitoring purchases, accumulating bid specifications to meet school needs, seeking bids and recommending vendors to be awarded the bid award.

This process requires multiple steps and should contain proper controls to assure the effective use of whatever is being purchased. A staff member may make the purchase request and have the purchase order signed by the budget manager. The completed purchase order is sent to the vendor and becomes a commitment by the school district to pay for the desired items. A copy is sent to accounts payable for entry into the computer-based accounting system. At this point, the purchase is encumbered against the designated account code in the manager's budget.

Purchasing interacts closely with the accounts payable function but is sometimes a separate unit within the business office, depending upon district size and volume of activity.

Bidding process: States usually adopt purchasing laws and administrative procedures for school districts that establish a dollar value for a set of goods or services that require a public bidding process. School systems are obligated to adopt school governing board policy to implement these constraints.

Schools and departments with specialized needs or equipment rely on the purchasing office to assist them prepare specifications and manage the bidding process. Bids must be published publicly for specific periods of time, opened at a given date and time, and the results made available to all bidders and interested parties. These steps are typically outlined in state law and the school district's policy and procedure manual.

After analyzing bids received for compliance with the specifications, the dollar value of bids is summarized, and a recommendation of the lowest, responsible bidder is made to the governing board. The board's approval constitutes a commitment to award the bid to the designated bidder.

Routine practices often result in smooth bidding processes, but complex technical equipment or services such as construction projects with alternative choices sometimes result in contentious consideration of the recommended bid award. In these circumstances, relying on well established procedures and clearly communicating with vendors and the board of directors is vital. It may also be necessary to consult legal counsel to make sure the recommendation for the bid award is legally defensible in case it is challenged.

The purchasing office issues a contract (called a purchase order) that authorizes the acquisition. This procedure is used to encumber the financial obligation against the appropriate budget code and monitor activities in accounts payable for ultimate payment of the completed order.

Some purchasing contracts may include public works that are provided by a contractor. Significant contracts for school construction are reviewed in Chapter 16—Capital Projects and Bonds. In any case, procedures should be developed to review and approve changes to the initial contract based on developments that occur during implementation of the project. These important adjustments should be reviewed and approved by the project manager and the supervisor of that person.

Non-bid purchases: Each school budget manager is obligated to manage the purchase process for items that fall below the bidding threshold. The larger the district, the less likely schools and budget managers will have funds to purchase outside of bids because the volume of activity often puts even routine purchases above the bid requirement value.

The Business Side of School Success

To address this challenge, many districts develop a warehouse to allow compliance with the bidding laws and then ask schools and departments to requisition items from the warehouse. This process essentially creates and internal business operation so that items "purchased" from the warehouse are charged to the appropriate budget code as requisitions occur.

Schools may use the district warehouse for acquiring bulk items purchased ahead of time in ways that meet state bidding requirements. The purchasing office typically manages the warehouse function. See more in Chapter 15—School District Operations, F. Ancillary Services for more information about this function.

Purchasing cards and other purchasing options: To facilitate smooth, timely acquisitions when bidding is not required, consider the use of procurement cards. These financial tools operate like personal credit cards but are issued to the school district and/or school. Each card is assigned to an individual who has reporting responsibilities to account for all of the purchases using the procurement cards. Purchases are summarized, coded to individual budget account codes and reconciled regularly.

Small cash funds are sometimes allocated to school sites or various work locations for purchases that must be in cash or are for small sums. Called the Imprest Fund, this money is refreshed with an expenditure report much as described for the purchasing card. Because this fund involves cash, its use is increasingly being replaced by the purchasing card.

Other procurement tools are evolving that use the same processes many people use for personal purchasing online. For example, Amazon Business Services has developed its personal shopping protocol in ways that may work for school districts.

When any of these approaches is employed, set firm limits, assure review, and address bid requirements for items that, when consolidated to the district level, may require adherence to formal bidding procedures. It may also be important to consider how to preference local vendors who support the district's schools; adopting procedures that eliminate their access to providing schools with products and services may have repercussions costing more than potential procurement savings.

Accounts Payable

School systems consume many goods and services, all of which must be purchased and paid for in a proper, business-like manner. The systems that all managers with budget responsibilities must employ to access goods and services initiates a process to validate receipt of the item, authorize payment, and pay the vendor.

Upon receipt of the goods or services, the recipient sends a signed copy of the invoice from the vendor to accounts payable with reference to the purchase order. When matched by accounts payable, the item is added to a payment schedule for processing.

This process increasingly applies the technology of a management system to handle approvals electronically without physical paper documents. Depending on the district's size, number of staff and school sites, robust technology systems will reduce error and facilitate keeping track of the purchases and payment schedules to avoid penalties for slow payment of the obligations. The number of staff involved in this process is a function of the volume of transactions and how user-friendly the management system operates.

Accounts Receivable

A more limited and infrequent activity relates to funds paid to the school district. Districts must design and manage a billing system to reflect obligations to the district from outside patrons or business and sometimes other municipal entities that purchase services from the district.

Intake procedures are essential for these funds. School buildings may often receive cash or personal check payments for monthly school meals, fees, or deposits on books or equipment. Procedures must ensure that at least two people handle such transactions at the school level. One person must receive and write receipts while a second person reviews the receipts, counts the money, and checks and prepares a deposit. The deposit to the banking authority must be frequent and include a report to the district's business office for entry into the accounting system. This internal control protects the people and the district.

Outstanding obligations for anticipated receipts must be monitored by the business office. Regular collection efforts must be undertaken and documented. Outstanding accounts receivable are reported as an asset on the district's balance statement.

Insurance and Risk Management

The CFO or business manager is typically the primary administrator responsible for developing a risk management plan and acquiring proper insurance for school buildings, buses and other equipment plus obtaining liability coverage along with errors and omissions coverage for the district's governing board and officers.

This function is more fully addressed in Chapter 14—Enterprise Risk Management: What to Insure.

Audits

At the end of each fiscal year, a summary of actual revenue and expenses is reconciled to the banking statement. The general ledger accounts for each fund are updated and used to prepare a consolidated year-end financial statement. This official summary of the fiscal year financial operations in all funds forms the basis for the annual audit and serves as a report to state and Federal entities that require this information.

This process and its implications and requirements are more fully discussed in Chapter 10—Audits and Related Issues.

Cash Management and Banking Services

The process school districts use to acquire banking functions varies among the states. A central banking function will, however, -be required to support the receipt revenue and the distribution of funds through payroll and to vendors of all kinds.

Banks may seek business clients using personal relationships, but school districts are wise to establish school board policy to establish their banking relationships. Key to that process is the administration of a periodic request for proposals to select a financial institution to provide banking services for a fixed duration. The location of the banking facility, how deposits may be made, and how all the services associated with making payments must be evaluated. Carefully enumerate the services desired and provide a way to assess the cumulative costs of service from each firm making a proposal in order to fairly assure the board and the community that the district's banking functions are properly and economically being provided.

In some cases, a county or city level treasurer may be the required "bank" for the school district. In this situation, building a relationship with the elected or appointed governmental treasurer and her/his office is important. In many cases, this entity receives local property tax collections and is the designated recipient of state or federal funds designated for the school system. To effectively manage the district's cash flow, learn how that office receives and posts revenue.

Integral to this role is the need to assure advance knowledge of cash flow so that sufficient funds are available to address the required payment of payroll, benefits, and accounts payable. Cash flow analysis is vital for managing investment decisions. See Chapter 7—Program Monitoring, Fund Balance, and Reserve Funds for more details on this topic. Appendix A provides a sample cash flow analysis.

School districts with bank accounts must establish procedures for control of blank check stock, the signature block on checks or warrants and approvals. This duty is generally the responsibility of the CFO or chief business official, but in some districts the superintendent may be required to review this important fiscal control of the banking function.

State regulations and prudent practices require timely and regular deposit of receipts received at the school or the district office. Procedures for this management function must be clear and contain segregation of duties to provide the internal controls that help avoid or prevent fraud (see Chapter 10—Audits and Related Issues for more information). To support security and protect staff from being subject to possible criminal attacks, it may be valuable to establish a cash pick up service from one of the well-known vendors who specialize in this function (e.g., Brinks).

Other Considerations

School district size: School district enrollment size will affect how many people will be necessary to properly operate the business office. The degree of specialization will be influenced by the district's location and ability to hire enough professional people to meet all the business office functions.

Many school districts have enrollment below 1,000 students, making highly specialized roles within the business office unrealistic. The functions required to be met in a small district are the same functions required for larger districts. In these cases, finding a generalist to fill the CFO role is essential. Specialized services and support can be obtained from the district's regional educational service agency or through contracted services.

As districts increase in enrollment, more schools exist, more transactions are required, and more people must be managed. Financial issues emerge with more complex interactions within the district, with vendors, and with other levels of government. Specialized talents in accounting, purchasing, and support service functions may lead to the creation of a Chief Operating Officer function to coordinate financial affairs, facility maintenance and operations, pupil transportation, nutrition services and other support functions like technology and human resources. Chapters 11 through 16 describe how these support services align with financial services.

Strength of staff: Knowing the strengths, interests and skills of leaders will help you make organizational design decisions. Capitalize on the skills of the existing staff and hire to fill gaps that exist or are anticipated to emerge.

Larger districts may have more access to talent within the community and are better able to design internal controls as checks and balances in operating functions. Smaller districts may allow more intimate knowledge of the community and the people living in it which improves customer service and allows faster responses to emerging needs. Finding ways to maximize both sides of this service duty will enhance the relationship of the school district with the community and its stakeholders.

Analysis for the future: Wise superintendents will build upon the knowledge, strengths and interests of all the leadership team members to anticipate future needs and build readiness for them into current practices and activities. For example, keeping an eye on local economic development will aid forecasting enrollment trends for program development and school growth. Also, the rapidly emerging role of technology tools is changing the way curriculum is designed and delivered. Is the school system anticipating the infrastructure needs to allow access to these emerging technologies?

Schedule leadership team meeting time focusing upon the future and evolving trends and obligations. This role is enriched by reading, attending conferences, meeting with community leaders, and sharing experiences with district personnel. Make this role an expectation for every leadership position.

Reporting Relationships

Determining the reporting relationships and duties of the business office personnel requires the assessment of the workload and the skills and interests of the existing staff. Because the enrollment size of the school district influences the number of schools and employees in the district, making this factor a primary driver for the workload in the business office.

A typical organizational structure will require one full time person devoted to managing and operating the payroll system. Due to heavy workload at certain times of the year, temporary hourly-paid staffing support may still be necessary.

The management and payment of bills through the accounts payable process is another position and is usually a separate person. Depending on size and workload variations throughout the school year, this person may be able to help manage purchasing decisions and work with preparation and conduct of bidding procedures when obtaining bids is legally required. When such overlapping functions are used, care must be taken to manage separation of duties by providing oversight by another administrator.

The CFO or chief business official usually devotes her or his primary effort to working with the superintendent and other senior level administrators on budget planning and development. This work requires investigation of spending patterns, knowledge of all fiscal factors that influence revenue and expense forecasts, and the school district strategic priorities. Budget development requires close coordination with staffing choices, compensation systems for use by the payroll office, budget format choices, and mandates imposed by state regulations. Often, each revenue source has spending restrictions linked to it. These requirements affect budget choices and decisions in ways that must be carefully explained to school boards and the public.

A smaller district may be required by resource limitations to consolidate various functions into one person. As district size increases the number of people adds complexity, requires more coordination, and regulatory exposure increases. Support functions and central office may no longer be co-located in one facility. Transportation, Maintenance, Custodial, and Food Service may need be managed within regions. These important considerations must be routinely examined to ensure efficiency.

Legal and regulatory obligations are the same regardless of the school system's enrollment size. For this reason, small districts are wise to foster positive working relationships with the regional educational service agency and/or larger neighboring district personnel. These relationships provide access to knowledge and guidance for meeting obligations.

Larger districts will often require more administrative managers for several of the above referenced functions. For example, the payroll office may require multiple people who specialize in various subsets of the staff. Benefits specialists are often also found in larger districts. Managing the medical/dental and voluntary benefits function may be more than a full-time role for a person. When multiple functional staff are required, oversight and management of the various sub-set functions is necessary.

Separate expertise and management leadership is needed for transportation, nutrition services (school lunch program and more), maintenance/custodial services and technology functions. Each area requires consistent and informed leadership than can be provided by one person.

Conclusion

No single organizational design is recommended because local skills and conditions must be adapted into the overall design. Create a business office structure that uses the strengths and skills of the individuals available to fill the various functional roles. The structure must respond to unique local challenges. Look beyond the CFO or Chief Operating Officer when designing the organizational structure. The strengths and interests of middle managers may indicate organization supports or opportunities for future assignments. If or when a position vacancy occurs, re-evaluate and adjust based on the current needs in alignment with the talents of the people involved,

Chapter 3

Budget Development Supports the Mission

This chapter will help leaders learn to...

Identify who is responsible for the budget.
Understand the need for a budget as a tool to attain goals.
Manage the budget planning process from start to finish.
Assure the budget decisions are sufficiently analyzed.
Know what to avoid.
Define and set direction to address challenges.
Seek to increase revenue.
Prepare for reductions.
Set the correct balance between leadership and community involvement.
Examine decision-making protocols.
Advocate for resources and priorities within constraints.
Communicate the budget to schools, staff, the school board, and the community.

Case Study

Jane finally gets her dream job, running a district. Now, it's time to lay out her vision. She does so first to the community. She's really pleased with the reaction to her vision. People like the options and the different choices she outlined. Then, she is surprised at a board meeting when some board members take issue with her community presentations. "I can't support these ideas unless you show us it's feasible."

The next day, Jane talks to Mary in the business office. Mary tells her, "We're going to be making difficult budget cuts this year. My guess is we'll have to reduce central office staff and teachers." Mary looks solemn, "I wish you had talked to me before you presented your vision to the community."

This conversation keeps Jane awake at night. She'd had fun sharing her dreams, but now she'll have to reduce them. Perhaps she'll need to keep her board engaged as well. Suddenly, her honeymoon period is over.

If you were the superintendent…
How would you have approached sharing your vision for the district?
How might you restart and reframe your goals within fiscal constraints?
What approach would you take to repair your relationship with members of the board?
What additional information will be needed and where might it be found?
How would you respond to Mary's complaint?

Who is responsible for the budget?

The superintendent is ultimately responsible for the preparation of the budget, its presentation to the school board and the community, and its proper administration. Setting the direction of budget decisions and making the fiscal plan as realistic as possible means the superintendent must involve all stakeholders within the district in the planning endeavor. The CFO and the business office need to know this direction to properly accomplish the technical work. Superintendent leadership must be consistent within the district and visible at key public stages in the process, especially when the budget is presented to the school board for approval.

Creating the budget development process means key stakeholders have sufficient input to the parameters and other aspects of the budget they've identified. The school board should participate in creating these parameters and formally adopt them early in the budget development cycle.

Sample school board-level budget parameters might include:

- ensuring that initiatives, programs and strategies introduced to improve student achievement reflect the board's student commitments and goals.
- complying with all state, federal, and local statutes and regulations.
- complying with relevant school board policies, including but not limited to budgeting for the board's own training, audits, and surveys.
- identifying all changes from the current year's budget.
- identifying major resource reallocations, including maximizing revenues that may have been overlooked.
- conforming to contracts and collective bargaining agreements.

Another approach to setting parameters might be to keep these values in mind if the budget may require reductions. Consider adding parameters that are:

- Strategic and intentional in the enhancement of programs, staffing or items based upon their value-added to achieving the previously identified academic ends/outcomes for students.
- Prioritizing enhancement of programs, staffing or items that add value to implementing the district's graduation's requirements and preparing P–12 students to meet those requirements.
- Promoting operational efficiencies.

Building an appropriate set of parameters is an important topic for school board discussion. Seek the board's guidance early in the budget development process to set the "tone at the top," focus the work of the administration, and support sound community engagement opportunities as the work progresses. Making sure the board adopts meaningful parameters in the beginning keeps a clear focus on resource decisions and is helpful in retaining your superintendent position, too.

When the school board provides the administration with parameters on process and content early in the schedule the potential for surprises is minimized. Stating obvious parameters about a legal, balanced budget creates proper expectations.

Whether investing in new programs or making necessary program reductions, describe how community input will occur. Be clear about when and how such input will be useful.

Why is a budget necessary?

The budget is a planning document. Whether cutting expenses or programs to balance spending with revenue or adding programs and expenses, careful planning must be evident.

During the planning phase, look for operational efficiencies, ways to eliminate redundant allocations, opportunities to consolidate budgets, reduce costs, and/or enhance revenue. The budget creates the plan for the district's actions and allows leaders to monitor and adjust to fiscal events.

Identify primary priorities for essential analysis and consideration early in the budget cycle. It is unlikely that all areas of possible interest can be analyzed in each budget development cycle, so keep a list of important areas to analyze in the future. Follow through on these plans in preparation for future development cycles.

Finding reductions to one area of the budget based on what isn't working well may be a primary way to introduce new initiatives. Program additions must be carefully examined to assure sustainability into future fiscal years, so it is essential to assure adequate future revenue or accurate implementation of what's being eliminated or reduced.

When does budget planning start, when does it finish?

The superintendent must constantly lean into the future. The best time to prepare for the next budget cycle is right after the CFO has made the last adjustments and the accounting books have been closed for the prior fiscal year. Plan several years into the future and consider emerging issues that may not yet be fully ready for attention or implementation.

The Business Side of School Success

Use a budget preparation calendar detailing the major events and the major players. Discuss budget preparation plans with the CFO and other members of the leadership team, then share the calendar with the school board to get their buy-in. Modify and adjust this plan based on the board's feedback.

An early start on the next budget cycle allows opportunities for community involvement and time to meet, analyze the input, and develop recommendations. Early input and analysis provide the lead time necessary to incorporate the planned changes into the work of the district.

Evaluate the existing budget parameters or begin to build them with the school board. Even if budget parameters have previously been used, re-visit them. This process gets the board talking about what they would like to see happen and sets the parameters for all the budget work. Engaging the school board in setting the parameters at the beginning of the process avoids missteps and miscommunication about their ultimate financial responsibility.

A viable budget development calendar will identify the time for key decision points. Schedule community involvement ahead of these milestone dates. Publish schedules with timelines that show who is responsible for each step. Consider legislative calendars and required state reporting or adoption deadlines. Adjust this calendar when conditions require changes. Use this planning calendar to schedule the work with administrators and the community.

Use the budget parameters as guideposts for the planning work. The initial planning assumptions, especially those that drive revenue calculations, must be clearly documented and shared with the school board and other stakeholders. These assumptions will provide early warning about potential issues. Additionally, the actions of others (e.g., legislative budget actions) may alter the steps associated with initial assumptions. Clarity in sharing these assumptions and noting when assumptions are updated and changed is an important action for making wise decisions and for effective communication with others.

Some states require districts to provide multi-year budget forecasts in each budget adoption cycle. This process, even if not mandated, makes sense in showing the longer-term impact of choices in the current budget year. For example, some programs may begin part way into a fiscal year and therefore not require a full twelve-month budget allocation; the carry-forward costs must be shown in the second year. Such actions demonstrate prudent stewardship and help assure the board that programs are sustainable.

Is the budget sufficiently analyzed?

Superintendents lead the budget review process and must make it an important component of the district's work by paying attention to it. But the detailed analysis and evaluation of elements within the budget likely falls to the CFO and the relevant other program administrators.

To guide this work, expect the CFO to make plans that include the following:

- Ensure analytical techniques produce reasonably accurate forecasts.
- Ensure the information to make essential decisions is available in a timely fashion.
- Clarify who will do each analysis and when it needs to be done.
- Conduct a zero-base review of at least a portion of the budget each year by assessing what would happen if this function were eliminated altogether.
- Extend the budget process for the next three to five years to anticipate future needs and test its sustainability.
- Manage the total number of staff based upon accurate student enrollment forecasts. Carefully review enrollment forecasts with the whole leadership team.
- Use performance indicators aligned with the strategic plan and objectives to review programs and departments and set resource amounts.
- Check for alignment of budget allocations with the strategic plan and district mission.

The superintendent must take an active role in budget development. Exactly how much time the superintendent devotes to this work is a function of the district's fiscal status, whether detailed budgets are new or routine, the CFO's experience, and/or if major unforeseen circumstances require action.

What should be avoided? How are the challenges identified?

A complete understanding of potential budget errors helps establish and sustain a budget development process that successfully meets the needs of the school district. Superintendents don't typically perform the technical work, but they are responsible to the school board for what is presented. Therefore, an important role for the superintendent is to test the validity and reasonableness of the assumptions being made by the technical staff. Since most revenue generating formulae rely on enrollment/attendance data, pay careful attention to these forecasts in the budget cycle.

Some of the more frequent potential errors budget system planners encounter are:

1. **Production and assembly errors**

   a. Because many people interact with the budget system, the underlying information systems may rely on data that is incomplete, inaccurate or not useful for planning, projecting, or estimating costs for the future. For example, because some people are not full-time employees (FTE), the ability to track the specific number and cost of all employees can be especially difficult but extremely important. Use care to review all staffing assumptions and FTE calculations.

   b. Analytical techniques do not appropriately consider relevant variables or appropriately weigh their impact. Variables that require review and understanding include:

   - rate changes
   - volume changes
   - productivity changes

- seasonality
- conversion from part-year to full-year
- trends

c. Lack of precision and consistency in accounting for costs or revenues contributes to a database that is not very useful for planning, projecting or estimating costs for the future. Watch for changes in accounting procedures that may skew historical data.

d. Poorly trained or inexperienced staff may introduce errors into the database, into analyses, into the assembly of the documents, and/or into reports used by decision makers. Ask questions about the data and scan trends to check for anomalies.

e. Analytical work is not updated or checked with the most recent data to confirm its relevance and accuracy.

f. Using the current budget to make projections often compounds errors. The errors that existed in the previous budget cycle may be maintained and magnified into the new budget. Verify projections.

g. Using inaccurate assumptions regarding the time required to implement program adjustments or changes.

h. Making inaccurate assumptions regarding what resources are required to accomplish agreed upon objectives.

i. Failing to provide adequate fiscal reserves, especially those needed to ensure adequate cash is available to sustain operations throughout the fiscal period.

j. The process for developing the budget is not understandable, does not identify who is responsible for each element, or does not set appropriate deadlines for the completion of various stages of the work. Even one of these factors may result in not having the data needed for timely decision-making.

k. Failure to identify and resolve all one-time adjustments.

l. Using resources multiple times. It is easy to assume an additional resource will be used to cover a financial issue. However, without clear longitudinal documentation, by the time the additional resources arrive the funding might be re-directed to cover other issues. Document decisions so that everyone who may have an interest in the decision is fully aware of it.

m. Failure to check and follow through on reduction plans. The implementation of reduction plans encounters a form of attrition that often reduces the amount of savings realized. If the next budget assumes 100% implementation without this result being confirmed, embarrassing errors are introduced.

n. Resist the natural tendency for fiscal staff to make overly conservative forecasts. Understand the assumptions by asking questions. Direct revisions if it is determined changes are warranted.

o. Inaccurately forecasting district enrollment creates revenue issues and may result in hard-to-reverse investments in staffing. If a forecast has been off by one-half of a percent total for all grades, examine why this occurred and revise the modeling process to adjust to experience. Adjust expenditure levels as quickly as possible.

Missing the impact of unique or alternative programs and their effect on overall revenue and operations. For example, charter school programs may include a revenue sharing relationship with the school district within which they operate. Seek to monitor and understand the relationship of such programs to the overall school district's budget plans clearly and carefully.

2. **Human dynamic errors**

    a. Communication breakdowns contribute to using the wrong data, applying the wrong adjustment, or overlooking important information.

    b. The absence of a system of incentives or accountability that expects staff to responsibly support providing accurate information in a timely manner.

    c. Failure of individual program administrators to fully understand or embrace the team concept and seek to embellish their efforts through competition or deception. Build a culture of trust by expecting all leaders to be honest; be sure to address issues where evidence indicates this virtue is not followed.

3. **Decision-making errors**

    a. Organizations and organizational leaders may erroneously ignore the impact of bad news or external factors that could have a negative impact on resources or costs. This blind-spot may occur when attempting to protect schools from changes in enrollment, state support, or mid-year corrections.

    b. The review process does not ensure critical information is presented and discussed at appropriate times.

    c. Decisions by policy makers are not communicated to those who assemble the budget.

4. **Efficacy errors**

    a. The budget is not aligned with the strategic plan and does not provide the resources needed to accomplish the most important objectives identified by the organization.

b. Inadequate consideration of multi-year impacts. A good plan for next year might be influenced by what is expected to happen in subsequent years.

5. **Implementation errors**

   a. Failure to give timely information to managers about changes made to their budget or limitations in the use of the resources available to them.

   b. Failure to provide adequate training to managers regarding expectations.

   c. Unintended consequences that were not predicted in the planning process identify themselves as new problems that derail aspects of the budget.

Ask the CFO what is being done, or could be done, to mitigate errors that may have been introduced into the budget during its development. Remember, the first budget upon becoming a new superintendent is inherited. Do not blindly follow this budget or simply build upon its assumptions without questioning the practices and policies that underpin its development.

Reductions or Additions?

Balancing the budget often presents a challenge to staying focused on student learning (see Chapter 1—The Mission is Student Learning). The best strategy to sustain the proper focus is to build this focus into the budget parameters and then reinforce it throughout the decision-making process. Persisting in building the budget to support student achievement may still require some alteration to past practices and thinking creatively about how to manage with less money. But the decision-making associated with these reductions must clearly be demonstrated to avoid impairing the district's essential teaching and learning functions.

An early task when preparing a budget is to look at revenue. Is the district receiving all the revenue it is entitled to receive? If not, find out why. This is the time to reconsider planning assumptions related to revenue.

The case study in Chapter 7—Program Monitoring, Fund Balance, and Reserve Funds demonstrates how a superintendent increased lost revenue by requiring staff to claim federal dollars for Special Education Summer School. Look through each revenue account and seek to maximize each one while simultaneously being cautious and avoiding over-optimistic, unrealistic plans. It is better to ultimately receive more revenue than was planned, but it is still vital to make sure all sources are properly evaluated.

In some states, attracting students from another district includes authority to collect tuition for nonresident student enrollment. Even if tuition charges are not permitted, the state allocation may be sufficient motivation to warrant seeking to increase out-of-district resident enrollment. This aspect of budgeting is too often overlooked, so analyze this issue with as much energy as is used finding efficiencies or reductions.

Using stakeholder engagement helps identify sources of reductions. Engage all employee groups by providing them with the parameters and the fiscal assumptions you are using. Working with program administrators, principals, and teacher and support staff leaders to explain the conditions leading to a potential set of reduction decisions.

Share the same facts with a citizen's budget committee or other advisory group representing your community. If no citizen advisory committee exists, plan well in advance to develop one and define how its membership will be selected (e.g., school representatives, board appointments, community roles, etc.,). Do not hesitate to make any data available to them. Be prepared to research their ideas thoroughly.

Expect members of the budget review committee to devote the time and effort to the task so they can ultimately make solid suggestions. Plan enough meeting time that provides sufficient information to develop suggestions in alignment with the budget development schedule. Invite representation from teachers and classified staff to these meeting so they can explain their perspective and outline information about requests to the citizen representatives.

When facing budget reductions, one suggested approach is to identify more potential reductions than will be needed. Identify the amount of savings or reduction associated with each item. Ask each committee member to evaluate the plans, add more for consideration or modify the items suggested. Then, have each committee member identify their proposed mix of options to create a balanced budget or to hit the reduction target. Be clear that the school board expects the presentation of a superintendent recommended, balanced budget, so the committee input is to the superintendent who will make the recommendations.

The superintendent's recommendations should include a set of proposed reductions that acknowledge the committee's input and ideas.

Cortner-Castro (2009), a school district administrator in Idaho, describes ideas and recommendations for managing budget reductions:

- Review and analyze current enrollment numbers and expenditures for the district, schools, and individual programs within the district and the schools. Compare data from the previous years with projections for the upcoming school years.
- Identify programs and personnel positions that cannot be cut because they are required or have specific funding (e.g., federal, state, or grant programs). Also identify supplemental programs and personnel positions that are in place for enrichment and are not required by the state and federal governments.
- Identify programs and instructional personnel positions that have the greatest effect on student learning and support transitioning into adult living.
- Identify areas of low student participation and high expenditures. Consider combining those areas to increase the efficiency of services and free up resources and staff to serve in other areas of need.
- Identify the administrative personnel and positions that are necessary and have the greatest effect on students and student learning. Determine

whether administrative assignments can be consolidated or reduced with minimal effect on student learning.
• Evaluate whether classes can be combined so one certified teacher oversees a program, replacing other certified teachers with paraprofessionals who can assist with individual needs and small group instruction.
• Evaluate whether positions can be eliminated, and the duties transferred to other personnel. Consider offering a stipend to compensate for the additional duties.
• Determine whether reducing the hours of some classified staff to part-time is possible to reduce expenditures for benefits.
• Consider reducing elementary school ancillary teaching positions and reassigning those duties to the elementary general classroom teacher.
• Consider reducing or cutting extra stipends for personnel, building supply budgets, or travel for staff and students.
• Review, research, compare, and evaluate school models that may reflect cost management. A four-day school week and flex schedules are models that some districts have adopted to assist with cost management. It is important to research the immediate and long-term effects of such school models on the budget, student learning, and the community. Obtain input regarding those models from stakeholders whose school districts have applied them. Evaluate whether those models would work the school district and community, keeping in mind the unique needs of the district and community.

Hard lessons have been learned through previous budget restriction processes. These experiences show that a variety of budget development approaches work, but almost any budget reduction process encounters resistance and challenge. Resistance should be anticipated. Make every effort to fully listen and understand the reasons for such resistance and design processes that mitigate these factors.

Some typical sources of challenge and resistance are predictable. The following examples provide insight into some areas of such resistance:

• Managers intentionally withhold information, or sometimes present misinformation, to avoid losing staff or resources.

- Managers avoid sharing information regarding how discretionary resources might be used. For example, some federal programs have significant carryover and managers may seek to use these funds as a cushion to cutbacks or as a safety net if a budget or management error surfaces.
- Managers sabotage efforts by garnering the support of special interests or ignoring implementation steps.
- Individuals can see potential reductions in someone else's department or program see those that directly impact them.
- Whenever individuals or teams review the needs of a specific area of the budget, they are more likely to see the need for more resources than they are to see the need for less.
- A "no extra work, I'm exhausted" argument might be presented to avoid attempts to reduce one function of the organization. Other parts of the organization will support this idea for fear they might be next in line for reductions.
- Historical context can slow down or stop nearly any conversation about changing resource levels. Phrases like, "we tried this before and it didn't work," "it took us twelve years to get this extra help," 'we've always done it this way," or "we've been cut every year" are indicators of this type of thinking.

Might the community become too involved?

The superintendent is directly responsible to the school board for budget recommendations and support for fiscal decisions. Seeking input and involvement about ideas and approaches enhances the process, but the superintendent must clearly communicate that these inputs will be reconciled into a superintendent recommended budget plan.

Clear boundaries that establish this parameter for the role of participants must be established at the beginning of the process. Using processes for budget review that are open to all comers avoids issues of selection, but a clear expectation must be made and must be repeated occasionally. For example, identify the schedule of meetings, topics to be covered, and when recommendations will be provided to the superintendent. Also, note when the superintendent recommendations will be made to the board of directors.

Public involvement in part or all of the budget development process requires that citizens commit to an investment of time and effort. This investment influences their perspective during subsequent steps in the process. Because of this phenomenon, care should be taken to provide clear guidance through a committee charter for staff and community members who participate in the process.. Review the charter regularly, especially when transitioning from one phase to the next.

Based on these issues, strong budget development processes utilize accurate and complete information and set clear expectations for the appropriate role of everyone involved in the process.

Making the Decisions

The school board must sponsor the budget development process and be informed about its ongoing development actions. Defining who gets to decide among various choices is an important aspect of the budgeting process. Be clear about this issue for every phase of the budget development process. A successful process strikes an appropriate balance between stakeholders and clarifies the role of experts, employees, associations/unions, parents, students, and community representatives.

The superintendent, after consideration of inputs from the staff and public, will present a recommended budget to the school board. This recommendation should conform to the budget standards and parameters established with the school board during the budgeting process. By the time the budget gets to this stage, there should be no surprises for the school board. They should already be aware of the challenges and how the budget addresses the board's parameters. The recommended budget should include the latest information on revenue and expenditures and highlight the changes from last fiscal year.

After the superintendent recommendations are received, the board has the duty to adopt the budget in public session, often after holding an input hearing prior to action. Budget committee members, staff, and other citizens are able to share their input at this stage, especially if they disagree with the superintendent's proposals. Fair, honest processes may reduce, but not eliminate, this form of disagreement.

Early in the process, the superintendent and the board must understand that the board may add to the recommended budget or change it before it becomes the adopted budget. If the board adds expenditures to the budget, it must be prepared to take something away of equal or greater budget effect. This understanding must be a clearly defined element in the budget action schedule. It establishes an important threshold that most school boards do not have the appetite to actually change the budget at this late stage.

Superintendents must listen carefully to the board's adoption debate. Board member expressions concern about the recommended budget may not change budget adoption actions, but such issues may be addressed in the next annual budget or through modifications within the current year's budget monitoring process.

Advocacy

Sometimes hearing directly from those who advocate for a certain position helps and sometimes this advocacy blocks the important review work that needs to be done. Timing and tone are the key to listening and addressing the views of such advocates.

Sound budget processes provide a legitimate opportunity for advocacy at the appropriate time. Too early and good options may not get developed for consideration. Too late and concerns may magnify or result in unintended consequences because key input was overlooked. For these reasons, it is important to clearly communicate when and where stakeholders will have an opportunity to present their recommendations to the superintendent or school board. Multiple opportunities for this kind of interaction are recommended.

Communicating the budget

Many school districts have recognized the need to develop a communication staff to address the many issues confronting schools. If such a staff exist, use them to guide every engagement step in budget development. This expertise will assist with advocacy inputs, information sharing, and describing parameters and assumptions at each phase of the budget development process.

Communicate clearly and frequently whenever assumptions are revised. Necessary changes in data or assumptions are crucial crossroads that present the potential to undermine trust and sow discord. Adapt the style of the communication to the needs of various audiences but be sure to use the same set of data or information for the school board and a different set for staff and community members.

What will the budget accomplish?

The budget is perhaps the most significant operational document to support the district's strategic priorities. What gets funded gets attention and should support the district's goals. Each budget year provides an opportunity to advance this work, so seek to accomplish as much as possible within the available resources. Staging the strategic work is necessary and the budget document is a powerful way to share how that process will unfold.

Budgeting is not a solo sport, so encourage participation in your budget development process. Levenson (2022) states that budgeting is the time to "keep student needs at the fore and embrace new ideas, approaches, and systems." For more ideas on improving your budget see the second edition of Levenson's book *Smarter Budgets, Smarter Schools: How to Survive and Thrive in Tight Times* (2022).

The budget must live within existing resources, but it must leave enough reserve to cover monthly cash flow needs, meet legal requirements, and demonstrate financial stability. Plan carefully to achieve sound operational results. Tools and ideas supporting effective fiscal monitoring are described in greater detail in Chapter 6—Accounting and Monitoring Fiscal Status and Chapter 8—Assessing School District Financial Health.

Conclusion

This chapter addresses numerous ways to integrate budget development into the core operational work that supports and implements the district's strategic priorities. View the process as continuous and iterative. As each step unfolds, it sets the stage for advancing the district's work and taking subsequent actions. Many important initiatives take multiple years to mature and demonstrate effect, so the budget is the way resources are deployed to accomplish those goals.

Use the process outlined in Figure 1, Chapter 1—The Mission is Student Learning to assess the work of these initiatives in each fiscal year. Sustained effort and resources are vital for students and their success. Engage the staff and the community in the process to build understanding and generate support for this vital effort.

Chapter 4

Revenue: An Integral Component of the Budget

This chapter will help leaders learn to...
Identify the sources of revenue available to the school district.
Understand the value in identifying all available sources of revenue.
Identify and use the different categories of local, state and federal funding.
Understand the importance of monitoring the status of revenue and how to assure the school district receives all the revenue it is entitled to receive.
Understand the importance of sound revenue assumptions and estimates.
Take steps to keep the school board and community updated on fiscal matters, including the status of actual revenues compared to estimated revenues.

Case Study

Gerry has been the superintendent of schools for the West School District for the past seven years. The school district serves 4,000 students, pre-k through grade 12. Approximately eighty percent of the students come from economically disadvantaged families. The high level of poverty and low property wealth in the community has resulted in an annual struggle to meet the academic and social needs of its students. Although academic achievement, as measured by state assessments, has been slightly improving, there is still a need for much improvement.

The Business Side of School Success

The upcoming school year will be financially challenging due to the projected increases in salaries and benefits for the faculty, staff and administrators. These increases will put pressure on the $70 million general fund budget. Moreover, like all the school districts in the state, the increase in the tax levy is capped at 2%.

During a budget preparation meeting, the school business official informed Gerry that a newly discovered analysis projects a deficit of approximately $4 million for the current fiscal year. In addition, the fund balance is already nearly depleted, so presenting a budget for next fiscal year with a tax levy at or below the cap will be impossible. Significant reductions in programs and services will be necessary to meet commitments and live within the revenue limitations unless the community approves an over-ride levy.

Gerry informs the school board and writes a letter to the community explaining the dire budget forecast and the probable program and service reductions for the upcoming school year.

Most parents in the community recognized that the children desperately needed these programs and services if they are to continue to see academic improvements. The next school board is packed with angry parents and other community members.

This situation caught the attention of the state education department and state comptroller's office. A subsequent audit by these state agencies revealed that revenue and expenditure budget estimates over-estimated actuals for several years leading to the depletion of the fund balance and a projected deficit for the end of the current fiscal year.

Gerry has no choice but to present a school budget to the school board and community that exceeds the statutory tax cap, a decision that requires 60% of the voters to approve the budget. The board opted for a community vote that failed to be approved. The painstaking task of making program and services cuts commenced.

Gerry thought to himself, "I really should have been more involved in the finances of the district. Now, what am I going to do?"

If you were the superintendent…

What information and data should Gerry request for review? Where might it be found?

Who should Gerry meet with to better understand the reasons for the school district's financial problems?

What information should Gerry have shared with the school board? When?

Why is it important for Gerry to facilitate the meaningful participation of stakeholders to address these problems?

How can Gerry ensure that the school district is receiving all the funding it is entitled to?

The conditions West School District faced happen often enough to cause concern and serve as a stark reminder that school leaders need to be thoughtfully involved in understanding district revenue sources and guide accurate forecasting. Accurate revenue estimates are important to maintain the financial stability of the school district. If revenues underperform estimates, the potential for a budget deficit exists. When the school district fund balance is sufficient (see Chapter 8—Assessing School District Financial Health), these resources are reduced to make up for the shortfall in revenue. The same effect occurs when expenses are not reduced when revenue doesn't meet the budget plan, a topic that is discussed in Chapter 3—Budget Development Supports the Mission.

This condition places upward pressure to increase taxes, reduce or restrict programs, or some combination of both actions. The fund balance is not a reoccurring source of revenue. Using a portion of it to offset the next year's expenses may provide a short-term solution to avoid program reductions or raising additional revenue (e.g., tax increases or new funds from other sources). Still, using fund balances is not a sustainable financial strategy.

Where Does the Money Come From?

Generally, three main sources of revenue exist in public school districts:

Local Sources: Property taxes are typically the most significant source of local revenue and, in some states, the largest source of revenue.

Other local, non-tax revenue sources exist. Examples include fees, purchased student meal fees, investment earnings, and rental income charged for facility use when allowed for outside entities.

State Sources: This revenue category is significant with the largest share usually generated from formula-based aid provided to all school systems in each state. It is often referred to as state aid or general apportionment. Major factors used to create formula-based allocations include district enrollment, property wealth measures, geographic considerations, personnel characteristics, and school size factors.

Flat grant models are used by some states to allocate equal per-pupil funding. Born (2020), states, "In a conventional format, the formula divides the number of primary and secondary public school students by the legislative appropriation" (p. 52). In some states, such as New York, flat grant aid is allocated with the same per pupil funding for all school districts meeting the state's criteria based on a formula using income and/or property valuation of the district.

The full funding model is an approach where the state provides the full amount of state aid with no local options for funding. The only state in the country that uses a full funding model, without any supplemental local funding, is Hawaii (Born, 2020).

State level categorical programs and expense-reimbursement-based aid comprise other sources of state provided revenue. Categorical program funding from the state is often focused on major educational initiatives required by either state or federal law.

For instance, special education funding usually relies upon a formula (e.g., using the prior year's December enrollment) with a mix of state and federal funding sources. Integrating other revenue sources into such a formula adds complexity to accounting and expenditure management (e.g., IDEA, the federal statute mandating such programs for special needs students and provides some federal fiscal support). Other categorical funding programs could include poverty-based, youth institutional programs, pupil transportation, and student nutrition services. These programs may be funded via a categorical formula or by using an expense-reimbursement model.

The nature of the economy and state legislative issues may create fluctuation on some sources of state funds. Monitor the state level policy conditions to stay alert for such changes. This potential is another reason to make sure the district maintains an adequate fund balance to offset the negative impact of such events.

Federal Sources: These revenue sources are driven by Federal law to address specific student needs or conditions (e.g., students with disabilities or Title I support for students from disadvantaged situations). Such allocations are often complementary to state funding and are awarded by annual formula-based grants through the state education agency (SEA). Federal regulations govern the grant making criteria applied by the SEA to these grant determinations.

Federal funds may also be tied to natural resources within the state (e.g., Federal Forest funds) or the presence of Federal land that isn't subject to property tax (e.g., military bases using P.L. 874 appropriations).

Federal categorical program revenue must supplement state and local funding and not supplant (replace) local or state budget appropriations available to all students. To ensure supplanting isn't occurring, these expenditures must be carefully managed to assure compliance with Federal regulations. These funds may be charged to a designated program code with the general fund or, in some states, may be accounted for in a separate, designated fund.

Local Revenue Sources

Property taxes: A major funding source is the annual school tax levied against the assessed property value of the school district. Paid by all property owners, the assessed property value is multiplied by a tax rate (sometimes measured in increments of .001, called mills, or $1 per $1,000 in assessed valuation). Some states limit the tax rate and some limit the total dollars that can be collected. The approach used to assess the value of property also affects these determinations. Often, some mechanism exists in state law that allows voter approval to over-ride the statutory limit.

The uneven assessment of property within the school district and the disparate amount of property wealth among school districts are challenges for school's reliance on property taxes. Uneven assessment practices and schedules cause some inequity among taxpayers. This issue is eventually corrected as the re-assessment cycle occurs. Low property wealth school districts must levy a higher tax rate to raise the same resources as wealthier districts can obtain with a lower tax rate. This disparate "effort" in terms of tax rate causes property-poor school system to live with less fiscal support than districts with property wealth.

A variety of interventions exist among the states to equalize the disparities in assessed valuation and limit overall tax collections. Some states collect a statewide property tax locally but transfer it to the state for equalized distribution through the state aid formula. Some states limit how much over-ride funding can be generated by local voters. Knowing how the property tax system works is an important revenue management requirement for superintendents.

Most states enact tax relief programs. These programs may include exclusions or reductions for veterans, volunteer firefighters, low-income families, senior citizens, or agricultural uses of the land. Many states have enacted legislation in various forms to place limits on property tax increases. This process is discussed in more detail in Chapter 5—Property Taxes: What You Need to Know.

Payment in lieu of taxes (PILOT): Many states authorize public school districts, in cooperation with local government, to agree to an annual amount of revenue from a commercial entity in lieu of that entity being taxed at the rate established by local government. This procedure is used as an incentive to encourage businesses to locate in the community, to provide local employment, and eventually to add value to the tax base when the PILOT expires. The terms used for this arrangement vary from state to state.

Alternatives to such programs include tax rate relief or deferral of including new improvements to properties on the assessed valuation roll for a designated number of years. For example, a current use exemption may exist to protect farmland from being taxed at a higher valued use.

Interest income: This category includes interest and earnings on money that is invested until needed. Typically, the types of investments are limited by state statute to avoid speculative investing.

Tuition: School districts may be allowed to accept nonresident students into programs at a tuition rate generally set by the school board or other governing entity. These tuition rates are often set to address the local property tax support provided by the citizens of the serving district. State and federal revenue are usually excluded from this rate determination because these funds follow the student's enrollment.

Rental of property: School buildings or unused space in school buildings may be rented to other school districts, charter schools, public libraries, churches, private businesses, or other government agencies. District patrons may also rent school facilities on weekends or evenings for allowed functions and pay a rental fee for such use.

Sale of property and compensation from loss: This revenue is generated from the sale of equipment, supplies, real property, and insurance recoveries. In most cases, proceeds from the sale of real property must be deposited in the capital projects fund, not the general fund.

Other districts and governments: This revenue is generated from performing services for other school districts. Cooperative services such as special education, data processing, summer school, health services, transportation, account for this revenue source.

Miscellaneous: Refunds from prior year's expenditures, gifts, donations, gate proceeds for events, endowment and trust fund income, and other unclassified revenues may provide additional local revenue.

Bond issues and other referenda: School districts are generally allowed to raise additional local revenue for specialized purposes using public votes. Bond issues are used for specific non-operating expenditure such as capital improvements, including new construction, busses and other capital assets. See Chapter 16—Capital Projects and Bonds for more clarity on this topic.

Some states also allow school districts to seek voter approval for dedicated property tax levies linked to specific purposes like technology, construction or school buses (Born, 2020). Laws regarding processes and procedures required to increase property taxes for these uses vary from state to state.

State Revenue Sources

General State Aid: Each state has provisions in its constitution that requires funding for education. For example, the State of New York's constitution requires that students receive a "sound basic education." Washington State's constitution makes education the state's "paramount duty," and New Jersey is required to provide a "thorough and efficient education" for its school-aged children. Other state constitutions may contain similar language.

State revenue to the school district is viewed as a state-level expenditure appropriated by the state legislature and managed by the state education agency or the state budget agency in accordance with state budget and fiscal policies and practices. The state level process for funding school districts begins with the development of the state budget by the governor and adoption by the state legislature.

Budget adoption at the state level relies upon the use of various formulae factors that are applied statewide for all districts. Which factors to use and how they are applied is often a source of significant policy debate in state legislative halls. The degree of support for these allocations depends upon the overall fiscal health of the states' economy within the political context of that state.

The significance of this revenue source requires superintendents, chief business officials and school board members to frequently engage with state policy makers. Because state budgeting is tied to state political and economic conditions, political decisions often influence state school appropriations and may reduce the adequacy of educational funding. Local leaders can be a significant factor in influencing the ultimate adequacy of such funding decisions. School board members, superintendents, chief financial officers and other education stakeholders often lobby state legislatures for sufficient appropriations and implementation parameters.

State appropriations are usually distributed to local school districts by the state education agency using individual school district metrics applied to formula factors included in state law and/or the state's appropriation legislation. In some states, city government is the recipient of these funds for its local schools. In this situation, the city policy and political process applies another resource allocation model to funding individual schools. Many school districts are distinct units of government, though, that receive state funds directly and allocate funds to individual schools through appropriations adopted by the locally selected school board.

The state funding cycle may not be well-aligned with the school district's budget development and adoption requirements. District leaders must monitor state level decision-making processes and schedules. When the state funding is not available in time to complete the local school district's budget preparation, the amount of such aid will be estimated, often with little confidence in an outcome. The choice of how conservative or generous to make that estimate adds complexity and uncertainty to the local school budget adoption process. Alternatively, the estimate could be frozen at the current level unless it is generally known that cuts or increases are expected.

Formula based aid: State funding through a formula typically considers various factors such as enrollment, income and/or property values, staffing characteristics, and/or geography of school district. These general apportionment formulae will be referenced by various names. For example,

The Business Side of School Success

New York State calls this funding Foundation Aid, Illinois refers to it as Foundation Level Aid, Washington State as its Basic Education allocation, California as a Local Control Funding Formula, and Virginia's Standards of Quality formula.

Each state budget appropriates the state share of the formula using the process described above. Some states may incorporate local revenue into the formula by deducting its amount from the full calculation of formula resources due from the state, thereby appropriating those "local" funds into the state's formula as a form of equalization across school districts.

Counting the number of students for formula use is another important variable used by states. Some states use a funding system based on "enrolled" students, while other states still use "student attendance" as the basis for funding.

Enrollment: Most school expenses are fixed by annual contracts or ongoing expenses that can't be changed based on whether a student is physically in class on a given day. Consequently, monitor student "enrollment." Students are not removed from the counting system unless they are specifically withdrawn by their family or legal guardian or until their absence is confirmed for an extended number of days (e.g., two weeks of consistent, unexcused absence from school).

Attendance: Financial systems that fund schools based on student "attendance" insert a variable in revenue that is influenced by factors often outside the control of the school system. In an "attendance" based system, funding is reduced by a student absence due to illness, truancy, or other factors, even though none of the contractual expense obligations for the school system are reduced by such absences. For this reason, attendance-based systems are less reliable drivers of school revenue from state allocation models.

Visit the state's education department website to learn about current issues and processes for how the state's aid formula operates.

Categorical aid: State designated special program funding is usually separated into programs like Special Education, Pupil Transportation, or School Nutrition Services. District's hosting a state facility serving incarcerated youth or special group homes may also be eligible for categorical funding. Each program is appropriated resources through a specific funding category, hence the term "categorical aid."

The special education formula aid may mimic the basic educational program foundation aid with enriched funding factors to address the more complex educational requirements and costs for eligible students. Some states fund a full cost formula while others integrate the increased funding through a formula that provides an "excess cost" allocation above the core state aid for all students.

Pupil transportation funding is another significant state categorical aid program that uses unique factors such as miles driven, distance from school, and additional factors attempting to recognize the presence of unique geographic conditions in the school district to calculate a revenue allocation.

Inadequate attention to the factors and criteria that influence categorical programs may cause districts to shift resources away from the core educational program supported by the general aid formula to address categorical requirements. This tension is an ongoing source of debate in the state's budget cycle may create pressures within the school district and invite litigation.

Another variation in the categorical aid funding is an approach that provides funding based on reimbursement of state-approved school district expenditures. This variation is sometimes used for special education, transportation and capital projects. Since this approach requires initial expenditures by the school district, the reporting system to claim reimbursement requires advance knowledge of the reimbursement criteria and then careful review of the reports used to claim reimbursement.

Superintendents are ultimately responsible for these claims, so it is vital to review reimbursement claim reports with the school business official and other appropriate personnel to assure their reasonableness. Because state funding is driven by the data supplied by the school district, failure to report or providing faulty data may create a fiscal crisis. Reimbursement systems also may create cash flow issues when insufficient fund balances are maintained by the district.

Competitive grants: Often, various areas of state government will develop initiatives or programs that contain opportunities for competitive grants. These opportunities may require relationships with local partners (e.g., the health district, law enforcement, environmental groups, etc.,). Stay alert for such opportunities and use relationships developed through community or civic engagement to maximize the district's access to them. Take care to make sure efforts to obtain such funds align with the district's strategic plan and priorities.

Federal Revenue Sources

Federal program allocations: These funds, granted annually, are used for specific purposes detailed in federal law and generally must supplement, not supplant, state and local funding for these services or programs. Funds are usually distributed to states and school districts through formula criteria.

Elementary and Secondary Act of 1965 (ESEA) was reauthorized in 2015 and renamed as the Every Student Succeeds Act (ESSA): This federal act provides funding through specific grants to supplement state and local funding. Title I, Part A, provides funds for services to schools with high percentages of children from low-income families. Titles II through VIII provide funding for a variety of specific services that include English Language Acquisition, Emergency Impact Aid, and more.

McKinney-Vento funding: Targeted funding is directed in support of children and youth experiencing homelessness. The separate McKinney-Vento Homeless Assistance Act was reauthorized in December 2015 by Title IX, Part A, of the Every Student Succeeds Act (ESSA).

These grants are typically awarded to states and then allocated to school districts based on their unique student demographics and characteristics. The U.S. Department of Education website will provide current details for these grants (https://www.ed.gov/essa?src=policy). Additionally, the appropriate state education agency website will likely provide information and guidance.

The Individuals with Disabilities Education Act (IDEA): This federal act provides funding for eligible children with disabilities to receive special education and related services. Part B provides funding for students with disabilities ages three through twenty-one (IDEA 611) and pre-school, ages three through five (IDEA 619). Part C formula grants provide funds to support early intervention services for children ages birth through two.

Like the ESSA program funding, IDEA funding is allocated through the state education agency (see https://sites.ed.gov/idea/?src=policy-page for more information). It is based primarily on the December 1st student headcount of the year before. Use care that all students with special needs have a legitimate individual education plan before December so they may be included in the next year's funding.

Other Federal Revenue sources:

Some federal revenue sources are unique to the conditions of the district's location or geography.

For example, Federal facilities that house large numbers of families may not be included within the state's property tax base and therefore create financial burdens to the local community. Impact Aid (PL-874) funding is available to replace the loss of local or state funds associated with this loss of property taxes. This revenue source may be significant in some districts, and because its source is tied to national military policies, it is complex. Districts with this circumstance must take time to fully understand its history and current challenges.

Federal Forest tax funds are tied to logging practices and the presence of federally owned forest land. Receipt of these resources may be hard to predict and linked to actions beyond the district's control.

Be sure to examine local conditions to determine what sources of Federal funds are available to the district.

Federal Grant Funds:

Some grants are made via competitive grant applications. The availability of competitive grants reflects Congressional appropriations and varies over time. The state education agency typically alerts school districts about these grant application opportunities. This funding avenue is one area where having staff devoted to grant writing may assist with a district's budget.

Obtaining federal funds for technology, emergency preparations, or disaster assistance may require special attention. Each of these grant sources will need to be tracked with a separate revenue code and will require separate expenditure reporting to properly manage the grant.

The criteria for school district budgeting of federal funds varies among the states. Regardless of how these funds are budgeted, it is important that they be addressed when preparing the school district budget. For a complete description of the federal grants available to school districts, visit the website of the U.S. Department of Education (see https://www.ed.gov/programs-search/local-education-agencies).

Federal grants may be administered by the state or directly by the school district. It is imperative that the school district have processes in place to ensure that accurate data are submitted to federal and state agencies in a timely manner to receive the entitled funding. Superintendents should meet periodically with their business officials and special education administrators to ensure these processes are in place. Also, the use of federal funding must be carefully monitored to ensure funding is being used for eligible students as supplements and not to supplant other budgeted appropriations.

Other Revenue Sources

Astute leaders will stay alert to the opportunity to secure other revenue sources of revenue. Philanthropic foundations have focused considerable attention on education and have been noted for making sizable grants to support strategic initiatives. Grant writing initiative may involve the entire school district's attention and must be carefully calibrated to assure alignment between the enticement of the grant, the district's strategic priorities, the actions necessary to deliver on grant requirements.

The Bill and Melinda Gates Foundation is one such entity that has invested significant resources in P-12 educational endeavors (see https://www.gatesfoundation.org/our-work/programs/us-program/k-12-education). Investigate the availability of other philanthropic foundations focused on P-12 education that may serve the school district's region.

State or federal agencies may announce grant opportunities for a variety of functions that may include elements of school district operations. Building out the infrastructure for wireless Internet connectivity is one such opportunity that is receiving considerable attention. The Federal Communication Commission's E-Rate program is a good example of this non-traditional reimbursement support for essential school district technology expenditures. See this link for more information:

https://www.fcc.gov/consumers/guides/universal-service-program-schools-and-libraries-e-rate

A reliable funding source for student support services is the Social Security Act which provides for reimbursement of costs for certain health support services provided to Medicaid-eligible students with disabilities (Medicaid Reimbursement). This reimbursement program is managed by both state and federal requirements. Taking advantage of this funding source requires detailed attention and careful management of the claims process.

Reimbursement for services provided to non-resident students or foster care children may be another source of revenue. Such funds are likely to be received from the school district of origin. It is important to be aware of reimbursement for non-resident enrolled students, incarcerated youth, homeless children and foreign exchange children. The processes involved to receive reimbursement for these services varies from state to state and must be reviewed with your business office staff to ensure proper, timely reimbursements are received.

Revenue Monitoring

All funds received are entered into the accounting system using a coding system, generally referred to as a system of accounts (discussed in Chapter 3—Budget Development Supports the Mission). The coding systems are present in each state and are similar in application with varying numbering systems.

It is important for superintendents to review revenue reports with the business official on at least a monthly or bi-monthly basis to keep tabs on how actual revenues compare with budgeted revenues and to assist with forecasting the following year's budget.

Program and fiscal monitoring are thoroughly explored in Chapter 7—Program Monitoring, Fund Balance, and Reserve Funds.

Conclusion

A thorough knowledge of all revenue sources available for the school district is an essential component of budget development and monitoring the district's fiscal situation. Tracking the progress of school funding through the state and federal appropriation processes takes time and effort. Advocating on behalf of the school district requires understanding how each of the revenue sources outlined in this chapter interact and connect with other governing bodies and the school district.

Superintendents will find being aware and conversant with each of these revenue sources will be valuable when setting the spending plans for the school system.

Chapter 5

Property Taxes: What You Need to Know

This chapter will help leaders learn to…
Understand the elements of the property tax levy.
Understand the definitions of the property tax rate and millage.
Understand the factors used to determine school taxes for individual properties.
Identify how assessed valuation is determined.
Understand how property tax levies are collected.
Describe the property tax exemptions and how they provide relief to taxpayers.
Understand property taxation caps and how they might impact a school district's budget and financial planning.
See how property taxation may create inequalities in funding between various school districts.

Case Study

Carlos has been the superintendent of a large P-12, suburban school district for the past five years. During his tenure, all questions regarding financial matters including taxation, have been deferred to the school district's business official who had been in the job for thirty years. The business official retired, and Carlos is beginning the process to hire a replacement. The hiring process has become increasingly difficult to conclude due, in part, to the long tenure of the retiree.

In the meantime, several residents arrived at a school board meeting to ask questions about their property tax bills. Carlos, having relied upon his seasoned, now-retired business official had not learned the details about how school taxes were calculated and applied to homeowners. School district residents were appalled when their questions weren't answered.

Carlos recognized that this situation might lead to a loss of support in the community as well as from members of the school board.

If you were the superintendent…

How would you find the information you need to know to develop your knowledge about taxation?

What are the important concepts of taxation that every school superintendent should know?

How would you avoid the embarrassment that Charles experienced at the school board meeting?

What alternative choices did Charles have to avoid being exposed as happened in this school board meeting?

Property Taxes: The School District's Largest Source of Revenue

Public schools receive significant funding through property taxes. How does a school district determine the amount to be raised from this revenue source? Who pays property taxes?

Taxes are generally levied against three categories of property. The first category is real property (e.g., land, permanent structures on the land, and some improvements to the land). The second category is tangible or personal property. The third category is intangible, property that has value, but because of lack of substance, has no value in and of itself (Baker, Green, & Richards, 2008).

Property taxes dedicated to support schools are most frequently a tax on real property. Because this revenue source is historically the most significant way schools have been financed, it is a separate focus of this chapter.

Determining the revenue to be raised from property taxes and amounts paid for individual properties

The revenue school districts raise through property taxes is determined by the assessed valuation of the real property in the taxing district. This value is determined by the town or county assessor, often a locally elected or appointed official. Each state authorizes this assessment process to regularly update the property values in-line with market conditions. Some tax rates are fixed by state law, so pressure to keep assessed values low exists even though most people hope to sell their property for more than its assessed valuation.

The amount of funds raised is determined by the tax rate, also referred to as millage (see p. 70). Some states control revenue by controlling the tax rate while others control the total amount of revenue that is to be collected, a methodology which makes the tax rate variable. When tax rates are fixed, revenue goes up when valuations increase. When the dollar amount to be raised is controlled, the tax rate will decrease when valuations increase.

Taxpayers are usually allowed to make property tax payments in two equal payments within the calendar year. A spring payment may occur in about April and the fall payment around the end of October. Many homeowners make these payments through their mortgage company which routinely provides consistent peak revenue in the month in which each fractional payment is due. Knowing the system and when funds arrive is important for making cash flow projections (see Appendix A for a sample cash flow analysis).

What is a tax levy?

The system used to determine the allowed tax levy varies among the states. Two primary models exist although numerous variations of each model have developed among the states.

Model 1: In this model the amount a school district may raise in taxes (i.e., the tax levy) is determined by first finalizing the expenditure side of the budget, i.e., how many dollars are needed to fund the programs and other financial requirements for the school year (see Chapter 3—Budget Development Supports the Mission).

This approach starts with building the expenditure budget and then subtracting the estimated revenue from state, federal, and other designated revenue sources (see Chapter 4—Revenue: An Integral Component of the Budget). Another requirement is to identify the portion of the fund balance that will be carried over from the previous school year to support the new program year's expenses (see Chapter 8—Assessing School District Financial Health). Once all estimated revenues and the allocated fund balance are identified, the amount necessary to be raised in taxes (tax levy) may be determined.

In this model, the following calculation format is usually applied:

A. Budgeted expenditures for the new school year using the anticipated expenditure level for current programs plus new investments.

B. Budgeted revenue for the new school year from state, federal and other sources.

C. Estimated fund balance from the current school year.

D. Portion of the budget due from a new tax levy (A-B-C=D).

Model 2: Another approach to determining the tax levy is to use a formula (usually enacted by the state education agency as authorized by state law) to identify the amount of local tax levy the school district is authorized to collect.

In Washington State, until 2019 this approach applied a percentage factor against the total state and federal revenue for the prior school year. This calculated amount became the allowed tax levy lid. Starting in calendar year 2020, the system switched to the lower of a maximum levy per pupil (indexed to inflation) or a maximum tax rate. The amount to be collected remains the lower of these two calculations.

In this methodology, the total value of the tax levy is used to determine the revenue for the school budget. It is added to the anticipated state aid, federal funds, and other revenue sources and serves as a limit upon the revenue the school district has available for its operations. Fund balance resources become one-time budget balancing resources.

What is the tax rate?

Once the school district's governing board sets the amount of the tax levy, the tax rate is determined by dividing the amount of the tax levy, calculated using whichever of the above approaches is applicable, by the school district's total assessed value of taxable property. The district-wide tax rate is then applied to the individual property parcel's assessed value to determine the specific tax to be paid by each property parcel owner. The higher the assessed value of the property the higher the amount of the annual school tax paid by the property owner. The same tax rate is applied to each property parcel.

Property tax rates are historically expressed in terms of "mills." One mill is equal to one-tenth of one percent, so 1 mill is equal to $1 in property tax levied per $1,000 of a property's assessed valuation. The millage rate is the number of mills applied to the assessed valuation. To express the tax rate more simply, some states express the tax rate in "dollars per $1,000 of assessed valuation." Using either the dollars per thousand tax rate or expressing the rate in mills generates the same tax levy amount.

The tax rate is the result of the interaction of the total assessed valuation of the school district and the level of revenue planned to be raised for the school system. This interaction is well described in a video produced by the City of Kitchener, Ontario, Canada located at:

https://www.youtube.com/watch?v=_pw2HJUMytY

This video is a useful way to understand how service levels expressed in terms of total dollars to be raised and the district's assessed valuation interact to determine the applicable property tax rate.

How is the assessed value of property determined?

Generally, the school district's tax base, or the total assessment of all properties in the school district, is determined by the tax assessor of the county, township or other municipal government agency. The assessor prepares an assessment roll of all real property within that jurisdiction. The assessment roll lists the value of the properties within the boundaries of the school district.

The assessment system used to determine the property value varies from state to state and sometimes even within the state. The total value of all property within the school district determines the tax rate applied to the assessed value of each property parcel within the school district. Property may be assessed at 100% of the market value or some fractional value applied consistently throughout the tax jurisdiction.

Because property values change over time and because annual updates of these valuations are unlikely to be feasible, valuation variance exists within the system. Generally, the assessor updates a section of the county or other jurisdiction every year on a defined cycle and adds improved properties shortly after improvements are completed (e.g., construction of a new home on a previously empty parcel of land).

Equalization ratios (ratio of total assessed value to a municipality's total market value) are applied when a school district's boundaries cover more than one town or county jurisdiction. Some states, notably Washington State, use a market assessment study to indicate the variance from actual assessments to market conditions. This ratio is applied to each county's assessed valuation to equalize the variance of assessment and market changes across the state.

Typically, the assessor certifies to the tax district (school district) the total assessed value and the total taxable value of property within each taxing entity. Various classifications of property may alter its ultimate assessed valuation. For example, a homestead tax credit may be allowed by state law for residential housing so that the valuation is reduced from its full market value. Other exemptions may exist for certain industrial developments or for agricultural land that may otherwise increase in value due to its proximity to a city or town. These exemptions affect the overall taxable property assessments and influence tax rates.

The problem of utilizing fractions of actual value is clear in California, where Proposition 13 limits assessed value to the value of property in 1975-76, with increases limited to no more than two percent a year. Property can only be reassessed at market value when it is sold. As a result, the assessed value of most property is substantially below its market value. Since property taxes are limited to one percent of assessed value, there is a substantial difference between the taxes collected and potential tax collections if all property were assessed at its true market value.

In sum, superintendents and their chief fiscal officers, must know the overall taxable value of the district's property in order to properly predict tax rates and forecast property tax revenue for each budget year.

The property tax collection process

School budget years are set up to cover a defined fiscal year (July 1 to June 30 or perhaps September 1 to August 31). As noted earlier in this chapter, taxpayers often divide their payments into two halves. City and county government usually budget on a calendar year basis so their annual property tax revenue matches the tax collection year. This condition causes school district budgets to include property tax collections from two tax collection years. Property tax revenue for school districts will be collected from the fall half (or fraction) of one calendar year plus the spring half (or fraction) of the second calendar year.

This split year calculation makes reconciling a full school budget year of property tax revenue hard to accomplish without knowing the collection rate and amount collected in each half of the calendar year. Typically, spring collections are larger because some property owners pay all their taxes at once, saving the effort to pay again in the fall.

The assessor and district treasurer can provide the relative information on taxes collected. What is the trend in collections as a percentage of the total?

Is the percentage collected rising or falling? Are late payments as large as uncollected taxes? These factors will provide information about how to estimate property tax revenue in budget planning.

Extra care must be taken to label the collections properly to avoid confusion from this inherently complex determination. Knowing whether a budget amount is a calendar year, or a fiscal year number will help avoid this uncertainty, but it does introduce a potential source of confusion for school board members or members of the public who may not work with this issue frequently.

Property tax caps

Property tax payments are not typically adjusted based on the capacity of the taxpayer to pay the tax. Since the tax rate is uniformly applied, high income and low income or fixed income citizens may all be paying similar tax amounts. Renters and residential homeowners feel the impact of this reality the most (Baker, B.D., Green, P., & Richards, C.E. 2008, p. 62). This regressive tax system may cause some citizens to resist funding schools. A tension between property taxes as a significant source of school funds and taxpayer impacts continues to be evident in all states.

The potential for market conditions to cause assessed valuations to rise quickly adds to this tension. The upward pressure on property values complicates the ways to limit taxpayer exposure to tax increases. It is important to understand the state's specific tax cap legislation since it will have a major impact on the school district's budget preparation process.

Many states have a fixed tax rate for a portion of property tax and have consequently introduced ways to limit the growth in property taxes or introduced programs that provide relief to certain categories of taxpayers. Examples of tax relief programs, often referred to as circuit breakers, in many states include:

> **Senior Citizen Exemptions:** Based on age and income, a portion or all of a property's assessed valuation may be removed from the tax rolls until the property changes ownership.

Disabled Veterans: Taxpayers who are veterans or have a permanent service-connected disability may be exempt from a portion or all of property tax payments.

Low Income: A process that links income levels with a property tax exemption may require filing Federal tax returns with the county. This exemption is sometimes called a "circuit breaker."

Homestead Exemptions: Based on varying criteria, this exemption may be applied to all residential taxpayers and is sometimes a fixed relief amount or a reduction in assessed valuation.

Special Programs: A tax reduction for volunteer firefighters or other designated groups (e.g., New York's STAR rebate program). Some states allow taxpayers to direct a portion of their property taxes to a designated charity or not-for-profit organization (e.g., Arizona).

Total Revenue Cap: In systems where fixed tax rates are the norm, the local taxing jurisdiction may be limited by state law for how much total revenue can be raised compared to the previous fiscal period. A percentage growth rate in total revenue will cap taxes and suppress the tax rate (Burrows, p. 72).

Another method that may provide relief from property taxes is a process that enables an individual to refute the assessed value of her/his property. Once the assessment roll has been prepared, the taxpayer has a prescribed amount of time to challenge the assessment of the property. The grievance or appeal is reviewed by a tax appeal board and may result in an altered valuation.

If the request is denied, the taxpayer may seek judicial review (called a tax certiorari proceeding) in the court of the county where the property is located. An alternative streamlined procedure to review the assessment may be available for residential property. In various states, and among municipalities within states, successful assessment challenges may require the school district in which the property is located to refund excess taxes paid because of the over-assessment.

Property wealth among school districts

Addressing the variance in property wealth among school districts is a policy challenge for school finance. Because the variance in assessed valuation per pupil varies widely, taxpayers in high property wealth communities may apply a significantly lower tax rate to raise the same revenue as a poorer property wealth community. This inequity among school districts directly affects the ability of low property wealth communities to provide sufficient resources to support high quality educational opportunities for their students.

For example, consider two school districts with vastly differing property wealth. District A is an urban setting with considerable industrial, manufacturing and commercial property that is taxed as real property. While the district has many students, this significant property wealth doesn't generate very many students for the district. Dividing the district's total assessed valuation by the number of students results in a property value for each student of $500,000.

District B on the other hand, is mostly agricultural land with a growing suburban population. Housing construction has been growing but the agricultural land is assessed with an agricultural property valuation exemption. Very little commercial property exists in the district as people drive into the city for employment and other needs. The assessed valuation per pupil for District B is therefore $200,000 per pupil.

Given this scenario, the tax rate to raise $1000 to support educational programs for each student will vary considerably:

District A $2.00 per $1,000 assessed valuation will raise $1,000 for each student ($2 x 500).

District B $5.00 per $1,000 assessed valuation will raise $1,000 for each student ($5 x 200)

This discrepancy in tax rate (called taxpayer effort) is significant and will likely result in District B settling for a smaller tax levy to address taxpayers' ability to pay. In their case, a $2 per $1,000 tax rate will only generate $400 per student to support the school budget while it generates $1,000 for the students in District A.

To address this inherent funding challenge, state appropriations have increasingly factored into the state basic aid formula consideration for a property wealth adjustment. When states seek to manage the tension among taxpayers and education advocates in a fair and equitable manner, a tax levy equalization program funded by the state may be necessary. This structural funding inequity is also at the source of much state level school funding litigation.

Conclusion

Property taxes are the main source of revenue for school districts. However, the property tax continues to lose its appeal due to problems with assessment practices. According to Brimley and Garfield (2002):

> Present problems of property assessment are largely the result of the predominately political system under which taxation laws have been made and administered. Elected county, town, or township assessors, often not particularly well qualified for their responsibilities, face the difficult problems of raising assessments because of inflation or actual improvements in the property, keeping assessments fair and equitable among all property owners, deciding on the relative worth of different kinds of property, and other equally difficult problems. (p. 125)

Property valuations do not necessarily indicate the ability of the taxpayer to pay the taxes generated by the valuation. This disconnect has given rise to tax relief plans, especially for senior citizens on low fixed incomes and low-income families.

Despite this growing resistance, most states continue to rely on property taxes as a central funding source for the operation of its schools. Efforts to equalize the effects of assessment practices and ability to pay adjustments moderate the resistance.

School leaders must know both the history and the procedural mechanism for the assessment, collection and distribution of property taxes to effectively plan educational budgets.

Chapter 6

Accounting and Monitoring Fiscal Status

This section will help leaders learn to...
Understanding the purposes that accounting plays in school finance.
Determine how the structure of accounting allows for analysis of school operations.
Value the usefulness financial reporting gains from accounting activities.

Case Study

Several principals complain to Diane about the accuracy of the fiscal system. In particular, they are worried about their school budgets. As superintendent, Diane listens to these complaints with concern and asks for an analysis of the spending by school.

As she analyzes the data, she is surprised by irregularities that become obvious to her. She requests three additional years of spending history. When she receives it, she is even more confused because several schools spending seemed to go up and down for no reason.

Diane shows Stephanie, her CFO, the spreadsheets and asks, "What's going on with these schools?"

Stephanie seeks time to study the results. "I'll get back to you in a few days. I need to research why this occurred."

When Stephanie visits Diane later, she came prepared to apologize. "I'm sorry for the confusion. We've posted the summer purchases two different ways at some of the schools. Sometimes, when we closed the books, we charged it to the prior year and sometimes we accrued these purchases into the current year. These summer purchases are supposed to be shown in the year when they will be used, but with different individuals making entries, fiscal staff interpreted the data in different ways. I've made a spreadsheet showing the amounts correctly, and I have a note to check this whenever we close our books in the future so that we don't make the same mistake again. And I will work with the affected principals to explain what happened."

Diane shakes her head. "Thanks, I thought I was going crazy for a while. Now, we can figure out if the amount we're providing the schools is adequate for our students' needs."

If you were the superintendent...
Why is it important that there is consistency is fiscal reporting?
What should Diane do to ensure that accounting doesn't have the same type of problem in other areas? Should she be concerned?
What additional information will be needed and where might it be found?
What should Stephanie do to resolve this issue?
Should she explain the discrepancy to the school board or auditor?
What implications exist for grants?

School district accounting encompasses the procedures used to record, classify, and summarize expenditures and revenue from all district activities or events. Accounting records must be organized so that the data can be accessed and analyzed. The data are maintained to document the historical spending and revenue experience of the school district. Other assets and liabilities are also recorded in the general ledger and used to develop a district fiscal balance sheet.

The accounting function enables school districts to organize their revenues and expenditures for purposes of implementing their financial plan and to maintain accountability and accurate reporting. Reports and financial statements are prepared from accounting records. These reports reflect the results of activities as of a given date (Adams, B.K, Hill, Q.M., Lichtenberger, A.R., Perkins, J.A. & Shaw, P.S., 1967, p. 260).

School districts are required to adhere to Generally Accepted Accounting Practices (GAAP) that provide uniform guidelines for the recording and reporting financial activities of the school district. GAAP standards are established by:

a. the Governmental Accounting Standards Board (GASB), formed in 1984; and,
b. the Federal Accounting Standards Advisory Board (FASAB), formed in 1990 in relationship with the American Institute of Certified Public Accountants (AICPA)(seeWikipedia,https://en.wikipedia.org/wiki/Financial_Accounting_Standards_Board).

For more information regarding GAAP and other accounting technicalities, refer to Government Standards Accounting Board at www.gasb.org.

The accounting process organizes and summarizes financial information regarding the activities and the school district's financial obligations. Hentschke (1986) puts it succinctly: "Accounting is the means of measuring and reporting these obligations" (p. 246).

The annual financial statement contains data that reflect the school district's financial position, operating results, and cash flows for the fiscal year. These financial reports are used by diverse stakeholders to assess the district's financial activities.

The names and uses of various funds may vary among the states, but school districts generally report financial data according to the following governmental funds:

The Business Side of School Success

General Fund: The school district's primary operating fund that records most revenue receipts and expenses for the operation of the district.

Special Revenue Funds: These funds come from specific revenue sources, such as federal and state grants. The funds are required to be used for specific purposes, such as school lunch operations, school bus purchases, or federal grant programs such as Title 1.

Capital Projects Fund: These funds are used to account for the financial resources used to purchase land, acquire facilities, construct new facilities or refurbish existing facilities.

Debt Service Fund: These funds are used to pay the principal and interest on the school district's long-term debt.

Fiduciary Fund: This fund is used to account for fiduciary activities in which the school district acts as a trustee and does include such funds in its financial statements. Examples are funds for extra-curricular classroom clubs, associated student body functions, scholarship funds, or labor union welfare trusts.

Other funds: A variety of special purpose funds may be established by statute to address specific requirements or more closely monitor activity.

School districts must ensure the proper segregation of resources in each fund. Accountability must be maintained as each fund is its own fiscal entity with its own set of accounts recording expenses, revenue (including cash), related liabilities, and balances. Each fund has a specific purpose with specific regulations, usually recommended by the state education agency and the state auditor working together with school business officials.

The accounting function

The school district's budget is a financial plan that supports its educational mission and goals, and its accounting system is the method by which the district monitors the implementation of its financial plan. The budget serves as a spending limit for the district. Districts generally have flexibility to adjust the amounts within the total spending limit for its various departments and schools; expenditures must not exceed the total appropriation. The accounting structure, including line items and spending categories, is reflected in the budget and will later be used in auditing the system for legal, appropriate, and responsible spending.

David Thompson and Craig Wood (2001) describe five purposes for the use of accounting in school districts. The first purpose is to "set up a procedure by which all fiscal activities in a district can be accumulated, categorized, reported, and controlled" (p. 111).

The second function is to assess the alignment of the district's financial plan (budget) with the district's educational programs. An accounting system allows the district to manage the use of resources and to assess whether they are adequate to meet the needs of its programs.

The third function is related to the requirements on the state and federal levels for fiscal accountability. Since federal funds are distributed to local districts through the states, accounting and reporting procedures are required for accountability purposes, using uniform budget codes and accounting standards.

The fourth purpose for accounting is budget preparation. Accounting allows for the organization of information necessary for a year-to-year comparison of revenues and expenses and of current year actual expenditures and budget performance.

The final purpose of accounting is to provide proper fiscal controls and accountability, which, in turn, build public trust and confidence.

Accounting systems develop a data base of all spending and revenue transactions that allows accumulate of totals and aid in the comparison of current period elements to budgeted or prior year transactions. The data base facilitates analysis among departments, schools, functions, and programs.

For example, a request to purchase supplies and materials or to enter a contract for services could initiate a transaction. When a request is made, the purchase order process is used to record it and track its progress. When the request is approved, a purchase order is produced and sent to the vendor, and the school district becomes liable for payment when the goods are received. Accounting systems may require the funds to be encumbered or reserved once a purchase order is produced and approved.

The Business Side of School Success

The accrual basis of accounting requires a school district to recognize expenditures at the time the liability occurs. All transactions are entered into a journal, which contains the original accounting entries. The purchase order provides evidence regarding the transaction. The entry in the journal is posted to the proper accounts in the general ledger which contains all accounts. Each individual account in the general ledger contains all the pertinent data for the transactions; account number, date of transaction, description, and whether the transaction was a debit or credit (Ray, et al., 2005). A comparison of assets to the claims against the assets is the foundation of the district's financial condition (Hentschke, 1986).

Most school districts are required to use a standard system for classifying and coding accounting transactions. Specific codes are used to provide a standard format for recording and reporting financial transactions. This standardization allows comparisons among school districts and informs more detailed analysis of school expenditures and associated revenue. Computer software allows many of these accounting functions to emerge from the source documents and facilitates analysis, budget preparation, and fiscal status reporting.

For example, the General Fund may be categorized by program (including sub-programs), activities or functions, object of expenditure and location. Programs might include General or Basic Education, Special Education, Vocation Technical Education, Transportation, General Support Services, etc. Functions or activities could contain major work types such as business services, the superintendent's office, supervision of instruction, teaching, counseling, library services, insurance premiums, utilities, etc. Each function is designated by a function code.

Major objects within the function, such as salaries, supplies, contractual services, travel, equipment, etc., have designated object codes. Coding may also designate the location so various sites can receive similar reports for their facility.

Revenue sources are also provided specific, unique codes to allow them to be summarized over time.

Budget preparation practices should be aligned with the financial reporting standards to facilitate accurate financial monitoring and reporting.

Formal financial reporting

Financial reporting can be internal or external. Internal reports are used by management to monitor the school district's finances and to ensure compliance with GAAP. These reports vary in accordance with the needs of management. In most states external reporting is generally a legal requirement. Additional reporting within each fiscal year for management purposes is discussed in Chapter 7—Program Monitoring, Fund Balance, and Reserve Funds.

School districts are required to prepare an annual, audited financial report. This information is presented to the board of education, the public, the state education department, and in some cases a state comptroller office.

School districts generally use an independent certified public accountant or independent public accountant to prepare an audit of the school district finances. Moreover, the Federal Single Audit Act requires that school districts that expend more than $500,000 in federal funds prepare a single audit that must also be submitted to the specific state and federal agencies. The Federal audit may be conducted by the same process as the normal financial report.

School districts must include the following information in the annual audit report, in accordance with GAAP and GASB reporting standards:
1. Management Discussion and Analysis (MD&A)
2, Basic Financial Statements
    a. Government-wide financial statements
    b. Fund financial statements
    c. Notes to financial statements
    d. Required supplementary information other than MD&A

The Business Side of School Success

State audit requirements will vary and may be obtained by contacting the state audit agency. Also, see Chapter 10—Audits and Related Issues for a more complete discussion of the audit process.

Fiscal Stress Analysis

Use the annual balance sheet after closing the books for each year can be used to conduct a fiscal stress analysis. Such an analysis can be conducted by the staff and presented with a report to the school board on the status of the prior fiscal year finances. Such an effort aligns with the benchmarking process outlined in Chapter 17—Strategic Issues.

The State of New York's Office of the Comptroller developed a formal fiscal stress analysis system for local governments, including school districts. The system (https://www.osc.state.ny.us/files/local-government/fiscal-monitoring/pdf/system-basics.pdf) uses both fiscal and environmental indicators and creates separate 100 point scores using them as follows:

Financial Indicators
    Year-end Fund Balance
    Operating Deficits/Surpluses
    Cash Position
    Reliance on Short-Term Cash Flow Debt

Environmental Indicators
    Percent of Economically Disadvantaged Students
    Student-Teacher Ratio
    Teacher Turnover Rate
    Change in Property Value
    Budget Vote Approval Rate
    Percent of English Language Learners

This model provides a template for adaption to specific conditions in other states and school systems. Whether it is required by the state or not, it represents a prudent approach in concert with multi-fiscal year budget planning. These indicators provide examples that certainly might be modified to incorporate locally important criteria into the stress test.

Conclusion

School accounting requirements have evolved over the years in accordance with guidance from the Governmental Accounting Standards Board (GASB). It is important that accounting procedures and protocols are standardized to allow for accurate and consistent reporting that facilitates comparisons and analyses from year to year.

State agencies generally will oversee the accounting procedures used in school districts. They also provide guidance and standardized methods, such as a uniform accounting system to assist school districts in managing their finances and keeping accurate records of transactions. These procedures are also necessary to ensure that expenditures are made within legal limits as approved by the voters. Most, if not all, public school districts have computerized financial accounting systems in place to perform the many transactions and recordings that are required.

Accounting allows the school district to structure and organize the district's budget and implement its financial plan. It also provides the structure by which state and federal entities, as well as the board of education and citizens, can evaluate a school district's financial status. Accounting processes provide the necessary procedures and data to enable an independent, certified public accountant to conduct the district's annual financial audit.

Chapter 7

Program Monitoring, Fund Balance, and Reserve Funds

This section will help leaders learn to...
Identify characteristics of effective program monitoring.
Explore various forms of program monitoring.
Understand the oversight role of the superintendent.
See an example of program monitoring.
How to estimate the district's fund balance.

Case Study

When Virginia interviews to be superintendent, she promises the school board she will do a review of every major department the first year if they hire her. When she is selected, she remembers the commitment she made to the school board and puts this step into her plan for coming on board. At her first school board meeting, she introduces her plan. The plan is received favorably, including her concept to complete reviews of the major departments.

She meets with, Connie, the CFO, and shared this objective. Connie gives her a pained look, "I've been trying to do reviews every year, but the managers always put me off. They claim they are busy and tell me to wait."

Virginia asks everyone she interviews during the last weeks of summer to name a department or school that is well managed and one that isn't. Almost without exception, the one mentioned as struggling is Special Education. Even parents warn her about this program.

Virginia meets with Teresa, the special education administrator. "Teresa. I know that Special Education is a difficult area. Why do you think it was mentioned by the schools, parents, and central office functions as struggling?"

"I don't really know. Sure, we spend a lot, but it's an expensive area," Teresa told her. "I chalk it up to how different we are. No one seems to understand what we do and why we do it."

Virginia thinks about Teresa's answer. "I'll need to dig into this further. How about we monitor your department first. I promised the board I would do some and it makes sense to start with Special Education."

Teresa is immediately cautious, "I don't know if we'll be ready. We've got our December count for the feds to do. And we need to update IEPs for a new school year." Teresa looks very uncomfortable.

"Look, I don't mean to make your life more difficult, but we need to do monitoring so we can understand our needs and advocate for them." Virginia takes a deep breath, "I'll schedule you in for the middle of November, that's the longest I can wait."

Virginia works with Connie and gets a high-level assessment from her perspective. In the middle of November, she and Connie meet with Teresa. Virginia asks, "I don't see any plans to do summer school. How much did the program generate in revenue last summer?"

Teresa tells her, "It's too difficult to meet all the reporting requirements. We chose not to file last year."

Connie adds, "We've not done the reporting the last several years. We used to collect a quarter million dollars each summer."

"Why ever not?" Virginia is perplexed, "Are you telling me you didn't offer a summer program? I don't think that's legal."

"Oh, we offered a program." Teresa responds, "We don't have the time or the staffing to submit claims for reimbursement of the work. I'm certainly not going to make the staff do extra. They're tired and exhausted by summer."

Virginia closes her eyes. When she opens them, they are locked on Teresa, "I'm going to suspend this meeting for now. You have two weeks to do the following. Find out from the state if we can claim last summer's work. Then, I want you to do your best to get your hands on the materials we need to make a claim. Finally, I need a plan for how you will prepare the employees to go into next summer doing the reporting required by the state and federal governments."

Connie clears her throat, "I believe the state may allow us to go back three years."

Virginia continues speaking to Teresa, "This is an important program, but make no mistake. We won't be giving the state a free pass on the revenue because they've made it difficult for us to do."

Teresa looks defiant but swallows her anger. She responds meekly, "We will be ready."

If you were the superintendent...
    How do you view the efficacy of this meeting?
    What benefit do you think Virginia gains by being involved in the review?
    Would you be satisfied with the signal being sent to the departments and schools?
    Does Virginia's role change over time?
    What additional information will be needed and where might it be found?

The superintendent's role in program monitoring

Being up-to-date about the district's fiscal status is an important superintendent duty. Make program monitoring a priority for scheduling and include all members of the district's executive leadership team. Knowing whether budget estimates are "on target" and where variation is occurring allows maximum leadership time to prepare for program adjustments and allows time to alert the school board, all district personnel and the community in a timely manner.

Further, the superintendent must emphasize that required reports to state or federal agencies be completed on time and accurately. To accomplish this requirement, develop a calendar of report due dates and identify the administrator responsible for filing the report. Set up a tracking system to ensure required reports have been filed. When the superintendent reviews these reports before they are submitted, their importance is validated for district colleagues. Take care so this review does not cause any reports to be filed late; set up a default system to send it to the appropriate reporting agency on time even if you cannot review the report until later.

Regardless of district size, the superintendent must be a direct recipient of program monitoring reports. This review may be a summary level conference that is appropriate for the level of detail needed. District size will cause this level of detail to vary but it is important to stay abreast of the review and be in a position to decide if the corrective action plan meets district needs. For large districts this monitoring role might be delegated to a deputy with the understanding that unusual circumstances will be reported to the superintendent when encountered.

Sometimes, a new superintendent will discover that program monitoring is not embedded in the district's culture. The superintendent has an important role in initiating this effort. Departmental managers and supervisors will be reluctant to shirk this obligation if they see that it is a superintendent priority.

Developing the program monitoring approach

Use a simple, summary level layout (salaries, benefits, supplies, equipment, travel) of the budget to begin developing the program monitoring process. For example, look at summary salary and benefit levels or an analysis of various functions by program. Add layers of complexity to the analysis to fairly represent the fiscal status of the district and its programs and activities. We recommend avoiding the use of account codes at the beginning, so the fiscal concepts involved can be identified.

Adding account codes will add dimensions not readily apparent to the casual observer, such as the ability to sort and find cost centers when creating specialized reports. The fiscal team must possess or develop the knowledge and skill to accurately monitor any program or entity within the district. We recommend fiscal monitoring at least once each year for every program. Major programs or programs with challenges should be monitored more frequently. Ideally, the monthly review will help identify which programs need attention.

The program monitoring process

Fiscal monitoring goes by many names. It is often referred to as Budget Monitoring, Budget Status, or Budget Review because it is often shown as a variance to the budget. The name implies that this review is undertaken only for the budgeting or accounting employees. Avoid this perception.

The fiscal staff pulls together an analysis of what the department has spent, compares the results to prior year information, and compares it to the budgeted amount. This work can be charted, and the information standardized to clearly display the district's current fiscal status.

But to be effective and useful, program monitoring must include a step not controlled by the fiscal department. It requires that the program administrator (or school administrative team) add their knowledge about what is planned in the future. This information is not held by the fiscal department and can only be shared by a knowledgeable program administrator or their staff.

One additional element is needed to make sense of the current fiscal status. The annual budget needs to be divided into monthly allotments. These allotments are predictions about how the level of resources the department or school will consume each month.

Many spending considerations occur in phases causing monthly variations that should influence this allotment making process. Consequently, creating monthly allotments is not a simple exercise of dividing the annual budget by twelve and multiplying by the number of months that have occurred.

Who should turn the annual budget into a workable plan that can be monitored month-by-month? Answering this important question requires superintendent action. Ideally, accurate allocation decisions will best be done collaboratively with fiscal staff and the program staff or school leaders.

The allotment process must be applied to both the spending and the revenue side of the budget. To be effective for future actions, knowledge about what is planned in the future needs to be compared to the anticipated resources that will be available. Knowing that sufficient revenue is anticipated to address planned spending is important; this step is significant to identifying if a shortfall in revenue is possible.

Whether a projected shortfall or surplus exists, the next step in a program review requires that the department or school enunciate the actions planned to mitigate the situation. The district will benefit when such plans are elevated to the executive level and shared with others as needed. Program monitoring may appear mundane but is overcome by the discovery of a potential problem so it can be addressed early.

Regular fiscal oversight and reporting builds trust by providing the superintendent and the public through the school board presentation with timely fiscal information. Make a clear, conscious assignment of responsibility for timely preparation of this fiscal report and follow through with the scheduled reports.

The Business Side of School Success

Revenue forecasting and monitoring efforts are critical components of efficient fiscal management. Carefully managing revenue estimates and evaluating monthly receipts compared to estimates is an important strategy to avoid a fiscal crisis that would not bode well for students, community, school board and the education leadership team. Such monitoring won't eliminate the potential for a crisis, but the earlier it is noted the more capable the response can be.

According to Parla (2020), school superintendents should take these steps to further their knowledge about school finance:

1. Periodic meetings between the chief business official and other appropriate personnel, i.e., human resources, transportation, special education, auditors (internal, external, and claims), and the district treasurer are essential to monitor the financial health of the school district. Regular, public reports about the fiscal condition of the district are important and sometimes required by state law.

2. If necessary, retain a consultant who specializes in school finance to provide an independent review of district procedures and systems. Reach out to agencies that provide support to school districts (e.g., the regional educational service agency or the state affiliate for the American Association of School Administrators). Also, conferring with colleagues who have strong school finance backgrounds provides valuable local knowledge and perspective.

3. Finally, and perhaps most importantly, keep the school board and educational community apprised of the district's financial condition. Strong, timely communication with stakeholders demonstrates transparency and builds vital trust. Remember: no surprises.

An example of program monitoring

It's mid-November. The school fiscal year began in August. With three months of data, it is time to evaluate how the district is doing. You ask the CFO to do a fiscal review and meet with you to go over the budget.

The CFO brings you a printout showing the expenses to date, plus any accruals and encumbrances that have been entered into the system. The report shows salary, benefits, supplies and materials, and equipment broken down for each school and every major department. Shown this way, the report is three inches thick. It looks like this:

General Fund: encumbered report run on November 17. Program A.

Budget Item	Budget	Expenditures	Future Spending (est.)	Balance
Admin Salaries	150,000	60,000		90,000
Ad. Benefits	30,000	12,000		18,000
Cert Salaries	1,000,000	400,000		600,000
Cert Benefits	200,000	80,000		120,000
Class Salaries	400,000	160,000		240,000
Class Benefits	80,000	32,000		48,000
Supplies	150,000	100,000		50,000
Equipment	20,000	0		20,000
Total	2,030,000	844,000		1,186,000

The above report is a puzzle. The missing piece is the Estimated Future Spending, which won't show on any report.

You finally ask the CFO, "How do I make sense of this?" The CFO tells you, "The programs and schools do their own forecasting. We've always held them accountable if they overspend." This response is weak, leaving the organization subject to too much uncertainty and the risk of overspending.

So how can someone accurately estimate the planned expenditures for you? Several different methods might work, but one important method would have the fiscal department encumbering all the payroll information. This action would help estimate the fiscal obligations for most of the staffing.

Once this addition is made (see below), many questions will remain, so it will be important to ask the CFO to talk to the program administrator. Here are some questions either the CFO or you can ask questions like these:

- What is planned…short-term and long-term?

The Business Side of School Success

- When will you be able to finalize your plans?
- What unexpected expenditures happened last year?

- Are these expenses likely to repeat themselves?
- How do you control hourly employees and estimate their costs?

General Fund: encumbered report run on November 18. Program A.

Budget Item	Budget	Expenditures	Future Spending (est.)	Balance
Admin Salaries	150,000	60,000	100,000	-10,000
Ad. Benefits	30,000	12,000	19,000	-1,000
Cert Salaries	1,000,000	400,000	590,000	10,000
Cert Benefits	200,000	80,000	118,000	2,000
Class Salaries	400,000	160,000	245,000	-5,000
Class Benefits	80,000	32,000	47,000	1,000
Supplies	150,000	100,000	39,000	11,000
Equipment	20,000	0	16,000	4,000
Total	2,030,000	844,000	1,174.000	12,000

The Estimated Future Spending column is completed. You now have some confidence that the budget is correct, that planned expenditures are within parameters, and leadership has a firm handle on this program.

Turn your attention to the next program and repeat the process for all programs in the district.

Cash Flow Analysis

The importance of having funds available to meet current obligations has been referenced in discussing the development of the budget (Chapter 3—Budget Development Supports the Mission) and in planning the property tax levy (Chapter 5—Property Taxes: What You Need to Know). It is also an essential component of capital projects management (Chapter 16—Capital Projects and Bonds). Forecasting future revenue and expenses on a monthly basis is also discussed in Chapter 8—Assessing School District Financial Health.

A sample forecast of revenues and disbursements by month is included in Appendix A. This form of analysis is an essential planning tool and underlies the important considerations for identifying the district's fund balance which likely consists mostly of available funds held in cash or investments.

The cash flow analysis is useful for determining how much can be invested in short term investments and how much must remain available with the treasury institution for payment of each month's required disbursements for payroll, benefits, and accounts payable.

Fund balance management

Public school district budgetary appropriations close at the end of the fiscal year. The fund balance represents the difference between expenditures and revenue for the fund plus other possible adjustments to general ledger accounts.

School districts, usually by action of the school board, may establish restricted funds by designating a portion of the fund balance for a specific purpose. Reserve fund categories vary by state. Examples of typical restricted reserve funds include:

> **Carry Forward Reserve:** Funds designated to reduce the subsequent fiscal year's expenditures (e.g., carry forward funds to reduce the amount to be raised from taxes).
> **Repair Reserve:** Used to pay for repairs of facilities or any equipment, which are unanticipated and therefore not done on an annual basis. Voter approval is required to fund this reserve and to make expenditures from this reserve fund.
> **Retirement Contribution Reserve:** Used to fund employer retirement contributions.
> **Workers' Compensation Reserve:** Used to fund compensation claims. This activity funds the administration of a self-insurance program in accordance with Article 2 of the Workers' Compensation Law.

The Business Side of School Success

Unemployment Insurance Reserve: Used to reimburse the State Unemployment Insurance Fund for payments made to persons filing unemployment claims.

Insurance Reserve: Used to pay for liability insurance and other insurance claims except for claims covered by other types of insurance, such as health, life or accident insurances.

Reserve for Tax Reduction: If a school district sells real property, the proceeds may be used for tax reduction, usually on a gradual basis.

Reserve for Debt Service: When a school district sells real property, this reserve may be established to pay off any remaining debt at the time of the sale.

Property Loss and Liability Reserve: These resources are used to pay for property loss and liability claims. This reserve is often only used by districts with a population greater than 125,000 students or city school districts. These reserves may be limited to 3% of the annual budget.

Tax Certiorari Reserve: Used to pay for tax certiorari claims resulting from a change in the assessed valuation of property. The amount allowed to be reserved must be deemed reasonable based on known, outstanding claims. Funds not used in the same year must be returned to the General Fund.

Insurance Recoveries Reserve: Used at the end of the fiscal year to account for unexpended proceeds of insurance recoveries.

Reserve for Encumbrances: When goods and services have been ordered and not received, or if the school district has not been invoiced by the end of the fiscal year, this reserve is used to encumber the funds necessary to pay the obligations which are carried over into the next fiscal year.

Reserve for Inventories: Used to reserve any portion of the fund balance that has not been made available for appropriation.

Employee Benefit Accrued Liability Reserve: Used to reserve funds for the payment of accrued employee benefits. For example, when employees resign or retire, they may be entitled, according to contract, to receive payments for unused sick or vacation days, or other employee benefits.

Capital Reserve: This reserve may be established by voter approval and the expenditures from the reserve must also be approved by the voters. It is used to pay for any capital projects or for purposes requiring the issuance of bonds.

It is important that school districts establish the appropriate restricted funds so that they are prepared to meet unexpected financial obligations or payments that may not be anticipated. For example, if a commercial property has its assessed valuation lowered through a successful court appeal, the school district may be required to refund the back taxes. Also, if many employees retire at one time, having dedicated reserves to fund their benefit payments in accordance with the collective bargaining agreements will avoid serious budget constraints.

The unrestricted fund balance provides the cash and other assets that will be used to manage the monthly variation between revenue and disbursements. A portion of this unrestricted reserve may be assigned for emergencies and/or unanticipated revenue losses. Depending upon various state laws or regulations, limits may exist for the size of the undesignated, unrestricted fund balance as a percentage of upcoming year's budgeted expenditures.

Estimating the fund balance

Diverse stakeholders will be interested in the anticipated fund balance for the end of each fiscal year. Bond rating agencies often view this data point as an indicator of prudent fiscal management. Employee group leaders may see fund balances as accessible funds during negotiation of the next labor contract. Patrons and the school board will see the viability of planning for emergencies embedded in meeting fund balance expectations. These often competing expectations demand care when making projections about the fiscal year ending fund balance.

When preparing monthly allotments for both expenditures and revenue, the monthly resources available rely upon the beginning fund balance. Fund balance is the difference between expenditures and revenues. Forecasting this balance is vital in budget development (see Chapter 3—Budget Development Supports the Mission and Chapter 4—Revenue: An Integral Component of the Budget). Monthly tracking of the available resources after obligations are

The Business Side of School Success

addressed is important to assure short-term coverage of expenses. Appendix A is a sample of how this tracking system might be presented on a monthly basis.

Examining the net fund balance will reveal whether sufficient resources are available for future spending actions. Identifying the beginning fund balance will occur after the prior fiscal year books have been closed and reconciled.

· Each month, a review of the fund balance in each fund is vital to the overall fiscal health of the district. Adding monthly revenue and subtracting monthly accrued expenses will provide a monthly indicator of fund balance, or resources available for the future months. This fund balance calculation should be reconciled with the cash on hand with the district's banker.

It may be helpful to review several years of historical data for comparison purposes. This review provides context and another reference point for the current status of the fund balance. Preparing a graph to track monthly fund balance provides a quick, valuable reference point that incorporates current behavior in comparison to prior year behavior. For simplicity, only a one year example of tracking fund balance is shown below.

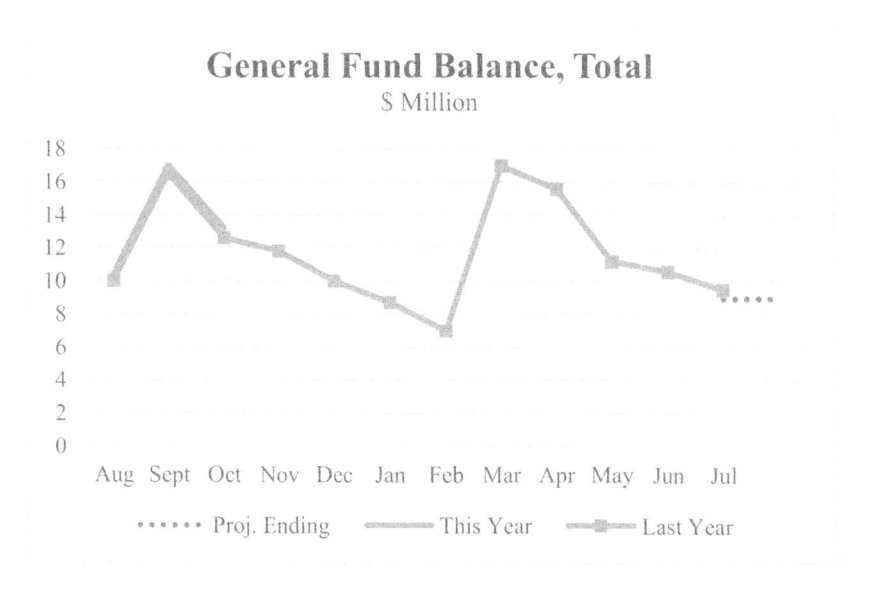

General Fund Balance, Total
$ Million

(Note: Each state has unique revenue patterns caused by state allocations, the collection calendar for property tax levies, and federal reimbursements. For this reason, actual district experience may not look like this example.)

What can be interpreted from this graph? First, note that the ending fund balance is projected to be slightly lower when this year ends. With three months experience, this district seems to be favorably meeting or exceeding its projecting ending fund balance. By April, actual data will have been posted so few months of forecast data will remain. At that point, confidence in the actual ending fund balance will improve.

As the fiscal year ends, some districts consider decisions about using any contingency funds to accomplish special or one-time projects before the fiscal year is over. Alternatively, if by January the review shows conditions to be worse than expected, time exists to implement a hiring slowdown, freeze spending by departments and/or possibly even schools, or avoid major investments planned for the second half of the year. Care should be taken to ensure any plans and steps are carefully thought out and explained to the staff, the school board, and the community.

Conclusion

Fiscal monitoring requires thoughtful effort and guidance from the superintendent and collaboration with fiscal and program leaders. Set clear expectations and adhere to scheduled review dates. Keep informed by receiving regular status reports, conducting fiscal reviews of each program during the school year, and asking questions along the way. This effort is worthy of leadership commitment because it improves certainty that unexpected (unbudgeted) expenditures and/or revenue shortfalls will be known well enough in advance so appropriate modifications can be initiated to sustain the school district's core educational mission.

Chapter 8

Assessing School District Financial Health

This chapter will help leaders learn to...
Identify why it is necessary to assess the district's financial health.
Know the key indicators and ratios that should be examined to determine the financial health of the school system.
Apply key indicators and other metrics to measure financial health.
Locate where to find the data designed to understand the district's fiscal health.

Case Study

Teddy is beginning his first year as school superintendent in a large public suburban school district serving pre-k – 12 students. During the interview process the school board and the search consultant did not discuss much about the school district's financial status.

However, Teddy researched to find out as much as he could about the financial condition of the school district. He asked questions about the district's financial condition during the interview process, but the answers he received were general and somewhat evasive.

Teddy really wanted to land his first superintendent position, so he didn't pursue the evasive responses to his questions. Still, knowing that he would face some fiscal challenges, Teddy accepted the position when it was offered. Teddy did not want to have any financial issues surface when he was too far into his new leadership role, so he needed to delve into the school district's finances on day one.

If you were the superintendent...
Where should Teddy begin his analysis of the school district's finances?
Who should he talk to?
What are the important data he should be concerned with?
What reports should he request?
How should he go about assessing the competency of the business office staff?

As spelled out in the previous chapter, assessing the school district's financial health should be conducted at planned intervals to detect issues and problems that may not be apparent. This process relies on current conditions to avoid the later emergence of fiscal surprises and identify systems flaws or leverage points that improve efficiency and accuracy of school operations.

A first, important step is scheduling monthly meetings with the district's chief business officer to discuss the overall fiscal condition of the school district. Create a clear understanding that a monthly fiscal status report will be central to this meeting; other topics will certainly emerge, but never avoid timely review of the district's current fiscal status.

Schedule these meeting closely after the CFO receives the latest monthly revenue report. During these meetings, also review the key messages about the district's fiscal status the CFO will present to the school board. Rehearse what will be said about the implications of the new information about the district's financial status. Be sure the CFO understands that transparency is the highest priority. With an overview introduction by the superintendent, the CFO will frame the board's understanding of fiscal information in alignment with overall leadership goals.

Working from a shared set of data and the district's current fiscal status allows expanded conversations that will include meeting, at an appropriate time, with the district's auditors to ascertain their independent perspective on district finances and procedures (see Chapter 10—Audits and Related

Issues) for a more complete treatment of this topic. Sometimes, it is also necessary to engage legal counsel in discussions of fiscal matters (see Chapter 13—Legal Counsel) for a more complete treatment of this topic.

These regular financial review meetings provide an opportunity to examine areas that are working well and areas where improvements will be required. This work builds on the program monitoring work described in Chapter 7—Program Monitoring, Fund Balance, and Reserve Funds.

Seek to create a climate of trust. Use the analysis of fiscal data to support decision-making. For example, establishing reasonable reserve fund levels, providing students with the programs and services they require to be successful, and addressing infrastructure needs all rely on a sound fiscal decision-making process. These efforts build efficiency and reduce costs in the long run. They also develop a foundation for trust in the district leadership, a necessary condition for focusing on student achievement.

Further, a routine set of fiscal status meetings supports a foundation for the development of an effective, mission-driven, multi-year financial plan. According to Everett, Lows and Johnson (1996), the following questions (1-14) will help with this assessment and provide direction in developing the multi-year financial plan:

1. **Does the school district need to use short-term borrowing?**

This behavior may indicate a pending fiscal problem. To answer that question, conduct an analysis to determine the adequacy of the district's cash flow by forecasting monthly expenditure and revenue expectations to simulate what may be expected to occur. Use the allotment process described in Chapter 6—Accounting and Monitoring Fiscal Status.

Does the district have enough cash on hand to pay bills in a timely manner during the low revenue months? Has the school district been notified by banks that limits have been placed on borrowing? If cash flow analysis (see an example in Appendix A) reveals deficits, develop a plan to improve reserve funds to adequate levels by a specific date.

Generally, fund balances and cash on hand are used to avoid short-term borrowing, but such actions may occasionally be necessary. If the answer to this question is yes, investigate why this action was taken. Has the credit rating of the district been reduced? Has the district previously failed to pay back loans in a timely manner or is it at risk of doing so now? Develop a plan to avoid this condition.

2. **Have year-end fund balances decreased or increased over the past three years?**

Decreasing fund balances may be a sign that revenue and/or expenditure estimates have been inaccurate or are out of alignment with each other. When actual spending exceeds revenue or when revenue doesn't materialize as planned, a decrease in the fund balance to meet financial obligations occurs. If the fund balances are increasing over time, determine the source of this growth. Was this outcome planned? If performance is significantly at variance with plans, improvements to budgeting assumptions must be initiated.

3. **Have budgeted expenditures consistently exceeded budgeted revenues?**

If yes, the district has been experiencing annual operating budget deficits which means inaccurate projections of revenues and/or expenditures. Such a condition requires alterations in funding levels to establish the proper balance between revenue and expenses.

4. **Is the school district involved in pending litigation that could have an adverse effect on the district's programs?**

Pending or emerging litigation and/or other forms of claims related to accidents, personnel complaints, special education, or civil rights issues may indicate the need for fiscal adjustments that could alter district priorities. Set proper reserves for such issues to avoid a significant claim interfering with district programs in a given fiscal year.

The Business Side of School Success

5. **Has cash flow changed over the past three years?**

Fluctuation in cash available by month could signal a problem with inaccurate revenue budgeting or changing expenditure activity. Perform a month-to-month evaluation of cash flow (see Chapter 6—Accounting and Monitoring Fiscal Status and Appendix A) to identify minimum levels of cash necessary to avoid short-term borrowing activity.

6. **Have expenditures per pupil increased or decreased over the past three years?**

Expenditures per pupil indicate the amount of approved operating expenses are needed to educate each student. Compare this trend with other local school districts of similar size and demographics and to state averages.

7. **Have payments to vendors been delayed due to cash flow shortages?**

If this form of delay occurs, a budget planning or cash management problem may be the underlying cause. One of the important reasons for reserves is to make sure vendors are paid in a timely manner. If cash flow appears adequate, a review of business office processes may be required to understand the cause of the delays. Apply best practices to improve performance.

8. **Has revenue from local sources decreased? State sources?**

It is important to stay connected with the monthly status of revenue sources, especially state and federal funding (see Chapter 6—Accounting and Monitoring Fiscal Status).

Monitor local economic conditions. If the economy weakens, a negative impact on funding allocations to schools could develop. Keep your "ear to the ground." Participate in local business organizations and the state professional administrators' association for up-to-date information. Work to build relationships with elected officials at the state and local levels to influence their actions and proposals related to school district programs and functions.

9. At what rate has the cost of employee benefits been changing?

Salaries and benefits are a significant source of budget increases. Review collective bargaining agreements with your business official, legal counsel, and those conducting the negotiations on behalf of the school board to ensure increases are accurately considered during the budget planning process. Gather historical information to be prepared for future collective bargaining negotiations. This assessment should be collaboratively completed by your human resources and business offices and shared with all involved in negotiations on behalf of the school district.

Chapter 12—Human Resource Leadership provides a more in-depth identification of issues and relationships to monitor.

10. Has the school district used its fund balance to meet annual expenditure requirements?

This behavior indicates expenditures have not been matched with overall revenues, possibly over several fiscal years. This practice is unsustainable and should be identified along with plans to modify the district's budget behavior.

11. Have the district's buildings and grounds (infrastructure) been maintained? Do significant needs require attention?

Meet with your facilities director to get information about the status of day-to-day maintenance of your building and grounds. Is this area adequately staffed? Overstaffed? Does a deferred maintenance list exist?

The district should have methods and procedures in place to ensure adequate upkeep of buildings and grounds. Annual maintenance must be funded by each budget cycle to avoid a growing list of deferred maintenance.

Meet with the facilities director (and possibly an architect or facility planner) to assess the condition of your schools and other buildings. Prepare a building condition analysis report and use it to prepare a capital plan if one is not already in place. Identify areas in need of improvements: windows, flooring, roofing, doors, blacktop and concrete, fields, boilers, HVAC systems, etc.

Chapter 15—School District Operations outlines issues for examination and attention.

12. Is student enrollment projected to increase or decrease?

Enrollment projections are necessary for both short-term and long-term strategic planning, including budget planning. Use prior enrollment data enhanced by an examination of regional demographic factors and community economic conditions. Consider hiring specialized assistance in student enrollment projections, especially if staff-based efforts have not been as accurate as needed.

Numerous issues outside the control of the school district will typically influence the enrollment trend. New technology may alter the number of workers necessary for long-standing local employer. Likewise, the emergence of new technology industries may be on the horizon using vacated manufacturing space. A significant issue like the Covid-19 pandemic intensified and confounded enrollment forecasting approaches.

Regardless of the cause, school leaders must monitor local, national, and increasingly international conditions to determine their potential impact on community school enrollment levels.

13. Are resources adequate to meet the academic needs of students?

Do gaps exist in providing adequately for the needs of your students? Make sure the district aligns its resource allocation plan to ensure programs are adequately and equitably supported. Use the program monitoring tools outlined in this chapter to modify or adjust actions to assure this resource alignment.

14. Are changes pending in state or federal regulations or laws that may require additional expenditures?

Be sure to monitor activities on both the state and federal levels to assess potential impact on the school district. What new initiatives are being discussed by the legislators? Will new unfunded mandates potentially be created? Local and state professional associations will be helpful in keeping you and your leadership team informed.

Prepare a summary report on recently passed legislation that identifies the positive and negative impact on the district's operations. Be sure to identify when these impacts will occur. Additionally, the school district's legal counsel may be asked to disseminate advisory reports regarding the changes in education law and regulations enacted or on the horizon.

Factors impacting the financial condition of school districts

Many different ratios can be used to analyze the financial health of a school system. Short, medium and long-range indicators must be used to conduct an effective and comprehensive assessment. Check with the state's education department and/or the state comptroller's office to identify the various ratios used to assess the health of school districts in the state.

While a variety of different metrics/ratios may be used for this purpose, the following are some common measures:

1. A school district's financial health can be measured by its ability to meet its obligations that have been planned and those that result from emergencies without disrupting the educational program. Measures of financial stability include the school district's fund balance as a percent of its adopted expenditure budget for the General Fund and the ratio of assets to liabilities, among others. Compare this information with county or statewide averages to get a good sense of your school district's position. Specific targets for such ratios will vary based on the district's tolerance for risk (Everett, et al., 1996).

The amount of unreserved, undesignated fund balance may be limited by state statute or by school board policy. An unreserved, undesignated (different terminology may be used such as unreserved, unallocated) fund balance close to zero is an indication that insufficient funds may exist to cover necessary expenses. Check state regulations and review historical data to identify an appropriate fund balance target.

When considering a bond issue or planning to obtain voter approval for such a bond issuance, the district's historical management of fund balances will be a consideration in the bond rating. A low bond rating translates into higher long-term interest rates for the bonds. Consistent management of the fund balance in a 3% to 6% range indicates thoughtful budget planning and cash management, two important tools in communicating solid fiscal leadership and justification for a sound bond rating.

2. Deficits result when expenditures exceed revenues and deplete the fund balance or other reserve funds. Review these data for at least three years to identify the district's trend. If expenditures consistently exceed revenues, a gap is created that requires the school district to use its fund balance to meet its financial obligations.

   When this action is intentional, programs and services may be preserved. This practice will reduce fund balance and create the potential for a higher than normal tax increase to maintain programs or the need for future reductions in programs that directly impair services to students and/or related school district operations.

   A budget deficit exists when expenditures exceed the voter or board approved expenditure amount, even if revenue is available to fund the excess expense. The governing board must adopt a revised or extended appropriation level to address this issue. Unaddressed, this issue will create an "over-spent" budget and audit or other legal issues for the district and its officers.

3. Fund equity is the difference between assets and liabilities. Fund equity includes reserved and unreserved fund balances. Reserved fund balances

are resources dedicated for specific uses such as encumbrances and employee payments for compensated absences. Unreserved fund balances are either designated for subsequent year's expenditures, thereby reducing the amount to be raised in taxes, or undesignated for use to manage cash flow variances.

4. The ratio of assets to liabilities, often called the current ratio, measures a school district's ability to pay its current obligations, including its ability to pay bills in a timely manner. The ratio is determined by dividing the district's assets by its liabilities. The standard target ratio is 2:1.

5. The balance sheet shows the school district's items that comprise the district's assets and liabilities and resulting fund balances. It is important to track the elements that summarize into the balance sheet to manage the school district's fund balance. Downward trends may indicate that the district is using its surplus to meet its financial obligations, but a review of the component parts of the balance sheet will indicate sources of the trend.

6. Two ratios that are used to monitor the district's financial soundness are derived from the balance sheet: the Operating Efficiency Ratio and the Ratio of Liabilities to Fund Balance. A more complete identification of key ratios that are derived from the balance sheet is located in Appendix B. Review these items with your business official and annual auditor.

Where are these data?

Several documents contain data to assist in analyzing your school district's financial health: budget appropriation status reports, financial statements, monthly treasurer's reports, cash flow reports, state and federal aid reports, and other revenue reports. These reports are derived from the accounting system and should be reconciled to the monthly financial statement(s) from the bank or district treasurer. Develop charts to compare data over time to assist in making projections for multiple years as part of the school district's main strategic plan.

Forecasting status

It is essential to develop long range financial plans as part of the school district's strategic plan. Most long-range financial plans rely upon three or four years of actual data. Historical data is useful to determine trends and should be used as starting points to project data for future years.

Looking forward requires examining current economic conditions and future forecasts that may affect both revenues and expenditures. For example, federal and state economic forecasts could alter revenue trends, since state and federal funding relies on the economy of the nation which impacts the state's ability to raise revenues such as sales tax and income tax. The prices of goods and services in an inflationary economy will place upward pressure on expenditure projections. Multi-year employee contract commitments with collective bargaining units and contracts for services must also be reviewed when making projections.

Revenue and expenditure projections, annual deficits or surpluses, reserve funds and fund balances are key elements of a financial plan. Multi-year financial planning requires the projection of these components for three to four years.

Projections help to determine the school district's financial status in terms of delivering services for operations and instructional programs. The projections must be weighed against the community's likely ability or willingness to support its schools through taxation. The trends that emerge will help the leadership advise the school board about plans to meet the needs of students and maintain community support for the school programs. Update plans to annually address recent experience, emerging activity, and anticipated new developments.

Conclusion

Wise school superintendents realize that they are responsible for the financial choices and viability of the school system. Still, many external factors that affect these conditions are beyond the superintendent's control. Consequently, building effective fiscal monitoring tools into the routine practices of the school system will alert leadership about issues that may require modification to plans or new responses to emerging conditions.

Strong educational programs focused on students and their success require resources. Both internal trust and community trust are enhanced when people see that careful planning, diligent monitoring and thoughtful adjustments are made in a timely manner.

Chapter 9

Co-Curricular Activities

This chapter will help leaders learn to...

Understand the policies, regulations, law and accounting procedures, including cash management regarding co-curricular activities.

Identify the characteristics of co-curricular activities including clubs and other student organizations.

Maintain and control these activities.

Know with whom to meet regarding the review and approval of activities fund policies and procedures.

Case Study

Jorge is the superintendent of a 12,000 student school district consisting of two high schools, two middle schools and ten elementary schools. The Art Club is a popular student co-curricular activity in one high school. Twenty-five students regularly participated in club functions which culminated with an elaborate, popular art exhibition each year.

After a successful annual show and exhibition, some parents complained that students had paid to attend a regional art show in the nearby city, but the trip had not taken place. The students were told their payments for attendance would not be refunded since the club's account was nearly zero.

Parents attended a school board meeting to vociferously voice their concern. This protest led to an audit of the club's accounts and revealed that procedures had not been followed and accounting for the travel funds was not properly managed. To make matters worse, it was discovered that the Art Club was actually sitting on a large balance, hidden by the practice of making activities for each new year start with a zero account balance. Parents were furious, wondering what had happened. By this time, the trip to the city had come and gone. Some parents were demanding that a makeup trip to another city be scheduled.

Jorge is not familiar with procedures for co-curricular activities and even worse, the business official viewed monitoring the fund's activities and procedures as a low priority. The school board is disappointed, and some members hold the superintendent accountable for this debacle. The school board is in the process of completing the annual evaluation of the superintendent, and Jorge fears this issue will have a big impact on his evaluation.

This incident could not have occurred at a worse time.

If you were the superintendent...
How would you approach this problem?
With whom would you meet to determine if proper procedures are in place?
What policies, regulations, and procedures would you propose to avoid the occurrence of another issue like the art students experienced?
What orientation and training expectations might help avoid problems like the art students experienced?
Would a mid-year audit of all extra-curricular activities make sense?
What additional information will be needed and where might it be found?
Should the superintendent set new expectations for carryover funds?

Co-curricular activities

Public school districts typically provide co-curricular or extra-curricular activities beyond the normal school day curriculum. These activities are generally approved, school-related activities that take place outside regular school hours. They encompass a wide range of student clubs and organizations as well as district-directed activities, some of which are connected to inside the school day courses of study.

Activity funds (also known as Associated Student Body funds) are generally established to manage monies used for these student activities. Student activity funds are fiduciary and associated with student organizations such as art clubs, chess clubs, foreign language clubs, school store, etc. District activity funds are considered special revenue funds and include activities such as athletics, book fairs, music programs, school plays, etc.

Parent or community based booster clubs provide support for certain co-curricular activities (e.g., the band, athletics, etc.). These clubs are not subject to school district control or regulation, but they must be monitored to assure that they adhere to appropriate means and methods for supporting school district co-curricular activities.

Characteristics

Classification of what activities constitute extra- or co-curricular activities will vary from state to state. It is essential that proper procedures for accounting for funds provided to or raised for extra or co-curricular purposes. Both student activity funds and district activity funds are reported in the school district's financial statements and are therefore also part of the annual financial audit process.

Over the years, unique organizations have attempted to be treated as "extra-curricular" endeavors even though they may not be connected directly to the school. Controversial situations and court rulings led to the development of federal regulations. The U.S. Department of Education (National Center for Education Statistics (NCES), 2003), provides the following clarification for schools designing policies for the management of these programs and the subsequent funding associated with them:

- If a federally funded public secondary school allows at least one non-curriculum-related student group to meet on school premises during non-instructional time, it has created a "limited open forum," the school may not deny the same access for similarly situated clubs on the basis of the content of the clubs' speech.

- "Access" refers not only to physical meeting spaces on school premises, but also to recognition and privileges afforded to other groups at the school, including, for example, the right to announce club meetings in the school newspaper, on bulletin boards, or over the public-address system. Non-instructional time is "time set aside by the school before actual classroom instruction begins or after actual instruction ends," and covers student meetings that take place before or after school as well as those occurring during lunch, "activity periods," and other non-instructional periods during the school day.

- The Supreme Court defines a curriculum-related student group as one that "directly relates" to the body of courses offered at a school. A student group directly relates to a school's curriculum "if the subject matter of the group is actually taught, or will soon be taught, in a regularly offered course; if the subject matter of the group concerns the body of courses as a whole; if participation in the group is required for a particular course; or if participation in the group results in academic credit." According to the Supreme Court (Board of Education v. Mergens, 496 U.S. 226, 236 (1990)), a "French club would directly relate to the curriculum if a school taught French in a regularly offered course or planned to teach the subject in the near future.".

- Schools retain the right to exclude groups that are directed, conducted, controlled, or regularly attended by non-school persons.

- Non-curricular student groups may have faculty sponsors without compromising the requirement that they are student-initiated. "The assignment of a teacher, administrator, or other school employee to a meeting for custodial purposes does not constitute sponsorship of the meeting."

- Schools retain authority to ban unlawful groups, maintain discipline and order on school premises, protect the well-being of students and faculty, assure that students' attendance at meetings is voluntary, and restrict groups that materially and substantially interfere with the orderly conduct of educational activities. But the Act does not permit schools to ban groups or suppress student speech based on unpopularity of the message or on unfounded fears that the group may incite violence or disruption. Where the material and substantial interference is caused not by the group itself but by those who oppose the group's formation or message, the disruption will not justify suppressing the group.

Maintaining and controlling co-curricular activity funds

The accounting of district sponsored co-curricular activities funds is complicated by the number and turnover of students and staff involved in these activities and programs. Student activities frequently involve cash transactions generated from snacks, ticket, and/or merchandise sales for athletic events, theatre productions, and other special programs, receipts and disbursements. Therefore, the chances for errors in mishandling cash can occur and may lead to fraud. It is essential that school leaders ensure proper procedures and policies are in place to safeguard and properly account for these funds.

It is necessary to ensure that clear, well understood lines of authority be established to maintain control of all financial transactions generated by the various outside-the-classroom activities. The school board should adopt policies that outline the management and operations of all funds. The lines of authority will vary from state to state.

The following is a general list of lines of authority (National Center for Education Statistics, 2003):
Board of Education: Sets overall district policy.
Superintendent: Responsible for ensuring the adherence to board policies.

Central treasurer: Maintains custody of all funds and disburses funds upon receipt of payment order signed by the student activity treasurer, faculty adviser and building principal. This duty is generally a responsibility of the district's business official.

Building principal: The activity fund supervisor charged with the responsibility of overseeing all activity funds to ensure all procedures are followed.

ASB Council and officers: Each club or activities budget and fund status is reviewed and approved by the student government structure in place for the school.

Faculty auditor: Reviews account statements for each activity to ensure proper accounting of funds. The balance on the central treasurer's report should match the balance on the ledger of the student activity treasurer.

Faculty advisor: Advises students in the planning of activities, reviews and signs all financial statements including disbursement requests. Deposit slips are signed by the student activity treasurer and the faculty adviser.

Student Activity Treasurer: This is a student selected by the students participating in the activity responsible for collecting all monies raised by the activity and depositing the funds with the central treasurer.

The National Center for Education Statistics (NCES) publishes financial accounting guidelines for state and local school systems. Based on this publication, these policy issues should be included in school board adopted policies for Co-curricular Activity Funds (see NCES website, https://nces.ed.gov/pubs2004/h2r2/ch_8.asp):

- All activity funds should be managed using the same fiscal year basis as all other school district funds.
- All activity funds should be subject to sound internal control procedures.
- All activity funds must be audited and subject to well-defined procedures for internal and external auditing.
- The activity fund bookkeeper or activity fund supervisor(s) responsible for handling and recording activity fund monies should be bonded by the district.

- One or more activity fund supervisors should be formally designated by school board action.
- The activity fund supervisor should maintain a checking account for the school site.
- Bank statements for activity funds should be reconciled as soon as they are received and reviewed by someone other than the checking account manager.
- Depositories for student activity funds should be approved by the board of education and subject to the same security requirements as those for all other district funds.
- All activity funds should operate so that no payments, obligations, or indebtedness are incurred unless the student activity fund (or account) has an equal or greater amount of assets.
- A system of purchase orders and vouchers should be applied to all activity funds. This system should require written authorization for payment and should be strictly enforced.
- A system that uses pre-numbered receipt forms should be adopted for recording cash and other negotiable instruments received.
- All receipts should be deposited in the form in which they are collected and should not be used for making change or disbursements of any kind.
- All receipts should be deposited daily. If this action is not possible, undeposited receipts should be well secured and then deposited promptly.
- A system that uses pre-numbered checks and multiple original signatures (no signature stamps) should be adopted as the sole means for disbursing activity fund monies.
- A perpetual inventory should be maintained on pre-numbered forms, receipts, and other documents to create an adequate audit trail.
- Using activity fund receipts to cash checks to accommodate individuals, to make any kind of loan, to pay any form of compensation directly to employees, or to extend credit should be strictly prohibited.
- Monthly financial reports on all activity funds should be prepared and submitted to the administration and the board of education. A full reporting of activity funds should be included in the district's annual financial statements.
- Student activity fund monies should benefit those students who participate in that student activity for which such monies were accumulated.

- A board-approved process should be specified for all fundraising activities, and any fundraising event should require advance approval.

While policies, procedures and accounting requirements for student extracurricular activities vary from state to state, it is important for school leaders to ensure that these activities are properly managed. Extracurricular activities can be difficult to oversee since they are decentralized and involve multiple personnel and students who may not have financial training. Still, school leaders, including school superintendents, are ultimately responsible for the proper functioning of these activities and adherence to required accounting rules and statutory requirements.

The funds generated by these activities are subject to risk, including fraud and embezzlement. Unscrupulous staff may design spending policies to suit personal needs and not the students' needs. Because the funds being raised for students carry a special meaning for students, parents and guardians, the hours spent fundraising for a special trip can quickly turn shock into anger if funds are not safeguarded.

Unused funds in one school year may accumulate to the balance of a club or activity. Often, the presence of such balances is not reported to the student leaders in the successive year. For example, if a club doesn't take a trip this year because they didn't raise enough funds, the funds will carry over to the next year. The presence of this prior year fund balance needs to be acknowledged: how will it be used? Over time, these tendencies may become imbedded into the fund and fund balances may dramatically increase. These balances need to be monitored so that procedures are designed to use any accumulated funds in appropriate, student-centered ways.

Co-Curricular Activity Travel

Student groups will often engage in events that require large group travel management. Many such activities are in the local area or region of the school district and such group travel is typically provided by the district's transportation department (see Chapter 15—School District Operations, B. Pupil Transportation). Tracking these expenses to the co-curricular function may be accomplished through a debit-credit transfer in the district's accounting system or funded by monies raised by the club or its affiliates.

Major events may require airfare or charter bus companies to provide the transportation. Contracts with reliable private companies may require that bids be sought, and bidding criteria be followed. Support for such efforts is necessary through the district's purchasing administrators.

Other travel costs such as hotels, meals, tipping, and registration are also normal and expected expenses. Assuring proper financial controls is the duty of the coach, manager, or trip organizer. Chaperone expenses are a legitimate expense for the function, but proper reimbursement procedures need to be followed.

In the event a planned trip is cancelled, a pre-determined process for refunds should be in place. Sometimes, cancellation fees apply and must be paid. This expense is a risk of the planned event. It is wise to establish commitments and refund procedures in advance of collecting the funds.

Conclusion

Student activities provide valuable ways for students to learn to apply many concepts and skills taught in the classroom. These activities have grown more and more sophisticated and complex as students have travelled to national events or even internationally. Proper financial management is essential to the overall management of these funds. Involving students in the fiscal and decision-making process is fundamental, but also adds complexity due to the annual turn-over of students leading the efforts.

Clear procedures and practices must delineate the role of students, faculty, and administration in the management of co-curricular funds. Fiscal management, including audits, add strength to the need for these policies and procedures.

Chapter 10

Audits and Related Issues

This chapter will help leaders learn to...
Know the difference among various forms of audits.
Understand the types of control systems and analytics appropriate for the district.
Understand the audiences for the audit.
Know the difference between a management letter, audit findings, audit recommendations.
Clarify and understand the role of the superintendent in the audit process.
Recognize actions that will prevent fraud and embezzlement.

Case Study #1

The independent auditor arrived on Wednesday morning to begin their regularly schedule audit of the district's prior fiscal year. After an initial meeting with Jerome, the superintendent, and Simone, the business officer, the auditors provided an outline of the scope of work for the audit and requested the superintendent and business official sign the letter of representation that they used to indicate that the records they would review were complete and accurately prepared by management. They agreed that Simone would be the primary district official to monitor questions and address suggestions from the auditor.

One key area the auditors would be examining was the school-by-school enrollment management system. Enrollment was the primary source of data driving the general state aid formula and therefore represented a data source with considerable financial implications. Another area for the audit would be timecard management to verify proper controls were in place for the calculation of hourly pay for various school staff.

Jerome and Simone commented to each other after the meeting that the auditor was professional but certainly not friendly.

As the audit began, the auditors met with the office personnel of each school to examine enrollment records and compare them to the school's monthly report to the business office. The business office used these reports to consolidate them into the district's enrollment report to the state for use in the apportionment formula. They also discussed the process principals used to validate timecards for the monthly payroll process.

Several principals and their administrative officer leader began contacting the business office with questions about the intent of the auditors. They were being told by the auditor to change their procedures and alter well developed district guidance. The auditor was intimidating and demanding immediate changes. What should they do?

Simone met with Jerome to review the complaints and questions she was receiving. It was her view that the auditor was going outside the agreed upon protocol. While the district viewed the audit as a learning opportunity and validation of their business and fiscal practices, the auditor was not expected to be altering district decisions without consulting with Simone and Jerome. Now they had to address this issue with the auditor.

If you were the superintendent...
How would you approach meeting with the auditor?
What role would your principals and Simone, the business official, play in helping you prepare for the meeting?
What questions would you want to explore in that meeting?

What would you do if the auditor's counsel differed from what you expected or knew the proper procedure to be?

Case Study #2

A new school year started with a need to manage numerous fiscal changes. The HR department controls people costs, while the fiscal department handles the non-employee expenses. Each month each employee's taxes are calculated. Payments to the federal government for mandatory benefits are collected from employees and held until paid to the government quarterly (e.g., withholding of income taxes).

At the beginning of the new fiscal year, some employees complained to the HR department that their benefits were incorrectly calculated. They talked to a supervisor in the department who explained that employer provided dollars for health care were non-taxable. This explanation was confusing, but the employees were assured their withholdings were properly calculated.

Eight months later, a staff member in the fiscal department spotted errors in withholding taxes and reported it to fiscal leadership. It was clear that the HR staff had incorrectly advised employees and perpetuated the earlier error.

When the error was corrected, increased money needed to be deducted from employee paychecks and the increases had to be designated to the appropriate time period for each employee. This situation led to angry employees and required slow, labor-intensive procedures to correct the error.

The liabilities booked for withholding tax payables had taken a significant dip beginning with the new fiscal year, indicating a potential under-collection. A review of the error and how it was missed identified the need for improved and increased staff education, especially for the individuals who made these mistakes.

The error should have been more readily apparent using an analytic technique to monitor the dip in total liabilities. For example, a chart of the total liabilities of the district each month would show changes and those changes should be explained by staffing variations or reveal the presence of errors.

The drop in the total liability account for taxes collected was nearly one million dollars each month. The reduction in liabilities was caused by a misinterpretation of the tax consequences to individuals, but it could have been caught at the beginning of the school year and been more easily corrected. More importantly, the anger expressed by affected employees toward the district would have been avoided.

If you were the superintendent...

What systems would you propose to catch an error like this?

If it is caught and corrected before the end of the fiscal period it isn't an audit finding, but should an error of this magnitude indicate more should be done?

What are the implications of this error for the HR team? The fiscal team? The district?

What additional information will be needed and where might it be found?

How might the reputational damage to the district and HR be rectified in the eyes of staff and their union?

Audits

Most school districts are required to have financial statements audited on an annual basis by an independent certified public accountant or a state agency assigned with public entity auditing responsibilities. At the end of each fiscal year, the district's fiscal staff prepares a summary of actual revenue and expenses that is reconciled to the banking statements and reviewed in accordance with accepted, predetermined standards.

An Office of the State Auditor is typically designated with the responsibility for the audit function for school districts and local governments. In some states, agencies such as the State Comptroller's Office in New York State and the Office of Fiscal Accountability and Compliance in New Jersey may conduct periodic program, internal controls, or operational audits of school districts in addition to the required annual audit conducted by an independent accounting firm.

In Washington State, the Office of the State Auditor is constitutionally established as an elected official who oversees a team of auditors to perform the annual audits and do specialized audits upon request or when conditions (e.g., suspected fraud) warrant extraordinary reviews. For example, this process in Washington State reconciles district accounting records with the financial report for the district provided by the County Treasurer who holds district funds. Other states may allow districts to use the services of a bank so this reconciliation process must tie into the district's banking records of receipts and disbursements.

Alternatively, the State Auditor in some states doesn't actually conduct the audits. Rather, the state sets the standards that school districts must use to retain a private, independent audit firm to conduct the district's audit. Regardless of the avenue for the audit, it must conform to a determination of accuracy according to GAAP.

Monitoring the state auditor's website helps school officials identify issues and trends that may affect the district. Early knowledge or awareness of these issues helps school leaders prevent such issues from occurring or be prepared to address them with the auditors. Use this information to identify potential risks for the district and initiate remedial actions as soon as possible.

The general ledger accounts for each fund are updated and used to prepare a consolidated year-end financial statement. This official summary of the fiscal year financial operations in all funds forms the basis for the annual audit and serves as a report to state and federal entities that require this information. Most audit functions rely upon the official management representation of these statements and seek to verify their appropriateness.

The purpose of an independent audit is to render an opinion that the financial statements are fairly presented and that they reflect accuracy and consistency with accounting standards. This independent review is necessary for the school board to have confidence in the accuracy of the financial condition of the school district. This report also informs the public, other state agencies, and bond rating firms that the district is operating in compliance with established standards and procedures. The person or firm serving as an external auditor would compromise the integrity of the independent audit if they also, for example, served as the internal auditor or the district claims auditor.

Any findings in the audit report are contained in a letter to the school board outlining the issues. These findings require a response outlining corrective actions that have been taken or that are planned to be taken. Subsequent audits will verify that corrective action was properly taken. Districts must make correction of all audit findings a high priority for completion before the next audit.

Before a finding is reported, the audit may identify weaknesses or areas of concern that management is asked to address. These issues are identified in a management letter from the auditor that is not a formal finding from the audit report. Failure to take timely action to properly address issues raised in a management letter may result in an audit finding in subsequent audit reports.

Audits are a significant, important source of organizational learning. In addition to validating school operations and data to the public, the audit helps teach school business office personnel and other school administrators how to address fiscal and operational accountability. A successful audit is a valuable tool in building trust and confidence in the school district by a variety of external parties (e.g., parents, district employees, taxpayers, state and federal officials, and holders of district G.O. bonds).

The CFO is typically the district administrator with most direct engagement with the auditor, but audit criteria require the superintendent to attest to the presentation of the financial data and share the results with the school board in a public meeting. Given the importance of the audit to public perception and trust, it is essential that the superintendent have financial understanding and know the auditing and reporting requirements in their state.

Types of audits

The most significant audit to a district is the independent external audit. Whether the audit is conducted by a state agency or with an independent, private firm, a contract sets forth the roles and assures auditors of the district's representations about the financial statements.

When contracting with a private firm to conduct the annual audit, be sure the selection process adheres to district's purchasing or contracting guidelines and addresses the following questions:

- Has this contract been with the same auditor for a long period of time?
- Should the district re-bid the contract? If the answer to the second question is yes, follow state guidelines in the process to award the contract.

Other types of audits may be focused on special situations or aspects of the district. These program audits may examine internal controls, claims, technology and software, capital construction, food service, etc.

Beyond the annual fiscal audit, other agencies such as the Internal Revenue Service, the state workers compensation agency, or various other Federal entities may choose to conduct an audit or review of district compliance. These audits may be routine, or they may result from a complaint or set of complaints filed with the agency by citizens.

The superintendent may need to request a special audit to address suspected fraud or other concerns related to corruption. Specialized auditors with forensic skills or a background in criminal activity may be necessary in these cases.

Performance or program audits may be mandated by the state as a tool to inform future executive and legislative actions. Such audits may be initiated by the state legislature, the governor, or the state schools superintendent. In some cases, such audits may result in a recapture of funds from the district due to over-payments by the state.

The Business Side of School Success

Management audits are another form of program review. Such an audit might be initiated by the superintendent using a consultant or a team of colleagues associated with the state superintendent's professional association. A management audit demonstrates a commitment to improving operations in advance of the fiscal audit and allows more discretion in acting upon the recommendations received.

New superintendents often accelerate the audit schedule to establish a bright line between administrations. Depending on the conditions, findings from such a transition audit clarify accountability and provide the new superintendent with guidance for action based on a clean slate. Waiting too long to conduct the initial audit may miss the window of opportunity provided by being new.

Internal controls

Internal control is a process designed to provide reasonable assurance regarding the achievement of business objectives. Internal controls are intended to meet four primary objectives:

- promote effectiveness and efficiency of operations that assure the prudent use of taxpayer dollars.
- protection of assets.
- ensure reliability of financial reporting.
- maintain compliance with applicable laws and regulations.

A variety of internal control assessments may be used, depending upon the context and circumstances. Use of internal controls will reduce the occurrence of errors described in Case Study #2 at the beginning of this chapter.

Analytics to evaluate trends: Analytics are a powerful tool when properly used. Analytical procedures should be used to identify unusual trends, activities, or transactions. Variables that lend themselves to such processes include student and staff FTEs, travel reimbursement expenses, petty cash activity, equipment purchases, etc. All unusual patterns or changes in trends should be investigated.

Separation of duties: Separation of duties involves splitting responsibility for bookkeeping, deposits, reporting and auditing so no one person controls the complete financial procedure. The further duties are separated, the less chance any single employee has of committing fraudulent acts. This effort protects all staff. For smaller districts with only a few accounting employees, sharing responsibilities between two or more people or requiring critical tasks to be reviewed by co-workers meets this need.

Accounting system access: Controlling access to different parts of an accounting system via passwords, lockouts and electronic access logs keeps unauthorized users out of the system while providing a way to audit the usage of the system to identify the source of errors or discrepancies. Robust access tracking also serves to deter attempts at fraudulent access in the first place.

Physical audits of assets: Physical audits include hand-counting cash and any physical assets tracked in the accounting system, such as inventory, materials and tools. Physical counting can reveal well-hidden discrepancies in account balances by bypassing electronic records altogether. Counting cash in sales outlets can be done daily or even several times per day. Larger projects, such as hand counting inventory, should be performed less frequently, perhaps on an annual or quarterly basis. It is important to establish a dollar value of those assets being tracked in this manner.

Standardized financial documents: Standardizing documents used for financial transactions, such as invoices, internal materials requests, inventory receipts and travel expense reports, maintains consistency in record keeping over time. Using standard document formats makes it easier to review past records when preparing reports or searching for the source of a discrepancy in the system. A lack of standardization often results in items being overlooked or misinterpreted in such a review.

It is important that every employee provide the required information for all transactions in a timely manner. Superintendents and other executive level administrators set the tone by personally making timely reporting. Do not tolerate employees who abuse or bypass established procedures.

Daily or weekly trial balances: Using a double-entry accounting system adds reliability by ensuring that the books are always balanced. Even so, it is still possible for errors to bring a double-entry system out of balance at any given time. Calculating daily or weekly trial balances can provide regular insight into the state of the system, allowing you to discover and investigate discrepancies as early as possible.

Periodic reconciliation in accounting systems: Regularly scheduled accounting reconciliations are essential to ensure that balances in the accounting system match up with balances in accounts held by other entities, including banks, suppliers, and others. For example, a bank reconciliation involves comparing cash balances and records of deposits and receipts between your accounting system and bank statements. Differences between these types of complementary accounts can reveal errors or discrepancies in various accounts or identify errors that may originate with the other entities.

Approval authority requirements: Requiring specific managers to authorize certain types of transactions adds a layer of responsibility to accounting records by proving that transactions have been seen, analyzed and approved by appropriate authorities. Requiring secondary approval for large (e.g., establish a threshold amount) payments and expenses beyond normal separation of roles is sometimes instituted to prevent unscrupulous employees from making large, fraudulent transactions with district funds.

Preventing Fraud and Embezzlement

Embezzlement is the theft or misappropriation of district funds placed in one's trust. Fraud is deceit, trickery, or breach of confidence perpetrated for profit or to gain some unfair or dishonest advantage. Corruption exists when two individuals are involved in the crime, either voluntarily or involuntarily, and may be the most difficult type of fraud to prove.

Various forms of inappropriate and/or illegal fiscal related actions include:

Conflict of interest: when a person who holds a position of implicit trust and has a competing professional or personal interest that motivates their decisions.
Bribery: offering, promising, giving, accepting or soliciting of an advantage as an inducement for an action which is illegal, unethical or a breach of trust.
Illegal gratuities: giving something of value to a public official because that public official does or fails to do some act.
Economic extortion ("Blackmail"): when an administrator demands payment from another party (e.g., vendor, donor, staff member, etc.,) in exchange for influencing or directing a decision.
Hacking and ransomware: when an outside person hacks into the district's fiscal system, corrupts data, then demands payment to release uncorrupted data.
Ghost employee: when an employee for the district has been terminated or a fake person created in the system. The fraudster changes the employee's address to their own or a different one and continues processing their payments.

A culture of transparency with strong internal controls protects the district and its staff from incidents of this nature. Separation of duties is one of the more powerful organizational responses to preventing these occurrences.

Another wise practice is to require fiscal staff to take two consecutive weeks of vacation. This simple practice helps avoid inappropriate behaviors that might require daily management to sustain. Appropriate use of vacations is a healthy practice for employees and improves morale.

Suggestions to manage the audit process

- Has the school board expressed concerns about any fiscal area?
- Should the audit contract be rebid? How long has the contract been in place? Administer requests for proposals for the auditor on a regular schedule to avoid overly familiar independent audits.
- Do concerns exist about a particular fund, process, or program?

- Should a special management audit be conducted to identify lingering issues or challenges?
- Require auditors to report results directly to school board. This focus keeps the relationship where it belongs. Board members must provide appropriate oversight of audits.
- Require that district responses to the audit, including corrective action plans, are promptly handled.
- Establish the tone at the top by acting with integrity and making the handling of money, transactions, and entries a serious business.
- Use a calendar and check list. The many required tasks are easier to do if calendar time is planned.
- Establish well thought out procedures for cash, especially petty cash.
- Use written procedures to set employee's expectations. Review and revise them regularly.
- Control access to district computer software and be clear about what change authority is associated with each person with access.
- Set up systems that make passwords complex and difficult to use. Periodically change these passwords.
- Track who makes changes or adjustments to your system so that problem-solving is easier, especially if suspicious activity occurs.
- Be vigilant by using a trust but confirm approach.
- Publicize a fraud hotline number and monitor it for issues reported.
- Ensure that someone is responsible for posting audit reports on the district web site.

Conclusion

An annual financial audit provides a vehicle to build community trust, improve district management and educate staff about proper ways to manage resources. Although some anxiety exists when an external entity examines district processes, encourage cooperation with the auditors and embrace the process as a form of professional development.

When issues arise (and they will) address them quickly and use the audit as leverage for positive change. Make sure that the "fixes" undertaken avoid creating new, unintended issues. Working with the auditors to resolve findings in a timely way works to the advantage of the district in future audits.

Make a complete, public report of audit results to the school board. Public reporting builds confidence that the district leadership supports openness and sound fiscal management. Ensure that the audit report is posted to the district web site.

Section II

School Support Services and Operations

Chapter 11: School and Community Partnerships: Maintaining the Public Trust

Chapter 12: Human Resources Leadership

Chapter 13 Legal Counsel

Chapter 14: Enterprise Risk Management: What to Insure

Chapter 15: School District Operations
- A. Maintenance and Custodial Services
- B. Pupil Transportation
- C. Food Service
- D. Information Technology
- E. Safety and Security
- F. Ancillary Services

Chapter 16: Capital Projects and Bonds

Chapter 11

School and Community Partnerships: Maintaining the Public Trust

This chapter will help leaders learn to...

Maintain the public's trust in the school district's financial operations.

Know why transparency is important in building positive relationships with all stakeholders.

Understand why it is important to lead meaningful participation of constituents in the financial management of the school district.

Manage relationships with the media and establish a professional rapport with the press.

Apply best practices to garner positive support from voters for financial measures requiring voter approval.

Identify and use channels of communication that provide accurate information and messages to the public.

Case Study

Harold began his first year as superintendent in a suburban school district that has been experiencing financial problems. The annual school budget vote had been defeated by residents for the past three years, even when one of the budget proposals presented no increase in taxes.

The Business Side of School Success

It was apparent that the poor financial condition and management of the school district contributed to an overall lack of faith and trust in the school board and district administration. Operating deficits and rising costs of goods and services as well as reports of upcoming reductions in state and federal funding would exacerbate this problem.

It is critical for Harold to win back the trust of the school community to successfully meet the challenges ahead.

If you were the superintendent...

Who should Harold meet with to determine the current financial condition of the school district?

What steps might Harold employ to create transparency of district finances and operations issues?

What strategies could Harold initiate to gain the public's support of the proposed budget?

How can Harold build a trusting rapport with the media?

What additional information will be needed and where might it be found?

This chapter focuses on the relationship between school, family, and community partnerships and the school district's finances. Transparency concerning the financial matters of the school district is essential to maintain positive relationships between the school district and the community.

These relationships affect how parents, other residents, community groups, and municipal governments located within the boundaries of the school district support and interact with the school district. These areas of community support are vital elements of a strong educational system. A timely auditing process is an effective tool to keep the community informed about the school district's financial condition, a topic discussed in Chapter 10—Audits and Related Issues.

Additionally, an environment of trust between the superintendent and all school district constituents emerges when the superintendent is enthusiastically visible throughout the community and accessible to its constituents. Effective superintendents regularly visit schools during the school day to interact with school staff and adult volunteers. They attend sporting events, diverse student activities such as music and/or drama performances, and school-based parent meetings to build strong relationships. These connections are vital to understanding what is happening in the school system and provide insights into how constituents are reacting to any policies or practices. Participating in a service club and/or serving on the board of directors of a community-based organization is another way for school leaders to build positive relationships.

Observe the work of other governmental units. If they have a measure on the ballot, publicize their election in school district publications. Routine notice of all elections avoids the appearance of being inappropriately self-serving when a school election issue is on the ballot. Helping other community organizations publicize their measures builds goodwill for the district and the superintendent.

A strong, consistent reputation for being a visible school leader both in the district and within the community shows respect for all elements of education and builds trusting relationships. When personal visibility and citizen engagement are consistently encouraged, public support increases. This support is especially valuable when a school funding issue is on the ballot.

Encourage and support the involvement of other district leaders in community organizations. This involvement extends the district's presence in the community and helps develop future leadership. Set clear expectations for what other administrators are expected to share in meetings with community groups.

The media

Establishing rapport with the media, especially the reporter for the local newspaper, is an important relationship for effective communication with the public. Even though the existence of long-established local newspapers is increasingly under attack, most communities still have some newspaper that covers local events and news.

The Business Side of School Success

Identify the specific news sources in the community and initiate a meeting with the publisher or primary education reporter. Use this meeting to develop a protocol for sharing information. Be sure to adhere to this protocol. Clarifying how you will work with the media is an important introductory step whenever a new reporter is assigned to cover the school district's affairs and will pay dividends when the inevitable sensational issue arises.

Establishing a time for meeting with the education reporter in advance of each school board meeting. These sessions will provide opportunities for the superintendent or other leadership staff to brief the reporter on the context and background for key agenda items. This effort is especially valuable when tight budgets require tough choices. In-depth briefings are especially important when a more complex issue, like a school operating levy or a bond issue proposal, is approaching.

Controversial issues and complex problems will certainly attract media attention. Adhering to timely background briefings and establishing relationships that encourage the reporter to contact the appropriate district personnel will help give the district's perspective, but these meetings won't stop adversaries or people with another viewpoint from being included in the story. The key is to have the district's message presented consistently and in a timely manner.

Television media coverage requires a different approach. It is less likely that the local television stations will assign a specific education reporter to cover the district. Consequently, less background will accompany the arrival of the television reporter. Still, making an on-camera statement is important to get the district's message into the public's awareness. This effort may require multiply repeating the same message, especially if the reporter is seeking a different or more "news-worthy" quote. Know the message intended to be given and stay with that message knowing that a reporter is not able to broadcast something you do not say.

Be cooperative and available when reporters are working against deadlines. This access is appreciated and will pay dividends when difficult circumstances or issues arise. Be truthful, confident, and timely in all media relationships. Make every effort to provide accurate information; if an error is made, correct it as quickly as possible.

Family & community involvement

Family and community involvement with schools forms an important partnership that enriches and improves student learning. This involvement also builds trust between citizens and the school system.

The superintendent sets the expectation for community engagement. Through collaboration with principals and other school leaders, the superintendent helps ensure that parents, teachers, students and community members are involved in productive and meaningful ways (Epstein, J. L. & Associates, 2019). For example, a district citizens advisory committee should have clear responsibilities, understand how decision-making occurs, and know their role in decisions. Some of those decisions may be advisory while others may vest with the committee. Clarity in responsibilities is vital to effective involvement.

It is wise to focus engagement and involvement of school staff, students, parents, community members and the school board on improving school performance. This focus requires that resources be devoted to improving academic achievement, increasing graduation rates, decreasing dropouts, improving attendance, and improving student behavior. For example, in a school with a large percentage of non-English speaking parents, strategies might be implemented to reach out to parents in their first language. Using interpreters at class and school meetings and disseminating information in the various languages using written documents and, on the school and district websites is essential to this effort.

When the community needs to vote

School districts need to obtain a positive community vote for various financial matters such as the school budget or renewing or increasing important local tax levies. Effective involvement of all constituents will assist in garnering this vital financial support. These efforts are essential to assuring the resources needed to meet the needs of all students (Epstein J. L. & Associates, 2019).

Wise leaders ensure the community is given the opportunity to understand the contents of the budget and participate in its development with the school board. For example, the State of New Jersey does not require a vote on the school budget if the proposed tax levy increase is at or below the statutory cap. Nevertheless, providing the community with budget details for the school district's programs and maintains the public trust in its school system because, at some point, a proposal to raise the levy limit may be necessary.

Some states require communities to approve the school budget by an affirmative vote. In such cases, the budget is presented to the residents so that they may have the information necessary to vote on it and the proposed taxes. In this phase the community can become informed about estimated expenditures, estimated revenues, the estimated unreserved and designated fund balance, the amount to be raised in taxes, and the property tax effect upon homeowners.

Some states require this community vote on the operating budget by a certain date. Other states establish the budget adoption calendar for the school board. In all instances, public hearings and public actions must be taken regarding adoption of the budget. Consequently, engaging as many stakeholder groups as possible in the lead-up to the recommendations is vital. Provide time for early review of the budget with Parent Teacher Associations (PTA/PTO), faculty and staff, community organizations such as the American Legion, service clubs, other fraternal organizations, and homeowner associations. These efforts will prepare the public for the final adoption action.

The budget presentation should be accurate and present the "numbers." It should also highlight the actions it funds to maintain and improve educational programs. Highlighting mandated expenditures such as retirement systems contributions, social security taxes, and unfunded mandates provides context on necessary elements of the budget. It is important for taxpayers to understand what they are supporting with their property taxes. Budget presentations should tell a story about the district's mission and vision for the children of the community.

Use the school district's educational vision to introduce budget presentations. Emphasize that the budget is a financial blueprint for the district's educational programs. The district's educational programs should be highlighted to emphasize the educational opportunities for children that the budget supports. Include easy to read graphs and charts to outline the financial data so that taxpayers can make informed decisions.

Strategies for getting voter approval

While many school districts continue to receive positive approval from the voters, changing economic conditions may make continued voter support uncertain. Given the uncertainty that school districts face each year regarding support for budget approval, prudent school leaders will be alert for ways to communicate positive news throughout the year, not just at budget adoption time.

State law usually prohibits the use of taxpayer funds to advocate for a particular position on elections or budget approval issues. School district leaders nevertheless have a duty to explain their work to advance student achievement and improve educational programs. Demonstrating effective, proper use of resources helps obtain voter approval. While these activities are not a direct attempt to persuade voters, action must be taken to share information without advising voters how to vote.

School districts can effectively plan activities to demonstrate how educational programs and activities support students throughout the school year. This effort must be consistently applied, even during times when financial elections are not scheduled. When finance measures are on the ballot, highlighting school programs and activities continues the district's routine effort to provide information essential for community awareness and understanding.

Care must be taken to not specifically advocate a "yes or no" vote on the budget. It may be useful to check with the district's legal counsel to clearly understand the relationship between information sharing and recommending a specific way to vote. Some important ways to share information are:

- Make informational presentations about the measure to be voted upon throughout the school district (e.g., at PTA/PTO meetings, special school board meetings, community organizations, etc.,).
- Publish an annual report to the community highlighting the district's progress toward student learning goals and student activities. Schedule this report to occur about a month before the date for an election on school issues.
- Make the district's Comprehensive Annual Financial Statement readily available to the public. Also make the Annual Budget and planning document which highlights goals and strategies to accomplish them publicly available.
- Hold a student awards assembly close to or on the day of the vote.
- Ask children to invite parents to become reading partners throughout the year and especially on the budget vote day.
- Enlist the support of the teachers' union to call other teacher union members in the district reminding them to vote. This calling must be done outside work hours and must avoid the use of district telephones.
- Hold musical performances around the date of the election; provide information during these performances.
- Display student artwork in the school (whether it is used for a polling place or not).
- Hold parent open houses during election season and display students' work.
- Present information about finance measures or the budget at all PTA/PTO meetings.

A community advocacy organization

Many districts encourage people who support school funding measures to form a political action committee (PAC) devoted to supporting the passage of the budget or property tax measure presented to voters. A separate committee, led by citizens, may advocate and support passage of the school finance measure. This committee can build upon informational sessions presented by district leaders and encourage a yes vote.

A levy or budget adoption support committee will likely be required to register with the state agency that monitors political activity. Just as any candidate or other support group must do, the committee will raise funds to support passage of the budget or levy measure.

The school superintendent will likely be involved with this support group, but only during non-work time. When speaking for the district, the superintendent provides information, but when working with the supportive committee it is permissible to exercise one's citizenship duties and advocate passage of the school finance measures. Superintendents must be clear to avoid confusion of which role is being used and when it is being used.

The budget newsletter or website

Districts typically provide regular written newsletters to the public. When a finance measure is anticipated, using this newsletter and the district's website to provide information is a valuable way to inform the public. The budget newsletter, in paper form or electronic format provides an opportunity for school boards to meet statutory budget notification requirements as well as being the basis for efforts by the community group to promote passage of the measure(s).

Budget and/or tax measure information can be made available in greater detail on the school district's website. Public funds can be used to inform voters but cannot be used to advise voters to vote affirmatively or negatively. Tax election or budget information should describe how funds are proposed to be used for school programs and to support student achievement. The following ideas may be included in both a newsletter and a website:

- Provide budget highlights, including educational programs that are new or are being maintained.
- Include the successes of the school district, such as awards, honors, and improved test scores.
- Include pictures of students and staff in classrooms using technology, playing sports, and participating in theater or special events.

The Business Side of School Success

- Provide information on the impact of a contingency budget on the school program.
- Include graphs illustrating the percentage of the budget that is allocated to administration, programs, and other functions.
- Provide graphs that compare the school district's cost per pupil, state averages.
- Include a graph that compares the school district's budget rate of growth to the state average.

It is also important to disseminate accurate, clearly understood budget information to the public. If data cause questions to arise, be sure to address those questions in the document and on the website. It is vital that an honest, clear presentation of fiscal measures be presented by the district.

When opposition groups develop

Not all citizens will support public schools or the taxes that are necessary to support them. It is typical for a taxpayer group to form with a goal of fighting school financial measures. Anticipate the opposition by building consistent actions to share information openly and collaboratively.

It may be possible to engage directly with the leaders of these opposition efforts. Always include a facilitator or respected third party to join such efforts to avoid mis-representations or mis-use of the comments and/or information shared in such meetings.

Some opposition groups have demonstrated a willingness to use misleading or slanted allegations based on the district's data. Take specific actions to clarify such actions in every possible place and way. A natural human reaction is to become defensive and respond to every objection. Exercise care by staying factual and calm. Enlist reliable community partners in this effort using the district's readily available data and descriptions. These allies may include the local business organization, other elected officials, civic leaders, and religious leaders.

Creating a citizen advisory committee is a long-tested strategy to address concerns and respond to opposition groups. This approach is especially valuable when planning a school capital construction program (see Chapter 16—Capital Projects and Bonds). Furin (2022) provides a summary of how the superintendent in an Ohio school district overcame opposition to taxes to solve a school facilities and educational program controversy by inspiring the work of such a citizen group.

Conclusion

Maintaining an open and transparent relationship with the school board and with all stakeholders in your school district is an important foundation for a superintendent's successful tenure. The superintendents who are visible throughout the community and accessible to parents, teachers, students, the media and other community groups and other governmental agencies increase their probability of success on many fronts, especially in gaining fiscal support for educational programs and services.

Student academic achievement and overall school improvement requires the meaningful engagement of all school district constituents in the educational process. These partnerships will enable the establishment of an environment of trust necessary to gain the support needed to provide the resources required to meet the needs of all students.

Devoting the time, energy and commitment to public engagement is a significant effort for the superintendent and pays rich dividends for school system success

Chapter 12

Human Resources Leadership

This chapter will help leaders learn to...
Identify how staffing decisions influence fiscal health and student achievement.

Define position categories, job descriptions and compensation structures.

Understand the benefit structure for all district personnel.

Recruit, on-board, support, and retain high quality people to serve the school district's mission.

Manage investigations and disciplinary matters.

Provide aligned professional development opportunities for staff.

Maintain personnel records necessary to document payroll, evaluations and other legal requirements.

Organize and lead the collective bargaining process.

Case Study

The Fallow School District has recently completed a difficult year that pushed the school year into early July as the result of a long teacher strike. A long-time board member resigned in a board dispute related to major shifts within the school budget. In the fall, four school board members were replaced with new board members.

The long-term superintendent retired June 30, creating the opening that Grady now fills. Grady wonders why he had agreed to move his family and take on this tough assignment, but that decision is now in the past. He faces the task of re-building trust within the community and even within the school system.

The new school board, including one appointed in September, rallied around the district's staff and seemed to have both community and staff support. But the teacher contract that resulted from the strike would be expiring at the end of the current school year. Grady is faced with developing a strategy for bargaining with many uncertain conditions challenging the school district.

The state's funding system provided essential support for many district programs. Fortunately, local voters had already approved a multi-year over-ride levy to augment the state and federal funding sources. But the state's future budget was being developed in tough economic conditions. Prospects for state budget cuts remain a concern. State law limited salary and benefit levels to that contained in the state's budget, but a loophole allows some discretionary increases. State funding levels will not be known until well into next summer.

In November, as Grady and the new board start budget planning for the next fiscal year, they have to consider how to make provision for the expectation that teachers and other employees will be looking for salary supplements above the state's limits.

Grady's prior experience includes participating in challenging bargaining sessions and serving as the chief spokesperson for the school board in his previous district's bargaining process. He'd learned that trust and credibility were vital to a successful bargain. Still, even with those elements in place, personalities and complexity made finding tentative agreement at the bargaining table a challenge.

Grady earned a reputation as a dependable, straight-shooting superintendent who valued teachers and the work of other school personnel. These strengths helped him get this new position. Now he faces new challenges with new people.

The Business Side of School Success

If you were the superintendent…

How might Grady work with the school board to set responsible bargaining parameters?

What other actions related to personnel guidance and leadership might Grady and his team take to address the overall climate?

What role should Grady play in bargaining?

What best practices would help Grady advise the school board and finalize a new teacher contract before the next school year begins?

What additional information will be needed and where might it be found?

Guiding the work of all staff members within the school system is a significant requirement for school leaders. Because education is a people-intensive endeavor, employee salaries and benefits typically focus eighty to eighty-five percent of school district operational costs. Consequently, the superintendent must maintain a close working relationship with all aspects of these functions to set the tone and direction for the district.

Many school systems organize the many elements of people services into a Human Resources (HR) department. We're using the term "human resources" to describe these functions, but we recognize that many organizations are moving in the direction of re-naming these functions as "people services" or "human talent." Regardless of the label, we see leadership of the district's people as perhaps the most significant responsibility of the superintendent.

HR functions include staffing, maintaining job descriptions and titles, position control, recruitment, training, employee benefit coordination and administration, retirement functions, labor relations, employee discipline/investigations and maintaining a multitude of employment records required for taxation and other purposes. Payroll processing to handle the timely and accurate payment of all employees may be organized either within HR or the business office. These activities and duties communicate the essence of the district's culture to its employees and set a tone for daily operations that extends into the collective bargaining context and ultimately to the learning conditions for students.

Much is written about the function of human resources departments; an in-depth examination of these issues is beyond the focus of this book. Still, because the significant influence of investing in people relates closely with school financial operations, we include points of reference for key issues and considerations that superintendents will be called upon to address.

Position descriptions, titles, and compensation levels: The HR department must design an integrated series of position descriptions, job titles and compensation levels that align with market demands, support recruitment, professional development and overall compensation equity for school personnel. Salary schedule information must be coordinated with the business office to ensure accuracy in payroll. These tools are essential to support operational management, budget development, and collective bargaining.

Superintendent knowledge of the relationships of these compensation structures is important for working with all district staff and for deciding important fiscal matters during budget-setting sessions.

Superintendents new in their position are in a unique position to notice compensation irregularities within the district. One way to correct these irregularities is to have a compensation specialist (either a staff member or via a contracted consultant) study these anomalies and offer written recommendations on how they might be addressed. It is an essential responsibility to ensure that all employees are fairly compensated for their work. Recommendations may take time to be implemented but proceeding carefully helps manage any shock waves and allows budget capacity to evolve.

Staffing allocations: Without a doubt, the staffing allocation process represents the most significant fiscal decision in the budget development process. Working with the human resources administrator, the chief fiscal officer and other program managers to allocate staffing positions is an essential way for the superintendent to guide the direction of the district.

To accomplish this set of decisions, the HR department is expected to know, understand and maintain a system that addresses every position and compensation level applied within the school district. Developing a rigorous position control system is necessary so all managers and senior leadership have the information to address requests for additional resources and/or avoid over-commitments that cause serious fiscal difficulties.

The HR and business office staff must ensure their records match to maintain the integrity of payroll and benefit expenditures and support accurate forecasting of expenditures for current and future budgets. These efforts are best incorporated into the position control system.

Employee benefits: One of the superintendent requirements related to people leadership is balancing the employee benefit package with other resource demands. In many cases, this issue creates a "tone at the top" that influences employee morale factor within the school system.

HR maintains employee benefit records for both certificated and classified staff. Frequent changes to benefit options are usually due to statutory and renewal requirements. These changes must be coordinated between the human resources and business offices to ensure the integrity of payroll.

Benefit programs affect personal lives of staff and their families in terms of health, safety and long-term planning, so this area of HR operations requires detailed, accurate attention. Key types of benefits include:

Sick leave: Full time employees typically generate a fixed number of sick leave and family leave hours for each month of work. This system is usually governed by state law and collective bargaining agreements. Often, the leave is transferable to a successor employer and may be subject to conversions to cash annually or at retirement.

Health and dental benefits: This benefit program has become increasingly complicated due to federal and state legal requirements. The district's array of medical and dental insurance vendors provides varying plans for different family conditions and personal situations. An annual selection process is then combined with an open enrollment period for employees. Selection of choices must be updated accurately to calculate the employer-based contribution along with an employee payment.

Mandatory benefits (e.g., social security, unemployment and workers compensation): Federal and state laws mandate certain coverages for benefits provided as a matter of public policy for all employees. Social Security (or a state-run pension in some states) and Medicare are perhaps the most significant of these programs; both require district knowledge and a deduction and employer-paid contribution tied to the payroll systems in each pay period. States that have opted out of Social Security still typically use an alternative state retirement system in its place.

State programs provide unemployment insurance and benefits for employees injured in the course of their work (often called workers compensation). States are adding programs, changing them and adjusting financial rates on a regular basis, so it is vital that the HR team stay current on these employer obligations.

Retirement systems: Employees who work at least a minimum determined assignment may be required to participate in a state designed and managed retirement system. The HR staff will need to know the eligibility rules and maintain liaison with the state retirement department personnel. Developing expertise in the nuances of the retirement program is an asset for managing the intake of new staff and the negotiations with those who may consider retirement voluntarily or due to some other disciplinary circumstance.

Diversity, equity, inclusion, and belonging: School systems seek to have their workforce match the demographics of their community. This effort demonstrates the district's need to know its community and the students being served. Students are increasingly seeking a learning situation led by staff who look like them.

Racial and cultural diversity alone may not be the only basis for assuring diversity. For this reason, strong efforts to persistently pursue inclusive engagement efforts across all district functions is vital. We raise this issue here, knowing it that this deep, broad topic extends beyond the scope of this book. Still, how school systems act to embrace all aspects of their community, and we note it as a significant area for HR staff and for superintendent leadership.

Recruitment: Finding talented, diverse teachers, administrators and other support personnel is increasingly important. The talent search is shared among many organizations, which makes recruitment into the school system additionally challenging.

The HR department takes the lead in these matters, but requires financial support to participate in job fairs, manage and support recruitment visits for finalist candidates for some positions, and building relationships with colleges and university sources of emerging talent. Examining the support system and the district's protocol for recruiting candidates is worthy of the superintendent's attention and knowledge. Assuring that proper fiscal support is put in place to align recruitment with other district strategic priorities requires superintendent sponsorship.

Employee assistance: The human resource executive is often involved in providing employment counsel to administrative colleagues and sometimes to individual staff members. This counsel may be related to leave requests, Section 504 accessibility requirements, career choices, illnesses, other personally sensitive matters. A strong HR executive will take the role seriously and understand its value in creating a positive culture within the district.

Additionally, the district is wise to establish a formal contractual arrangement with a third party employee assistance provider. This service is a valuable tool to support district personnel and their families. It is essential that this service be accessible without prior district consultation in order to preserve privacy for staff and to maximize its usefulness.

The superintendent sets the tone that values (or not) the importance of providing support to the stressful work within the school system. This task is best shared across the culture, but key leaders will influence its importance. Even one setback in how a difficult employee matter is addressed or avoided can take years to overcome. Providing avenues for employee assistance and support is one important tool to avoid such setbacks.

Discipline and investigations: Unfortunately, not all employees exercise wise or responsible judgment in the conduct of their professional lives. Sometimes, these missteps extend into their personal lives with an effect on their professional credibility. Regardless of the cause, superintendents must make sure that processes are in place for fair, timely investigations of allegations about staff members.

Usually, a leader in the human resources area is delegated with the authority to conduct such an investigation, but this assignment may vary based on the person who is the subject of the allegations or other circumstances. Sometimes, initiating an external investigation or a process managed through the district's legal counsel may be warranted.

Collective bargaining agreements and legal conditions surrounding contracts and employment usually direct the due process considerations for investigations and the consideration of disciplinary actions that may be taken. Integrating ultimate actions with the business office for financial or liability insurance coverage considerations is a necessary step in reaching appropriate resolution for these complex and emotional actions.

Professional development and other training requirements: The human resources staff will want to work closely with the teaching and learning leadership to align professional development, especially for teachers and educational support staff, with the district's instructional strategies and goals. While the specific professional development topics must derive from the instructional leadership, the HR department may coordinate these professional development activities to assure proper application in the salary structure.

Similarly, human resources must work with various operational departments to design relevant growth options for district staff. Investing in the growth and development of all district personnel makes sense for creating a strong, effective school system. When professional development activities are conducted for employee classifications (e.g., administrative personnel, trades, custodial staff, food service, etc.), the community and its students are well served.

Record maintenance: A clear, reliable system of maintaining current and historical records for all district personnel is essential to the management of current activities (e.g., hours worked, sick leave balances, etc.,) and to accurately address future potential claims. Diverse legal requirements often contain fiscal penalties if the district ignores and doesn't develop appropriate records retrieval protocols.

Additionally, former employees may call upon the district at some future point to verify employment dates, seek resolution of a retirement question, or address other related issues. Because wages and benefits have taxable effects for individuals, having access to ex-employee records for at least seven years is essential.

Labor relations and collective bargaining

The chief human resources administrator is directly involved in collective bargaining and labor relations. HR personnel administer the collective bargaining agreements (CBA) as a liaison between administration and staff. HR may interpret provisions of the CBA for faculty and staff and to assist in settling an employment dispute.

The lead HR administrator often guides bargaining and assures that HR personnel support district negotiators during the negotiation process with various employee unions. The chief financial officer or budget official must be an active participant in this process. Since salaries and benefits constitute the largest percentage of school district expenditures, this function is extremely vital to maintaining the district's sound financial position.

Most collective bargaining agreements contain a process for resolving disputes that might arise in the administration of the contract. Called the grievance procedure, a senior HR official may be crucial to the proper management of grievances. This process may seem contentious, but it also may be viewed as a healthy safety valve to identify ways to resolve issues in the interests of all parties. Wise leadership will see grievances in this healthy perspective and take the process seriously.

It is often useful to consult legal counsel in resolving grievances. For a more detailed discussion of this relationship, see Chapter 13—Legal Counsel.

The superintendent's role: The superintendent is instrumental in setting the tone for labor relationships. Collective bargaining processes receive significant attention, but the real work and the best results in bargaining come from creating day-to-day alignment between policy and action. Valuing people who teach and perform all the other support roles essential for effective classroom learning to occur is essential to creating a positive tone. Bargaining matters may always contain divergent perspectives and differing solutions. Regardless, the best bargaining climate emerges when trust and respect are generated through effective, fair daily administration of the school system.

The tone at the top is a significant factor in building essential trust and respect. Consequently, superintendents have two primary roles when it comes to collective bargaining. The first role is to personally engage with labor leadership in regular sessions that allow issues and potential problems to be identified before they become festering sores.

Establish regular labor-management consultations that allow relationships to develop in advance of the formal collective bargaining process. Questions about contract intent, emerging issues and evolving factors in the legislature, the community and the district can be examined together. These sessions give everyone a shared set of facts to consider and encourage creative problem solving to occur within the current contractual framework.

If some modification of contractual language is determined to be helpful, nothing prevents the development of a memorandum of understanding or even a contract amendment to be created in labor-management meetings to avoid a festering issue from becoming a larger impediment in contract negotiations a year or two down the road.

Building a strong labor-management relationship with each employee organization builds a stronger district culture so the daily work is focused on students and their development. Another important result, if it can be obtained, is to help the employee association leadership share in the fiscal stability of the district for the longer term. Achieving this shared understanding leads to long term stability, a feature that is beneficial to all stakeholders in the district's mission.

The second major role for the superintendent is to design and lead an effective team during the formal bargaining process. Engage principals and other educational managers in a process that identifies areas in the contract that might be altered to improve school administration or better support the teaching-learning process for students. Seek input from all affected stakeholders and create a list of potential contract changes that might be considered with the labor unit.

The superintendent is not usually a direct participant in the bargaining process. Our experience indicates that staying one step back from the direct process preserves the superintendent's ability to be more visible when finalizing the agreement. For this opportunity to be most effective, the superintendent must meet regularly with the bargaining team, guide the strategy, and keep the school board posted on the status of bargaining.

The school board: Superintendents know and must remember that the management team is representing the school board in these contract negotiations. Input and bargaining recommendations from school management must be reviewed with the governing body. The school board is responsible to set the bargaining parameters, so the board must clearly be engaged in reviewing and understanding the direction management wishes to take with respect to the bargaining process.

The superintendent must help the school board know and understand the role of collective bargaining, how the process works, and prepare the board to handle potential interference or pressure to alter adopted parameters. This effort requires consistent communication updates to the board about the status of the bargaining process.

Setting parameters: Before bargaining begins, lead a review of the collective bargaining agreement (CBA) with school principals and other administrators. Examine labor-management meetings to identify issues that have occurred in the past year or two. Identify potential improvements to ease administrative complexity and better serve students. Use this review process to identify a few, key proposals to bring to the bargaining table on behalf of the community through the school board.

Knowledge about the bottom line for an agreement is a key bargaining practice. Some proposed principles, finances or processes from employee groups may violate fundamental values or beliefs of the school board or management team. Knowing these "hot button" issues and limits is essential in determining the best alternative to a negotiated agreement (BATNA). The long-standing negotiating guidance from Fisher, E. & Ury, W. (1981, 1991) is useful and informative to help you and your team understand setting your parameters.

Study interest based bargaining processes. Engage district leaders, including the school board, and the leadership of the union/association. When each party is clear about their interests, the other are better able to find solutions to their interests in ways that work for everyone. Hire a facilitator to help all parties develop interest-based approach to bargaining. It is a useful process to find workable resolution of issues, but it does take a commitment from all parties to work successfully.

Another vital aspect of the parameter setting process is often primarily led by the CFO; assess the cost of the current contract and the identify prospective fiscal of the district in light of anticipated proposals or interests from the employee groups. Salary and benefit items are not the only expense drivers; be sure that clear protocols are in place for the determination of both the short-range and multi-year impacts of ideas and proposal are considered.

Whatever parameter setting decisions for fiscal and management rights issues are made, it is vital that they be clear and re-visited throughout the process. Be prepared to discuss and share the long-term viability of proposals and areas accepted in the agreement. Forecasting the multi-year fiscal or operational implications for some concepts is essential.

Remember that the negotiating team is representing the school board in the bargaining process. Compare the final agreement with initial parameters in order to affirm and continue support from the governing board.

The bargaining team: Design of the bargaining team is directly related to the superintendent's role in monitoring and guiding the bargaining process. Bring knowledgeable, trusted administrators to the table representing the school board. Select a spokesperson for the bargaining team who has or can readily develop trust and confidence with the labor side of the table. Whether this is an internal administrator or position specifically designed to fulfill this role or is a contracted spokesperson for the board, make sure that you know the tone and style of the spokesperson. He or she will be your voice to the labor side of the house in the bargaining process.

The process: The district's bargaining history sets the context for whether a traditional proposal-counterproposal style is used or if alternative such as interest-based-bargaining are possible. Work with the union leadership to design the bargaining approach. Studying negotiations tools in concert with the labor leadership can help solve problems, address issues and carry-over into effective decision-making principles throughout the school system.

Using the labor-management process ahead of formal bargaining is a good way to engage both labor and management in determining how bargaining will occur. Joint educational sessions with management and labor leaders can lead to the development of more sophisticated and effective bargaining protocols. Joint educational sessions may build relationships and introduce trust-building bargaining strategies like interest-based bargaining that might better serve the community.

After the bargaining is complete, consider joint explanations sessions to the administrative team with labor leadership. Such an effort demonstrates a collaborative tone and sets an expectation that the transactional history of bargaining is being replaced. Be careful to make sure that this process is jointly developed.

Tips based on experience

The authors have all experienced many hours of bargaining involvement, both at the bargaining table and as advisers to the bargaining team. We share these tips from our combined experiences:

- Always respect the process. Take care to explore options but adhere to the agreed upon procedures and timelines.
- Always respect the people, even when conditions may test that respect. The burden on leadership to act with care is huge and isn't always returned in kind. You will be expected to forget aggressive behavior from employee representatives, but if you reciprocate, your behavior will be remembered.
- Document and date all proposals and cost estimates. Conditions may change and evolve with new information, clarification or policy decisions. Proper documentation may avoid future conflicts. Date and time stamp all proposals.
- See the bargaining process as a problem-solving process and use it to focus the strategic initiatives of the school district. Seek solutions that serve students by addressing mutual interests of employees.
- Seek to schedule labor-management meetings on a regular basis throughout the school year. Identify emerging issues and seek to resolve them without delay.
- Be prepared to go to the bargaining table as the superintendent in rare circumstances, usually as an agreement appears achievable; the presence of the superintendent to make an assurance or present a settlement proposal may be useful in some situations.

Conclusion

Careful, respectful human resources policies and practices set the tone for school success. Education is people intensive. Successful leaders see the value of openly and honestly addressing the interests of school personnel to effectively serve students. This essential fairness in day-to-day HR management sets a positive tone for bargaining and builds confidence that employee interests will be respected and useful in serving student interests.

Chapter 13

Legal Counsel

This chapter will help leaders learn to...
Know what to examine when selecting district legal counsel.
Know who should call the district's attorney and when.
Work effectively with your district's legal counsel.
Understand the nature of the Attorney-Client privilege and how to protect it.
Be sure you are getting what you're paying for.

Case Study

Nancy is in her first year in the 17,000 student Aloha School District. She was hired after a long, disruptive teacher work stoppage and difficult budget issues in its wake. The school board members are mostly new, having been replaced in the election that followed the strike. She'd begun to rebuild trust because everyone understood that a return to the disrespectful treatment of teachers by the school board was a key source of the previous conflict. Still, everyone was cautious as Nancy is young and had only been a superintendent a few years in her smaller, previous school district.

Several events throughout her first year gave all parties an indication that Nancy is clearly student oriented, focused on improvement, and respectful yet flexible in finding workable solutions to long-standing district issues related to class size, school construction and staffing. As she faces her first bargaining season with the teachers, she is hopeful, but worried.

One of the chief challenges was contract language many neighboring districts had adopted with their teachers' associations that added supplemental compensation to teachers beyond what appeared to be state established salary limits. Nancy is interested in finding a way to accomplish this outcome within the financial limits of the district. The school board is willing to consider this idea, so she convened a meeting with her lead negotiator and the school district attorney, the same person who had advised the district throughout bargaining, including during the strike.

The attorney is adamant that the solution Nancy is considering is not legal. Nancy realized he was one of the impediments to the previous contractual unrest. After much discussion, Nancy asks the attorney, "How have our neighbors managed to adopt these practices without legal repercussions?"

Her counsel responded, "They just haven't been held accountable by the state review process. You could go to jail by using these questionable efforts as a model."

But Nancy persisted that supplemental salary clauses had now been in place for several years. It was increasingly hard to defend objections to them that were not, in fact, realistic.

Finally, Nancy firmly told her counsel, "We need to become competitive for new teachers and retain our veteran staff. We will be creating affordable proposals like these for our teachers. Your role is to draft defendable language for us that will survive regulatory review."

If you were the superintendent…
What happens when you don't find your counsel's advice appropriate or useful?
Was Nancy appropriate to confront her attorney?

What options might she have considered?
What methods can you think of to give the district insight into the law?
What additional information will be needed and where might it be found?

Almost every facet of schooling has some connection to the law. State and federal legislative bodies consistently revise or add to the statutes guiding the work of school districts; rarely are any laws repealed.

Consequently, working with an attorney who specializes in school law is a prerequisite for every school superintendent and the district's senior-level leadership team. Finding the right cultural fit with legal counsel is as important as obtaining consistent, reliable legal counsel. If new to the district, meet early on with the district's legal counsel to get oriented to the status of legal issues. Whether new to the district or not, regular sessions with the school district's attorney are a worthwhile part of a superintendent's leadership routine.

The working relationship

When to call for help: Regardless of district size, establish a process with district level administrators and school principals addressing how to go about seeking legal counsel. With in-house legal counsel, access maybe regulated by the chief attorney. If outside counsel is used, designating a senior level administrator to be a point of contact for administrators who think they may need legal counsel is a wise way to manage costs and monitor legal questions.

In many cases, an experienced administrator will already know the legally, educationally appropriate action to take. This outcome emerges from prior legal consultation that doesn't need to be repeated. Unrestrained access to counsel can be expensive and overly complicate otherwise proper and prudent administrative actions. Having and following previous legal counsel will simplify actions and assure administrators that they have backup if necessary.

Staying in touch with legal counsel is especially necessary regarding special education law. The special education program director must know and carefully adhere to many timelines and other legal details to properly serve students and families and avoid costly legal remedies caused by errors.

Ongoing relationship practices: Numerous school functions require frequent review and consultation with legal counsel. Contracts with vendors, especially construction contracts or other complicated business relationship contracts, require legal counsel to protect all school district interests. Make sure procedures are in place via your business office to assure such review is completed prior to board approval and signatures.

School board policies and procedures are essential tools for management of many aspects of school life. The dynamic nature of legislative and administrative procedures by the state and federal governments, as well as updates from ongoing judicial decisions, make legal counsel necessary as new or revised district policies and procedures are considered for adoption. The state school board association may provide model policies and procedures for district action. Even though these model policies may have been reviewed by counsel, adapt them to local conditions based upon a legal review by counsel familiar with the district's operating principles.

Personnel issues are a major source of potential legal liability and conflict. Obtaining early counsel when adopting policies, developing employee contracts, and providing educational development to administrators about personnel matters is a valuable way legal counsel can support work that focuses on student achievement. It is essential to engage counsel in review of collective bargaining language and then the creation of employment contracts. When issues arise, and they will, early consultation about the case and how to respond in a legally defensible manner will save heartache and financial expense later in the process.

Grievance and other labor disputes about how to interpret contract language arise when unique circumstances or inappropriate behaviors occur. Wise legal counsel will have seen a variety of cases and know how case law applies to the situation. Avoidance of counsel in these matters is asking for trouble, so be vigilant in seeking and following legal advice when facing such matters.

The Business Side of School Success

One issue the superintendent faces is the potential tension that may emerge with legal counsel. As the case at the beginning of this chapter notes, counsel may sometimes evolve into trying to make administrative or organizational culture decisions that belong with district leadership. Superintendents and senior level administrators must maintain responsibility for decision making and remember that legal counsel is just that…counsel.

In general, it is valuable to respect and trust appropriate legal counsel. Most decisions will follow the advice of counsel, but superintendents must always evaluate the risk of modifying counsel or rejecting it to achieve other goals. Exercise great care when choosing this path, as this choice is risky and could lead to unwarranted legal difficulties.

Wise counsel will understand their role and support the district's work by sharing alternatives and identifying the potential risks of each one. If this relationship is developed, the district will be well served by its counsel. If evidence of weakness in this relationship exists, select new legal counsel (see the "Selecting Counsel" section that follows).

Attorney-client privilege: The confidentiality of counsel that is typical in the legal system typically is provided to the district and its administrators who seek legal counsel. Still, this "privilege" has limits and constraints.

One essential element of attorney-client privilege is that both parties must respect and honor it by not sharing any discussion of the issues covered by the "privilege" with anyone who is not properly a party to the issue. Because the public nature of school systems puts pressure on the superintendent or board members to share information with others (e.g., citizens, media, non-involved staff members, etc.,), care must be taken to understand what can and cannot be discussed outside the counsel provided.

Talk with the district's legal counsel if attorney-client privilege might be a concern or a requirement. Ask for parameters and follow them tenaciously.

Selecting counsel

An established, long-serving legal counsel may already exist. This counsel may be a district employee or through a long-standing relationship with a local law firm. Either way, a new superintendent will make an early assessment of the relationship provided by the district's legal counsel. A veteran superintendent will be wise to periodically evaluate such a relationship.

Assess the range of expertise the district's counsel brings to the work. Ask questions like these:

- Is the existing counsel a generalist or does she/he possess a particular special background such as personnel or construction law?
- What range of access to specialized counsel does the general counsel provide?
- What is the track-record of the firm or person in the role?
- Do the issues at hand require access to diverse areas of specialty?

Superintendents are well served to monitor the relationship with legal counsel over time and avoid making a snap decision about the adequacy of such counsel. If a determination to retain new counsel or take another approach arises, evaluate the range of available options. Consult with the school board early in this process as the district's counsel may have a well-established relationship with board members. Talk with neighboring superintendents about their experience with firms providing effective counsel for school systems. Consider the district's unique circumstances and how adding or changing counsel might enhance the overall risk management for the district. Also, consider hiring specialized counsel to augment the general counsel's role, especially if time consuming or challenging situations have emerged.

Most states allow discretion in hiring professional services like legal counsel, so it is unlikely that a bid or RFP process will be useful or appropriate for this role. Interviewing several firms will be beneficial, especially if the local bar is competitive. Always seek counsel with experience in educational legal matters.

Be clear about the client

Because superintendents work closely with the district's legal counsel this relationship may become cloudy when the superintendent's contractual interest and the district's interest conflict. The attorney representing the school district must keep this relationship crystal clear. The district's attorney is not the superintendent's attorney. Superintendents desiring legal counsel about their employment contract should obtain their own attorney.

When or if interests diverge (e.g., superintendent contract negotiations), the superintendent must acknowledge this separation of interests. If the superintendent needs legal counsel, it must be obtained from a different law firm than the one serving the district's board of directors.

Conclusion

Wise superintendents retain and rely upon a positive working relationship with the district's legal counsel. Finding the right relationship may require some adaptation by both the attorney and the superintendent, but finding the proper balance is vital to a successful school district. Seek and retain counsel that supports the mission and values of the school district. Superintendents must retain executive responsibility for the decisions and direction of the school district. Avoid shifting this burden for difficult leadership decisions to legal counsel.

Chapter 14

Enterprise Risk Management: What to Insure

This chapter will help leaders learn to...
Establish an enterprise risk management (ERM) program.
Understand the inherent risks connected with leading the school district.
Create a crisis management team.
Understand the need for disaster recovery processes.
Obtain an insurance broker to help manage residual risks.
Establish a comprehensive insurance program to help manage risks.

Case Study

Eugene Smith is a veteran school superintendent with five years getting to know the people of the West School District. The district safety officer, Mona Craft, calls Eugene to let him know that a serious accident has occurred on the interstate highway near West High School. A chlorine tanker has tipped over and created a chemical cloud that is drifting in the direction of the high school serving 1,200 students.

Ms. Craft advises Superintendent Smith that, "We have implemented the emergency evacuation strategy that's been created for situations like this."

Superintendent Smith recalls the recent ERM assessment meeting that included just such a risk in its planning session. He confirms with Mona that the school has been alerted and is responding. Next, he calls the crisis leadership team together in accordance with their safety protocols. But now what?

If you were the superintendent...
What actions would you have taken to prepare for an accident such as this?
How should the crisis leadership team operate?
What steps will you take to lead the district during and after a crisis such as this?
Who does Eugene call first? Should he immediately go to the high school or be present as the incident command meets?
What additional information will be needed and where might it be found?

Often, the purchase of insurance policies to cover school operations, transportation, worker safety, and many other risks associated with conducting education is viewed as a sufficient level of preparation for risk management. But risk management is more than selecting an insurance broker and paying annual insurance policy premiums.

Enterprise Risk Management (ERM): what is it?

Like many sectors of society, complex issues are often inappropriately examined in "silos" where valuable expertise is not effectively shared. In this condition, systemic perils as well as potential ways to mitigate organizational risks may not be identified. ERM is an important tool to examine all facets of the school district operations to identify risks that might be understated or missed entirely by each of its "silos."

ERM emerged in the business community as a way to identify and strengthen an entity's response to the risks that emerge from its activities. Mark Beasley, a professor leading the Enterprise Risk Management Institute at North Carolina State University notes that:

The objective of enterprise risk management is to develop a holistic, portfolio view of the most significant risks to the achievement of the entity's most important objectives. The "e" in ERM signals that ERM seeks to create a top-down, enterprise view of all the significant risks that might impact the strategic objectives of the business. In other words, ERM attempts to create a basket of all types of risks that might have an impact – both positively and negatively – on the viability of the business. (Beasley, Mark. "What is Enterprise Risk Management (ERM)?", July 2020, p. 4).

Applying ERM techniques to schools involves engaging the leadership team in understanding the inherent risks associated with its educational endeavor. Identifying and implementing actions to remediate these inherent risks is fundamental to knowing what residual risk remains. This knowledge directs what structures, policies, procedures, and other protections need to be in place to address these residual risks. In developing risk awareness, the district's leadership team will be able to identify actions that might be avoided or purchase the financial protection necessary to restore services and facilities in the event one of the risks materializes.

Increasing awareness of the complex array of risks facing public schools makes using the principles of ERM valuable. A wise district leadership team will spend quality time evaluating the natural, physical, legal, health, educational, social, and political risks facing the school district. Take the time to identify these risks as specifically as possible, examine ways to address the risks, and determine the residual risks that remain. Inherent risks are best identified in advance and should be shared with the school board along with mitigation strategies being taken to address. The residual risks will inform the level and nature of insurance coverage the district should secure to protect the district from fiscal exposure to risks that cannot be mitigated.

How might ERM be conducted?

Superintendent leadership is vital to creating a culture that places teamwork and integrity as essential values. The "tone at the top" matters. To that end, the ERM function must be sponsored by the superintendent setting an expectation for each function within the school system.

The Business Side of School Success

When departments within the district work as separate functions, systemic risks will be missed. To reduce this potential risk, at least annually, the superintendent should convene a meeting of the leadership team to examine the district's risk profile. The teaching and learning perspective might examine areas of risk that could prevent schools from being conducted as planned (e.g., the COVID-19 pandemic, weather, a chemical spill on a local railway, etc.,). Operations staff managing the heating, ventilation and sanitary systems of school buildings will also identify key risks to the safe and predictable operation of the school system. Finance, human resources, student transportation, nutrition services, and special programs serving students will all add important considerations to this effort. A more complete view of system risks emerges when each function understands the risks in other "silos."

One important skill for performing this assessment of potential risks is the identification of the underlying assumptions each specific function uses to perform its routine work. Once the core assumptions are identified, the risks associated with each function become clearer to all leaders.

Finally, the team must examine the overall environment in which the school operates to explore the interaction effects of each functional set of risks. What minor threat in one area could completely disable the operation of another function?

With a complete list of these "inherent" risks, the team can examine how to remediate the risks. Ask questions like:

- What actions are routinely taken to eliminate or reduce the risk?
- What happens if the risk materializes?
- What response mechanisms are in place to address the risk?
- Do response mechanisms need to be developed or refined based on this assessment?
- Do other agencies or vendors help mediate risks or create more risk?

The resulting identification of "residual" risk represents the risk the district undertakes simply by operating as a school system.

How are the inherent risks managed?

Awareness: Identifying the risks is a key first step in assessing the district's readiness to respond or manage risk. Using the process identified above and shown in Figure 2 below is a positive first step.

Training and practice: Schools have long conducted the periodic "fire drill" so students and staff know how to evacuate the building if necessary. This long-practiced skill is a good example of how to address risk, but it needs to be expanded into new areas. For example, the horrible emergence of school shootings has altered the landscape so that the fire drill concept has expanded into the active-shooter drill. Specific plans need to be developed and practiced on a regular basis to alert the students and staff to the risks and to prepare them for a response, especially when a natural evacuation response is not the correct response.

Adding new wrinkles into these routine drills is an important way to upgrade "practice." For example, simulate a real fire with the blockage of a planned exit route so students and staff must adapt to actual conditions. With shooter drills, for example, the choice to exit the building or lockdown may require an on-site assessment of the conditions causing the event.

Another approach to training is engaging principals and key district support staff in a tabletop exercise that requires thinking through actions that would be required for certain threats or risks. These exercises create the opportunity to identify gaps or problems that might otherwise be overlooked.

Crisis management team: Many events require support or a response from police or fire agencies. A crisis is typically not the time for debates and extensive group problem solving, so the emergency responders rely upon and train using an incident command process. The "command-oriented" lines of authority used by incident command procedures may conflict with more participatory decision processes used within school systems.

Work with emergency responders to understand their incident command protocol. Advance knowledge of these processes must be combined with clear identification of the lines of authority and the roles required for crisis management team members. These efforts will improve responses and allow for shared educational sessions with police and fire fighting personnel. When people know the language and structure of an incident command process, response effectiveness improves, and lives may be saved.

Disaster recovery planning: Emergency preparedness planning is a cross-functional requirement that intends to protect people first and then physical assets. A leadership team approach might be led by either the HR Director or the CFO, depending on the willingness and skills of the people in those positions. Including representatives of all employee organizations, building principals and other district level administrators (e.g., school supervisors plus maintenance and operations, pupil transportation, and school nutrition leaders) in this effort is essential.

Using the ERM process, identify the high-risk threats to the school system. The COVID-19 Pandemic that began in 2019 highlights how planning for a serious health threat might be high on the agenda. Natural disaster potential or other situational relevant accidents also require advance preparation and response practice. Potential risks are plentiful, but some areas that require attention include:

- Cyberattack on data files or computer operating systems.
- Loss of communication access via telephone and/or internet.
- Weather impacts (e.g., hurricane damage, ice storm, etc.).
- Fire damage or wildfire incident.
- Chemical spills or other traffic related catastrophe in proximity of a school or support facilities.
- School bus accident.
- Employee behavioral incident.

A variety of planning approaches are possible, depending on the type of incident that might happen. A school shooting will require strong relationships with the local police department(s) and knowledge of incident command protocols. A pandemic might rely upon the same principle but require guidance from health authorities at the local and state level. Disaster preparation allows the school leadership to build relationships with the appropriate emergency responders, primarily law enforcement, fire fighters, EMTs, and public health officials.

Recovery procedures may involve obtaining emergency assistance from county, state or federal sources designed to offset the unique expenses associated with the response process. Re-building damaged equipment, facilities, and vehicles is a separate and fiscal-oriented responsibility. Still, such efforts will dominate the school system leadership at all levels and must be anticipated in advance, perhaps even to be able to open schools to students and staff.

Use practice events such as planned table-top exercises or even physical walk-through drills to rehearse emergency responses and build systems capabilities. Thinking about these cases in advance will identify system needs, communication protocols, and areas where further investment and refinement of procedures are necessary.

Purchase equipment or supplies: The assessment of risks may result in an identification of gaps in necessary response equipment or supplies. Access to supplies for a multi-day emergency, safety equipment, and other tools for handling events may require funding in a budget cycle. ERM actions build knowledge and support for such fiscal discipline.

Putting it all together

Creating a team representing all facets of the school district to monitor risks and highlight them for the leadership team is a smart superintendent action. Further, at least annually, share this work with the school board in a public work session. Keeping the board and the community apprised of potential risks and how the district is preparing to respond to them makes sense. It is also helpful to demonstrate that residual risk remains a part of the school system's educational enterprise.

ERM is a continuous process based on knowing the district's strategic objectives. Clearly identify risks and evaluate their significance and then decide what actions to take. These actions must be communicated to all and monitored for success. And then the process is repeated. Beasley (2020) shares a graphic explanation of this process (see the following Figure 2).

Figure 2
Source: Beasley, Mark. 2020, p. 5.

Insurance: An important tool to address risk

Policies, practice, and investment in equipment and other physical assets combine to provide important tools to address the most potentially damaging residual risks. ERM planning activities will help the response if a risk event occurs, but they won't provide the financial backing needed to accomplish restorative work. That's the role for the district's insurance program.

Several options exist for retaining the insurance expertise necessary for a proper evaluation of the risks facing the school district. Evaluating prior litigation, the number of people employed, and the total square footage of all facilities owned and used by the district and its condition will be among the factors used by the insurance team to obtain quotes for coverage.

Scaling insurance coverage with core coverage and umbrella plans is a useful way to engage multiple carriers, spread the risk, and manage costs.

Insurance premium payments are typically annualized so this review of insurance coverage is a function that must be conducted in time to estimate insurance budgets for each fiscal year.

Key to developing an adequate insurance portfolio is using the ERM program in concert with an insurance professional who can help structure the insurance program that will provide the financial support for restoration or response efforts. A Request for Proposals (RFP) approach is an appropriate way to solicit proposals from the insurance industry for the person or team to advise the district about how to structure its insurance program. Consider selecting an adviser who is not compensated through a commission from insurance premium payments to a company who provides the insurance. The practice avoids building a conflict of interest into the advice that is provided to the district's leadership team.

The purchase of liability insurance programs for actions (or sometimes inactions) of school employees is vital to the district's financial protection. Of course, avoiding such claims is the best practice, but human errors do occur, and liability may fall upon the district for such actions or inactions of its personnel. Adequate insurance limits will be determined by local conditions, something that the ERM process will help identify. This coverage is reassuring to district staff and represents a wise personnel practice, too.

Other major insurance coverage will address vehicles owned by the district, including school buses and all the other vehicles used for district business. Facility damages caused by fire, natural disasters, vandalism and other actions is another vital part of the district's insurance coverage. Finally, Errors & Omissions (E&O) coverage for district leaders and the board of directors is important. Each of these components might be enhanced by providing some appropriate form of umbrella coverage to protect against an abnormally expensive event or incident. Actively consider the deductible included in these policies to help manage premium levels; a higher deductible amount will reduce the premium, a decision that may be determined by the district's overall financial condition.

The Business Side of School Success

Worker safety programs entail another form of insurance, typically called Workers' Compensation. Some states (like Washington State) provide this coverage through a state agency funded by a tax paid by employers based on employer payroll levels. Larger districts may choose to self-insure. Smaller districts often acquire scale and lower rates by forming cooperative insurance pools administered by their regional education support entity.

Some states allow employers to seek this coverage for worker injuries from the private sector. In this situation, consider adding the selection of a Workers' Compensation program would best be handled in coordination with the insurance consultation approach already suggested.

Conclusion

The educational process is not risk free. Protecting students, district personnel, and the public participants is paramount. To provide services in the best possible manner, the school superintendent must make sure that risks are identified and actions to mediate those risks are implemented. This continuous effort relies upon processes seeking diverse perspectives and the engagement of all elements of school district operations

Chapter 15

School District Operations

Many operational support functions assure students have safe, productive places to learn. Effectively providing support services allows greater focus on teaching and student learning. The diverse nature of school support services involves many decisions that influence the educational and fiscal health of the school system. Well managed and funded support services play a direct role in keeping the district and the community focused on students and their success.

Because many of these support functions interface with resource allocation and operational requirements, many districts align the leadership of these functions with that of the business office. This reporting arrangement elevates the organizational support for support services but may lead to tension with other departments resulting from support services being close to the budget developing officials. Superintendents must manage this tension and make decisions in light of the district's mission.

The success of maintenance, technology, custodial, nutrition, school security, and transportation services influence the school climate for students and staff. The more each department leader is aware of the role played by other departments in the success of students, the stronger the district culture will become. For this reason, the major operational departments typically found in school districts are reviewed in this chapter.

The Business Side of School Success

It is intended that this overview assist both veteran and new superintendents in finding the important balance in providing both educational program funding and vital support services.

A. Maintenance and Custodial Services

This section will help leaders learn to...
Know the key components of the maintenance and custodial departments.
Identify key areas that need to be considered.
Understand what questions to ask about contracting for such services.
Knowing what questions to ask about a district operated program.
Apply tips for superintendents.

Case Study

Scott arrived in his new district after a competitive superintendent search and selection process. On his first day in the office Scott visited with the members of the management team. He asks each of them to identify any problems or concerns that are challenges for their functional area of responsibility.

Six months later, Scott is surprised to learn that the Maintenance and Custodial supervisor is being cited by the district's auditor for allowing employees to borrow equipment from the district. According to the auditor, this practice contributed to a department culture that permitted staff to ignore district rules, regulations and policies, and set a tone that internal controls were unimportant. The practice also violates a state constitutional clause against making a gift of public funds. The supervisor is now accused of fraud as he has been one of many employees who has used district cars and equipment for personal use.

Scott must place his Maintenance and Custodial administrator on administrative leave pending an investigation. Fortunately, because Scott was new to the district, he was unaware of the lending practice and wasn't personally implicated. Conversely, this abuse has happened on his watch and citizens are asking questions about his knowledge and why it has taken six months to discover this abuse.

If you were the superintendent…
What questions needed to be asked to reveal this situation when you first came to the district?
What opportunities did Scott miss?
Was the auditor the only way he would know of a problem?
What could have been done to prevent this situation?
What do you do now? What resistance are you likely to encounter?
What technology could help resolve this issue?
What additional information will be needed and where might it be found?

What superintendents need to know about maintenance and custodial programs

Administrators who were teachers and previously served as principals typically have first-hand experience with the impact of a proper maintenance and custodial program on an effective learning environment. Conversely, and unfortunately, when these programs fall short of expectations conditions for students, staff, and the public suffer.

Many of the district's support services reveal more to the community than activities within the classroom. If this visible area is poorly performed, what assumptions might the community make about what is happening within the school where many citizens can't so easily observe?

Given the important role that facilities and their care require for successful educational programs, superintendents must examine the level of support and service that exists in the district's support services. These functions benefit from wise planning and resource management. Providing a clean and safe environment for children and creating a physical setting that is appropriate for learning actively supports teaching and learning and respects the community.

The maintenance and custodial functions are charged with protecting the community's substantial interest in district facilities. Doing so in an effective and cost-efficient manner requires access to accurate and timely information about the conditions of each school site and appropriateness of facility management efforts that are applied across the district.

To begin, conduct a site review of each school building with the district's maintenance and custodial supervisor. Inspecting the current condition of the school buildings will provide context for subsequent meetings and reviews of documents and proposals. Look for indications of damage or unsafe conditions. Treat this initial review as though you are a district patron deciding about sending your child to these schools. Examine the halls, the offices, the classrooms and the grounds. Do they appear to be carefully and thoughtfully maintained?

Another tactic is to set up a group of citizens who are willing to review all the facilities. Request this group to inspect the schools and issue a report to the superintendent. Share this report with the school board and use it for budget development and to take remediation actions.

Meet with the building principal and district level program administrators to identify things that are working well and areas where improvements are sought. See what program leaders have to say. Is the leadership concerned about the image of the school projected by its maintenance? Does a deferred maintenance list exist? If so, what projects or needs are listed? Do plans exist to address the backlog?

Next examine the required reports sent to the local health department, the state education agency, and the federal government. These reports may include annual or periodic reports on asbestos, air quality, Polychlorinated Biphenyls (PCBs), pesticides, carpet and rugs, disaster planning, hazardous materials handling, heating, ventilation and air conditioning (HVAC) systems, pest management, water quality, playground safety, radon, storm water runoff, and underground fuel tanks. Ensure that an inventory of these

The Business Side of School Success

various reports is prepared that highlights their key points and identifies where copies may be found. Produce a schedule for when such reports are due to be renewed and identify the administrator responsible for each report.

This schedule may already exist, but if it doesn't, make sure one is compiled. This inventory should be comprehensive (many of the reports are to be signed by the superintendent) and updated whenever there are changes or if a new requirement is added. Identify the district's weak areas and ask for a plan to improve the situation.

Superintendents will want to stay abreast of developments with the district's facilities because of the significant impact these facilities have support of the educational programs. Among the key questions to ask periodically, especially as a new superintendent, include:

- When will this inventory of reports be accomplished or when was it last updated?
- Who is assigned to take the lead on each report?
- What is the anticipated cost to repair/replace/fix the most concerning items?
- When will the deferred maintenance plan be updated?

Use this analysis to maintain an up-to-date list of timely facility investments or to highlight the impact of previously deferred maintenance projects. Present a plan to address at least one or two items a year to the school board during the early phase of budget development.

Consider emphasizing these areas to be studied in a facilities review:

- Are buildings spreading COVID-19 or other respiratory illnesses? Indoor air quality is a focus, both for students and staff. There should be an increased emphasis on changing filters and upgrading HVAC systems.
- Do barriers to learning exist that can be identified and resolved?
- Have regulatory agencies identified facility issues that require action (e.g., asbestos abatement, lead in the drinking water, etc.,)?
- Are facilities accessible for all students, staff, and citizens?

- Have district facilities been remodeled to address issues related to seismic conditions, flooding, or other potential natural disasters typical in the community?
- Are safety and security issues being addressed in facility retrofits or remodeling?

Key points to be considered

Strive to run an efficient maintenance and custodial program that meets the school community's needs. If changes are required, develop a plan that seeks to accomplish these changes in an incremental manner. Large fiscal impacts may overwhelm the district and render efforts frustrating, but making incremental progress is more affordable and demonstrates action. Use a multi-year fiscal plan to describe this effort.

Still, some facilities situations may have deteriorated so badly that bold action is demanded. If the district is facing such a dilemma, develop a multi-year capital improvement plan might be used to support a dedicated capital property tax levy or bond issue (see Chapter 16—Capital Projects and Bonds). Include stakeholders in the early phases of planning. Use a citizen planning committee and be sure to involve the school board early and often as the board will ultimately need to finalize an action plan for facility improvements.

Deferred maintenance issues

Given persistent financial constraints, routine and required maintenance of basic mechanical, electrical, and facility envelope systems is often deferred because the consequence of this expense avoidance decision won't be immediately apparent. Eventually, though, the accumulation of such delays will take a toll on the condition of facilities. If no preventative maintenance schedule exists, call for the development of such a plan. Even a small step to start preventative maintenance will pay-off with reduced future costs.

An assessment of major systems with an accompanying schedule defining when required maintenance is to be performed will add long-term benefits and save money over time. Development of a comprehensive list of deferred maintenance should include a cost estimate and a presentation of the schedule to the school board.

When combined with a preventative maintenance program, a financial plan to address critical deferred maintenance enhances the student learning environment. Such efforts also reassure the community that their investments in capital facility improvements will be maintained for the expected life of the investment, a vital element in obtaining voter support.

Contracting for maintenance and/or custodial services

When seemingly unsolvable internal issues or low service levels exist for the maintenance and/or custodial services functions, contracting with a third party is sometimes viewed as "the answer." Without a careful assessment of the underlying causes for issues, a contracting solution may just shift the problem without a high probability for improvement.

So, before formally considering contracting with a private firm to provide maintenance and/or operations and custodial services, ask focused questions about the current state of operations. Such questions might include:

- Do clear program standards of service exist?
- Is the current program meeting these quality standards?
- Does the existing management team have the expertise and skill to do an excellent job?
- Are complaints handled promptly and successfully?
- Are facilities and equipment appropriately in place to support the expected work of the maintenance and operations program?
- Is there a clear process to communicate concerns and issues? Are responses timely and complete?

Depending on the assessment of these conditions, a move to hire a firm that specializes in providing comprehensive support services may be prudent. This approach may rankle existing staff, require delicate union negotiations, and/or generate negative community responses. Exercise care to understand your community culture before considering this option.

Key questions to consider when evaluating the contracting decision include:

- What deficiencies or costs might be addressed via a contract for services?
- Do labor agreements or state laws govern how or if a contract for services can be used? How will these constraints be addressed? Is it realistic?
- What services would be covered by the contract?
- How long would the contract be in place?
- When is the next opportunity to make changes or negotiate a better deal?

Moving forward with such a plan requires creating a clear, concise document outlining the expected working relationship, the services to be provided, the duration of the program, and how it will be evaluated. Solicit proposals after adequate notice and thoroughly evaluate the responses before recommending a vendor to the school board.

Be sure that district counsel reviews any proposed contract, including renewals, before it is presented to the school board for approval. With help from legal counsel, ensure that a performance bond is part of the contract.

Custodial services

As health and safety issues have taken new prominence in a post-pandemic world, the school custodian role is increasingly visible and important. Many of the people involved in providing this service are residents of the community and have key relationships throughout the community. They will be key communicators about district conditions to many district patrons. Make sure these staff members are well informed about district services, expectations, and work plans.

Custodial services are mostly provided when school personnel and students are not present. Consequently, these staff members have more than normal autonomy. Create clear expectations for sensitive and routine supervision combined with clear descriptions of areas to be cleaned and procedures for the work. Provide consistent opportunities for teaching these staff members about the cleaning expectations and provide proper safety equipment and products to accomplish the task. For example, an investment in equipment can improve morale and output, help contain labor costs, and create a clean, safe learning environment for students.

Custodians provide the day-to-day cleaning services as well as minor building repairs. Custodians are generally supervised by a head custodian who reports to either the director of facilities or perhaps also the building principal. This shared reporting responsibility needs to be acknowledged to avoid confusion. The head custodian, with the school principal and the director of facilities, should jointly plan work to be completed on both a daily and a long-term basis.

Longer-term projects to be completed by custodians can be conducted during weeks when schools are closed to students and the public for holidays or recesses. Remember, that these staff already have routinely required work that must be completed during the interim, so be sure to allow enough time to complete additional assignments.

The superintendent should monitor the maintenance of school buildings by periodically meeting with the facilities director and the principal. Superintendent site visits add detail and first-hand observations to these sessions. The school facilities director coordinates with school principals to make sure district schools are being properly maintained.

Depending on school board policies or collective bargaining agreements, the role of the school principal in supervising the custodial services may vary from school district to school district. Despite the reality that school custodial activities are not the principal's top priority, principals will play an active role in overseeing this function and ensuring their buildings have a clean, safe environment for students and staff.

An effective maintenance and operations supervisor will understand the principal's competing interests and that building condition correlates with student achievement. Seek to find a balance and an appropriate sense of teamwork to support the principal's focus on teaching and learning.

Custodial staffing considerations

The number of custodians needed to provide the service required depends on the size of the building, the age of students served, and the overall condition of the building. Younger students are more apt to be involved with activities on the floor, so extra care needs to address floor cleanliness. An older building that has not been maintained may require a larger staff because more repairs may be required. Additionally, custodial staff in a school building can be a function of a collective bargaining agreement.

Ray, Condoli, & Hack (2005, p. 254) provide a frequently used formula to equitably determine custodial staffing assignments:

Enrollment / 250 = Number of full-time positions (N1)
N1 x 16,000 square feet = Square feet covered per position (N1)

Total Building Square feet – Allowance above = Remaining square feet
Remaining square feet / 25,000 = Number of part-time positions (N2)

Total custodial staff = N1 + N2

The checklist on the following page illustrates a partial list of custodial duties that could be included in an inspection form. The inspection should be done at least weekly and signed by the head custodian and principal. Areas requiring attention should be discussed with the custodian in charge of the area inspected and corrective action taken.

Partial List of Custodial Duties

Area	Yes	No	Comment
The outside appearance of building			
Evidence of no hazards or unsafe			

equipment on play areas, athletic fields			
The office is clean, well-organized			
Restrooms are clean and working, free of odor, and supplied with toilet tissue, soap, waste containers, and paper towels			
Floors, walls, and corners are clean, well-maintained, and free of excessive wax build-up; walls are clean and free of graffiti			
Ceiling tiles are replaced if needed			
Classrooms are clean, dusted, and orderly			
Comfortable room temperatures are maintained			
Vents and air returns are clean			
Report observed needs for maintenance work			

Other operational considerations

Tools to support successful maintenance and custodial functions must exist within the district. Among the many ways to support these sometimes overlooked school supports are:

Computerized work order systems: Work order systems are used to document, track, and acknowledge work requests from appropriate staff. Numerous computer software packages are available for this purpose. The software is used to log the request, set a priority, assign the task to a person or department, confirm the work completion, and track associated costs.

This process may be handled manually, depending on the school size and technological support. However, for large school systems, work order systems that are computerized and part of a computerized maintenance management system are more efficient. These software applications have become affordable and "user-friendly," making training easier. The software may be integrated into other systems or be stand alone. We prefer an integrated system if the department has sufficient resources to overcome the training for a change.

Environmental considerations: Be mindful of all laws or regulations regarding the use of environmentally sensitive cleaning products in public and nonpublic schools. Confer with the facilities director regarding any state or federal websites containing this information.

Training: Many federal and state regulations require training on the part of custodial and maintenance personnel. While these requirements are continually changing, some of the key compliance areas include:

1. Personal protective equipment
2. Occupational illness and injury
3. Integrated pest management
4. Indoor air quality
5. Hazard communication
6. Chemical safety
7. Asbestos awareness and management
8. Bloodborne pathogens

Larger districts may require a position for environmental health and safety to assure compliance with legal and regulatory requirements for product usage and the associated employee training requirements.

The Business Side of School Success

Tips for superintendents

- Maintenance and custodial operations issues are complex, and weaknesses are often not easily resolved. Seek steady improvement based upon program strengths.
- Establish standards of service and monitor progress toward their use.
- Develop and use a plan for routine and required maintenance. Create a comprehensive list of deferred maintenance issues with fiscal estimates. Begin to address deferred maintenance issues.
- Prepare a comprehensive schedule of required reports, due dates, and establish a notification system that ensures compliance with these deadlines.
- Visit school regularly and pay attention to the physical condition that introduces the school to all visitors. Is it safe? Does it show pride in care? What suggestions can be shared with the principal and/or facilities director?
- Include funding packages that address facility services needs and address deferred maintenance in each budget cycle, even when overall budget reductions may be necessary.

B. Pupil Transportation

This section will help leaders learn to…

Understand what needs to be known about the pupil transportation program.

Know the key concepts that need to be considered regarding transportation services.

Identify the questions to consider to fully understand and manage effective in-house operations.

Identify the questions to ask if considering contracting.

See the importance of understanding the transportation service function.

Case Study

Brittany has been superintendent for six months when she gets a call from her Transportation Manager at three in the morning.

The Transportation Manager tells her, "Sorry to wake you. But I think we should drive the routes this morning. We have an inch of snow in town, but I'm worried about the foothills. I've called in the Maintenance Manager and he's taking the routes to the north. I'm going to do the routes to the east. Then we'll do the south and west routes. I'll give you another call at about 4:30 to make a recommendation."

Brittany tells her, "I've got the routes to the west. Let's each drive our areas and try to make it to the Transportation office by four. That way I'll understand what we're facing and be able to answer the calls that will inevitably come to my office."

The Business Side of School Success

Brittany quickly gets dressed. She makes sure she has chains, flares, blankets, gloves, and warm clothing with her and starts driving her route. Listening to a radio station she learns that traffic is moving at a snail pace in the city about fifty miles away. As she climbs the foothills to the west, heavy snow pelts her car and visibility quickly drops to near zero. She realizes there's no way to complete her route, so she turns her car around and slowly makes her way back to the Transportation office. She pulls her vehicle into the lot and sees that her Maintenance Manager has beat her back.

"How did your drive go?" he asks when she enters the office.

"Terrible," she replies. "Let's find out what the other districts in the area are going to do before we make our decision."

A car pulls into the lot. The Maintenance Manager says, "Here's the Transportation Manager now. It will be interesting to compare notes on what she found."

If you were the superintendent...
Why might it be a good idea to share the driving of the routes with other managers?
Do you know who will handle this responsibility?
What technology can make this job easier?
What methods are available to check what neighboring districts are doing in the middle of the night?
What additional information will be needed and where might it be found?
This case study involves a decision for a late start or cancellation. What about this decision-making process will make your communication easier?

What superintendents need to know about pupil transportation

Most districts are required by state law to provide student transportation services (district operated or through a contractor). The district's transportation manager must exhibit a unique mix of skills that include understanding educational priorities and customer service combined with practical knowledge about leading a large fleet operation. The manager should have knowledge about district policies, state laws, rules and guidelines, age and condition of the fleet, scheduling, and mobile communication needs.

A superintendent who is new to the district will wisely make an early contact with the transportation program administrator to verify she/he understands that service and safety are high priorities. Such awareness will also help the manager communicate about the unique challenges and requirements of transportation in service of the district's students.

An effective pupil transportation manager will have a thorough understanding of driver qualifications, routing considerations, the status of bus safety inspections, procedures for bus safety drills, and complaint logs. The district assumes considerable risk and liability by putting a bus fleet on the road, so these factors are essential tools to manage risk and serve the community in a proper fashion.

The transportation program must balance between a customer service orientation (to students, families and schools), efficient business practices, and technical/operational know-how. Some parents will demand services that exceed the to-and-from school transportation standards the district has established. Tight, well-written policies will guide how the school transportation routes, bus stops, and schedules are established. These policies and procedures must consider state funding requirements as well as respond to local conditions and preferences. Make sure that transportation services criteria are reviewed in public school board sessions, are understood by all parties, and adopted by the school board.

When complaints arise, and they will, it is appropriate to expect that the transportation manager be the initial administrator to handle them. An appeal process that allows a request for review of administrative actions should be included in the program standards. Typically, such a request initiates an initial review by the transportation manager. If still unresolved, the complaint process might provide for one administrative review, and if still unresolved the ultimate determination for resolution resides with the school board.

Thoroughly prepare board members for this quasi-judicial review. Ensure that transportation policies are reviewed frequently so that dynamic community conditions are identified and addressed by the process. The transportation manager must regularly apprise district leadership when conditions are at variance with established standards.

Special education transportation: Students with special needs require unique transportation support. The special education director and the pupil transportation director need to work collaboratively to ensure every child who needs transportation services gets them safely and efficiently. This service is often door-to-door service and requires special vehicles and extraordinary driver preparation. For some students, a specialized aide may be necessary to assist the driver. Because of student Individualized Education Program (IEP) decisions and program availability, the district may transport students with unique needs to special programs offered by another district.

School day schedules: Sequencing routes so that one wave of buses can transition to another wave often means that elementary and secondary school start times may need to be staggered. The investment in buses is a significant fixed cost and affects the annual operating costs of pupil transportation. Wise district managers therefore want to maximize the use of buses and minimize the number of them to adequately serve all students while still leaving the system with flexibility.

In large geographic areas with significant transportation obligations, the district may be required to have multiple school start times. The start time and length of school day are educational issues, but this issue affects transportation costs that may alter the amount of funds available for educational programs. Educators, especially principals, need to understand how transportation duties intersect with these decisions. Some key questions in this tension are:

- How do school start times interact with community traffic patterns throughout the day?
- How might changing school schedules impact transportation?
- What is the length of time students must spend on the bus? How does this compare to board adopted policies?
- What supports, if any, are required helping students get to and from the bus pick up points?

- How are students guided at the school drop-off point and getting back on the correct bus for the trip to the local area drop-off point?

The answers to these questions affect overall transportation costs and may require an increased need to devote limited resources to transportation rather than to direct educational programs and services.

The start and stop times for elementary, middle, and high schools play a significant role in transportation scheduling and cost management. The emerging conversation about moving secondary school start times later in the morning, for example, triggers all of the above questions and more. This issue is an excellent example of the way investments in student achievement are affected by the support service functions required to serve students and families. We don't intend to fully explore this debate here, but addressing this issue requires bringing parents, educators and operations personnel together to study the research and examine potential solutions.

Mid-day transportation runs (often used where half-day kindergarten programs exist), changing bus stops, changing attendance boundaries, and before and after school transportation (getting students to school early and home late) are other areas where superintendents must balance the needs of many with the needs of a few. The interests of entrenched stakeholders must carefully be considered before making changes. Try to keep a multi-year view in mind when resolving these challenges. Developing clear service standards is essential to the evaluation of changing demographics and housing patterns in the district.

Special program considerations: Serving students who may be homeless and under coverage of the McKinney-Vento law, as well as other programs that require out-of-district transportation of students is another area with transportation complexity. Prepare to examine this issue by working with the coordinator of special programs for the homeless or legal counsel to ensure that the district's transportation program serves these students properly. Managing this issue is part of the commitment to receive federal funding.

The Business Side of School Success

Student discipline: Student behavior before, during, and after the bus ride is often an issue that requires collaboration between school site leadership, the bus driver, and parents or guardians. Typically, standards for safe behavior on the school bus are part of the student rights and responsibility statement that evolves from "in school" behavior guidance. Provide a means for the transportation team to engage with school principals and others to develop workable practices for this important safety issue.

Operational considerations: Another challenge to some school districts is how the location of transportation facilities impact operations. Buses require a maintenance facility and large parking areas that are centrally located and secure. Sometimes a satellite bus storage facility is used to efficiently serve an area remote from your central transportation area. Geographic conditions and availability of appropriate siting for such facilities is a complex factor that varies by district.

Developing a cooperative program among districts can produce economies of scale for repair and maintenance. Also, especially in urban areas, working with the regional public transportation system may benefit students and allow scheduling flexibility for the diverse school program requirements.

Evaluating transportation services

Many aspects to the transportation program can trip up a superintendent. Make a realistic appraisal of the district's current reality. Build upon this starting position and make improvements every year to get closer to an ideal state.

If a review of the program hasn't recently been conducted, conduct a comprehensive program review to use as a guideline to improve your transportation services. Consider studying these areas in such a review:

- Has the district established comprehensive policies and procedures for transportation services, including those for eligible ridership? Is the district in compliance with those policies?

- Is the district in compliance with all applicable local and state administrative regulations?
- Do the employees responsible for transporting students meet all standards and qualifications set by the state?
- Does the District or the vendor have supporting information showing that all drivers meet minimum training qualifications? Does the district have the necessary credentials required for employees to perform their duties?
- Are required pre-trip safety inspections on district buses documented? How does the district conduct and review vendor bus pre-trip inspections?
- Are vehicles monitored and securely safeguarded?
- Are vehicles maintained and replaced according to state guidelines?
- Are reports, inspections, and maintenance data complete, accurate, and submitted in a timely manner? Are required bus safety drills conducted and documented?
- Are equipment and supply inventories monitored and accurately recorded?
- Are fleet management services provided efficiently?
- Is fuel usage effectively controlled?
- Are bus routes and supplemental transportation scheduled efficiently?
- Are hazardous routes identified and updated at least annually?
- Is accurate information submitted to the state as required (e.g., routes, riders, and operational costs)?
- Does transportation operate within budgetary constraints?
- Is transportation provided adequate resources to fulfill its goals?

Key issues to consider

Efficiency aside, nothing can sidetrack a superintendent faster than a bus driver's failure to adequately inspect their bus at the end of a run. When this happens, and if a child falls asleep at the back of the bus and is overlooked, all the district's goodwill evaporates. Hours will be spent grappling with the fallout of such an event.

Make sure the driver training protocol requires each driver to fully inspect the bus at the end of every bus run and especially when returning to the storage location. If possible, use technology (e.g., a switch at the back of the bus) to ensure that bus drivers adequately conduct this inspection at the end of each route. Make sure that policies and procedures support dealing with bus drivers in a consistent and fair process.

Increasingly, conditions have evolved and intensified pressure on attracting an adequate supply of people willing to serve as bus drivers (e.g., the COVID-19 pandemic). Recruitment of drivers requires thoughtful exploration of community conditions, salary and benefit levels, and other working conditions. Filling the pipeline with new drivers is challenging due to the unique training requirements that must be met before putting a driver behind the wheel with students. A strong relationship between the HR function and the transportation department leadership is essential to managing the driver availability issues.

Screening potential drivers for their driving safety records is essential. Consider the appropriateness of drug screening as part of the selection process. Periodic screening of existing drivers may also be a sound risk-reduction process; it will likely require negotiating the process with the drivers' union or association. Monitoring new and existing drivers for traffic violations and/or drug and alcohol usage is increasingly necessary.

Given the selection process and training efforts, school buses and drivers generally have solidly positive safety records. Still, accidents will happen. Make sure a crisis response team has been developed ahead of time so a response to the immediate conditions of the accident can be addressed. Conduct after-accident reviews and adjust procedures, maintenance or systems as required. Support a culture of safety that avoids accidents through ongoing education, practice and safety inspections.

Manage the tension between conducting an efficient transportation program, meeting the needs of the community, and parental or community requests. Make sure routing and road conditions are evaluated and reviewed at least annually. Don't wait to adjust routes if conditions change inside a school year. Listen to parents and drivers who may have suggestions for improvement but exercise care in making changes only when they can be applied to all students equally and conform with sound judgment and district policies. When changes are needed, try to accomplish them with the least disruption possible for students and families.

Establish a clear and workable protocol for addressing emergency weather conditions affecting the operations of school. Whether it is snow, excessively cold temperatures, flooding, hurricanes or other natural disasters, each community will want to make sure a proper alternative plan exists. Some weather happens after students are already at school, so providing alternative procedures for getting students home will be important. Other procedures must be in place to anticipate upcoming weather to determine if it is prudent to hold school.

Early morning decisions are likely for emerging weather events. Weather is dynamic, but decisions often require lead time to implement. It may be frustrating to decide before 3:30 AM and then see district patrons look out the window at 8:00 AM to second guess the decision. This is particularly difficult in districts that serve large geographic areas with different microclimates.

Make sure a transportation official drives the routes, especially those known to have difficult conditions in weather emergencies. Use these observations to inform decisions about whether to conduct school. Establish clear, workable communication plans with local media, especially radio and television stations, but posting decisions on the district's website may be the fastest way to communicate current plans to the community. Some districts contract with a meteorologist to provide localized weather forecasts and assessments to aid in the decision-making process.

Weather delays may require extending your school year. Schedule extra days in your school schedule to prepare in advance for this eventuality.

Contracting for transportation services

Evaluating the advantages and disadvantages of hiring a specialized firm to handle district student transportation services requires clarity in the standards of service required and a thorough financial assessment. The ages of the existing fleet, the skill level of district maintenance and support staff,

The Business Side of School Success

facilities, the availability of sound routing decisions, and personnel practices may lead toward consideration of contracting for transportation services.

Before embarking on such an analysis, be clear that about the current reality of the district's transportation program. Ask these questions:

- Does the current program meet quality standards?
- Are program adjustments and fiscal management appropriate for the community?
- Does the current district management team have the expertise and skills to do an excellent job?
- Are complaints addressed in a careful, considered manner? What evidence exists to support this assertion?
- How are the district's facilities and equipment affecting what the capacity of the Transportation program to meet its required levels of service?
- Might a contractor capitalize the bus fleet to improve safety and better meet service standards?

Building a case for change must directly connect to service standards and the prospect of freeing up funding for investments in educational program improvements. Parents, school staff, and affected transportation workers may resist district consideration of such a change. To the extent possible, work with community and staff members to evaluate the current reality and involve stakeholders to identify the case to make a change.

If a change is determined appropriate and viable, a contract for services should be advertised for bid among various firms who will compete for the district's contract. Some factors to consider in setting the bid criteria will be:

- Establish clear service expectations and standards.
- What is the planned school day schedule?
- How long will bus routes be for students?
- What maintenance and training programs will be provided?
- What will happen to the existing district personnel?
- Will staff salary and benefits be improved or reduced?

- Who will own the bus fleet and where will it be housed for storage and maintenance?
- What is the duration of the contract?
- What's services and supports will be covered by the contract? Can schools contract out field trips separately or must they use the district's chosen vendor?
- How will annual changes and pricing be established? Will it be done by formula, or will it be negotiated?
- What requirements will be in place for the status of the program at the end of the contract period?

Be sure that district counsel reviews any contract, including renewals, before being presented to the school board for approval. Ask counsel to ensure that a performance bond is in place for the vendor recommended for the contract.

Tips for superintendents

Transportation services support families and the school's educational program. This unique service introduces risk and complexity to school operations. New and veteran superintendents alike must attend to this program as a visible school district presence in the community.

Driver education and service for students and families is important. Procedures to set standards, address complaints or service requests, and operate safely will serve to build confidence in the school system.

Take the time and make the effort to understand how the transportation system serves the community.

C. Food Service

This section will help leaders learn to...
Develop the necessary knowledge about the food service operation.
The knowledge needed to address key issues about food service.
Identify questions to thoroughly examine district managed operations.
Identify questions to ask whether seeking a contracted service is appropriate.

Case Study

JoAnn is frustrated as the Director of the Food Service operation at the district. Her last several supervisors she's didn't appreciate her department's contribution to the district's mission. To her, they seemed discourage teamwork and went out of their way to make her work harder. Schools were being built in her district where the kitchen is designed into the basement and at the back of the school. Locating the vending machines is easier for students than finding the food service area. In several high schools, the school store is allowed to compete with food service by ordering pizza and re-selling it out of the store.

The principals believe the student store is an important way to teach students how to run a profitable business. Still, the store isn't charged indirect costs, such as heat, lights, office support, etc. Additionally, the store is located at the entrance to the school and operates contrary to federal guidelines for the National School Lunch Program.

JoAnn's problems seemed to compound themselves. The kitchen managers didn't cooperate with her leadership because she was often undermined by her supervisor. It has been several years since her program showed a profit according to the district's methodology. She has no money to buy new equipment, and the hours of most kitchens have been cut. The program is required to pay for all maintenance, and recently she'd learned that the accounting department is going to also hit the program with an indirect cost charge, so she'll have to pay for personnel, payroll, accounting, and other support services provided to the program.

What will the fiscal people do next to make her life more difficult?

If you were the superintendent...

What questions would you ask JoAnn?

Do you think it is possible or appropriate for a food service operation to break even or show a profit? If so, under what conditions?

What direction would you give to the departments who charge food service for the work they provide?

What additional information will be needed and where might it be found?

What overall direction would you provide to JoAnn?

What superintendents need to know about food service

Whether new to the district or as part of an ongoing effort to learn about services provided to students and the community, regular meetings with the director of nutrition service and/or the director's supervisor, and the superintendent are important. Superintendents who build relationships with leaders of support service functions extend their influence and gain valuable perspective about overall district operations. Since many students are direct customers of the school meal program, knowing how it operates is an important consideration for superintendents.

A program review for the food service program provides valuable information to keep current and meet emerging health and nutrition standards. Such reviews are best undertaken by a team with expertise in all aspect of food service. This would include kitchen operations, personnel, menu planning, purchasing, and delivery. The review may vary depending on the nature of the district's current operational approach.

The Business Side of School Success

As with maintenance and operations and pupil transportation, private vendors operate in the food service domain so evaluating the district's current reality may create tension around the question of staying "in-house" or "contracting." As noted in the previous two sections, conducting a clear, thorough evaluation of the current operations provides an important baseline for consideration of options. It is vital to understand the existing system before seeking to make a change.

If a food management company already provides management of the food service operations, make sure that they operate in compliance with the federal, state, and local rules and guidelines. The ultimate burden for this compliance rests with the district. A contractor may be able to utilize purchasing power and subcontracts with other providers to reduce expenses. Often the contractor will also be responsible to employ and manage the food service staff and be responsible for the compensation changes over time. Make sure such a contract clearly delineates duties, responsibilities and pathways to correct defined deficiencies in all aspects of operations.

The National School Lunch Program (NSLP) is a federally funded meal program most districts embrace. It provides standards to serve nutritionally balanced, low-cost or no-cost breakfasts and lunches to children each school day. Many students and families rely on this program for much of their access to wholesome food, so this program may also extend into summer sessions.

The NSLP provides access to free or reduced priced meals for students of eligible families. Ensure that the administration of the program knows the rules and regulations and secures and maintains proper records documenting family/student eligibility. Meal composition standards and procurement of food sources are regulated and must be well documented. Errors in records may result in a loss of revenue and/or the repayment of inappropriately claimed funds.

This program makes school districts eligible to receive USDA food commodities and surplus agricultural food. Whether district managed or by a contractor, verify the proper use of this feature to support the district's operations.

The food service program has many characteristics of a separate enterprise, so it is often planned as self-sufficient with expenses covered by specifically dedicated revenue sources. Some states run the program from a Food Service Fund which adds some fiscal management complexity but highlights the requirement for revenue to cover expenses. In these situations, a transfer of funds from the General Fund may be permitted with prior board approval. In some states, this action must be included in the voter approved budget.

Establishing the prices for school meals and ala carte items is an interesting decision included in the school board action to adopt the annual district budget (or before the budget is adopted so that you may communicate any changes well in advance to parents). Review this recommendation carefully with the food service manager before taking it to the board for approval. If the prices are set too high, students may not opt to use the service; if meal prices are too low the program may not have sufficient funds to operate without drawing upon educational resources. Compare prices projected by neighboring districts so that prices remain consistent in your area.

Key points for consideration

Management of the district's food service program includes compliance with state and local health rules and other program requirements. Many of the issues that must be taken into consideration go beyond those affecting a regular business enterprise. This non-profit program invests revenue beyond expenses into equipment or other needs. It must also meet federal guidelines. Meals must be attractive to hard-to-please consumers and respond to competition from internal and external sources. Local health regulations must be addressed, and staff must possess food handling licensure.

Another key factor to keep in mind is that a high proportion of the food service staff are likely citizens of the school district. Listen to what they have to say about food service and other aspects of district operations; in all likelihood, they will also be sharing their observations in the community.

The Business Side of School Success

The food service staff may be part of a union. Take care to address this portion of the district's staff in equitable ways and avoid minimizing their role and influence.

Contracting for food service

Given the enterprise nature of the school nutrition program, consideration of selecting private vendors to guide the service is often undertaken. Before seriously entertaining the idea of putting the program operations out to bid to select a contractor, ask these questions about the district operations:

- How is the quality of the program? It is best to operate with first-hand knowledge of the menu and products being served.
- Is the program operating in the black?
- Which kitchens are improving?
- Does the management team have the expertise and skills to lead an excellent program?
- Who is responsible for food safety and training of staff?
- Will the optics of a district operated program out-perform hiring a contractor?
- How are space, electrical power, and equipment influencing the effectiveness of the program operations and staff capabilities?
- Does a management system track participation rates for each school? Is this data charted and reviewed regularly by management?
- How well is food marketed by your program?
- Are you maximizing alternative ways so students can quickly get what they want instead of standing in long lines?

After this examination, if a decision is made to seek a private management service, be sure to examine these questions:

- What elements of the program would be covered by the contract?
- How long would the contract be in place?
- When will cost factors be re-negotiated?
- Will inflation factors be built into the contract? Which ones?
- Will clear channels of communication be identified?

- Will opportunities exist to rectify complaints or problems?
- Does a clear pathway exist for feedback?
- Will the contractor put up a performance bond?
- Make sure the district counsel reviews the contract, including future renewals, before signing.

Tips for superintendents

- Sample the food by eating meals with students or staff. Ask kitchen staff to sample it also.
- Are school staff buying their meals from the program? Why or why not?
- How are student participation rates at each school? Examine trends and ask questions. Don't automatically accept the first answer for why rates are declining. Persist to discover what is really going on at that school, then ask the kitchen manager (or supervisor) to address it.

D. Information Technology

This section will help leaders learn to…
    Understand what needs to be known about information technology services.
    Identify essential elements of the program to guide decisions.
    Maintain security and privacy of students and staff.
    Plan for future technology needs.

Case Study

A district laptop program was instituted for all high school students. The laptops were purchased by the district, checked out for appropriate software, and then distributed to students with an expectation that they would be used by students at home as well as school.

As part of this process, a district staff member, without authorization, activated a feature on some of the computers that would take pictures of students apparently to help retrieve stolen laptops. Eventually, this feature was known and used to discipline at least one student. Over 56,000 photos were taken and stored by the district.

This invasion of student and family privacy resulted in what turned into a class-action lawsuit against the school district that became known as the Web-Camgate scandal. Amazingly, the district didn't settle this matter out of court, so the court found the district in error and entered a financial judgment that was mostly covered by the district's insurer. The employee who took the actions was not able to be identified, which further damaged the already marred reputation of the school district.

The superintendent called for an investigation by a reputable information technology security vendor. As a result of the investigation, insufficient information was discovered to justify anyone's loss of employment. The investigation further documented errors in judgment, lack of controls by IT management, and the need for a clear privacy policy regarding district-owned computers.

The professional reputation of district managers and ultimately the superintendent was stained, and the district was compelled to pay a significant insurance policy deductible as well as increased future insurance premiums. These factors combined to undermine the community's confidence in the district.

You are appointed as the new superintendent.

If you were the superintendent...
What could have been done to prevent this situation?
What questions might the prior superintendent have asked to reveal this situation more quickly?
Could you work now to identify a person(s) of responsibility, or leave it alone and move on?
What additional information will be needed and where might it be found?
What do you do now to protect the district and yourself?

What superintendents need to know about information technology programs

Technology reliance has increasingly found its way into almost all district functions. Information technology (IT) departments support financial systems, student information systems, and instructional software at the teacher and student levels. A trust-based, collaborative relationship in the use of technology ensures that decisions and overall strategy for its use align and are appropriately explained to constituents who make broader budgeting decisions and also those who use the equipment and systems.

The Business Side of School Success

Because superintendents rarely have experience working directly with information technology, they must rely upon colleagues with technology-based expertise for guidance. Superintendents will be expected to integrate an overview of the district needs with technology-specific knowledge. Wise superintendents will find reliable, knowledgeable IT leadership and work thoughtfully with that counsel to make informed decisions about technology purchases and guide its use.

School board approval is usually required (and should be sought if not otherwise required) for a district's technology initiative or the subsequent large purchase of equipment and software that accompanies this initiative. The information technology department should work with related systems/equipment users to identify and recommend how best to support the curriculum, students, business, and operational functions of the district.

The district should rely on its this collaborative process to build a three-to-five-year technology plan. The plan should focus on the following issues:

- technology planning and policies.
- equipment and infrastructure.
- finance.
- identify what software will be supported for staff and students and what will not. Be sure to have a clear policy for non-supported software.
- technology operating systems and functional software selections.
- maintenance, security, and support. How are data, operating systems, and backup files secured?
- professional development and training for users.
- how various systems integrate with each other.
- the sequence for planned upgrades and replacement of equipment and software.
- project management.
- the uses of technology by teachers and students as a learning tool.

Once developed, the technology plan should be incorporated into the budget development cycle (see Chapter 3—Budget Development Supports the Mission). Due to the large expense of equipment and systems purchases, consider using a dedicated capital technology levy or phased investments from the district's annual operating budget to stage implementation of the plan.

Virtual schooling options: The COVID-19 pandemic accelerated the demand for technology networks and systems to sustain school operations when in-person teaching was not possible. Even districts with minimal capacity for virtual school had to respond quickly. Fortunately, one-time emergency funding was often provided, but the external limits of internet access, limited wi-fi access, and lack of staff experience led to unanticipated challenges.

One ongoing impact that has emerged from the pandemic is the expectation among many that virtual schooling and virtual meetings will continue to be available. While most people do not want to eliminate person-to-person interactions, hybrid learning models that allow both in-person and virtual access are increasingly likely to become "normal."

This experience and its resulting benefits will be incorporated into the benefits and expectations of in-person access to teachers, administrators, and learning systems. Planning to upgrade and expand systems and supports for this effort must be incorporated into the district's information technology plan.

Remote learning introduces new threats for student and staff safety, too. It is important that systems include appropriate tools to monitor chat environments for younger students and avoid new vectors for bullying, inappropriate content, and other avenues of misuse of the technology. Everyone will need to be on guard to detect and report such issues of abuse.

Beyond the technical and hardware access issues, developing the skills to teachers, support staff, and administrators to use the technology for teaching and learning is necessary. Identify in collaboration with the instructional program leadership and affected staff members what kinds of learning opportunities they need. Provide a systematic, ongoing approach to this professional development effort.

The Business Side of School Success

Security and privacy: Parents, students, and staff expectations about access to technology systems, support, and curriculum will continue to expand. At the same time, frustrations will increase for everyone who will be required to remember login information to access multiple systems (fees, grades, etc.,). These related expectations require persistent monitoring and implementation of emerging tools to assist users. Facial recognition and two-factor identification methods are improving secure access and convenience, but implementation of these features often requires additional cost and workload impacts.

Likewise, bad actors increasingly see school districts as "soft targets" for ransomware and other demands that will be disruptive and expensive. Building strong firewalls to protect district users will require a relationship with proven technology applications and vendors. Persistently remind users to exercise judgment and caution to avoid being tricked by phishing attempts or other ways to open up the firewall to malicious parties.

A key guiding principle to reduce cost and risk is finding and using industry standard applications that can be implemented with no or minimal district requested modifications. Enterprise applications (e.g., finance and human resources software, student information software) may become overly customized resulting in higher costs to support. Be cautious when choosing these modifications. The hidden cost of this customization is revealed when the vendor upgrades the system, resulting in a need to re-program the customization factors. Exercise leadership discipline to adapt systems, district practices, and processes to the software to avoid this unnecessary and hidden expense driver.

Emerging issues: As personal access to technology evolves, expectations grow for the district's use of technology and the related supports (e.g., wi-fi installations, practices for smart phones, etc.,). This process creates additional challenges that require district leadership to rely upon the information technology leadership to incorporate into district planning and implementation actions. Challenges include:

- Reliance upon classroom management as a teacher priority – educators and parents may inappropriately expect technology to solve the problems that have always been present in the learning environment (bullying, etc.,).
- Balance access to avoid allowing students too much screen time without access to human interaction or physical activity.
- Manage the potential risk of access by non-authorized users to student information and student access to inappropriate content.
- Digitize a formal records management (storage and retention) or operational data store protocol that allows efficient access to historical data.
- Evaluation of rogue systems or low-cost personal tools that can slip through the district's approval process and result in enormous cost increases to IT staff who may be called upon to support or remedy errors created by these applications. Create a policy to manage this issue and continuously remind all staff about exercising care.
- Managing and monitoring the use of vendors to address district needs. Exercise care to avoid being the victim of an "over-promise and under-deliver" incident that leaves complicated systems for district staff to support.
- Being wary of slick sales presentations. Always ask questions related to the best fit for the district. Why is this contract being considered? What risks are associated with this proposal? Ask the district's manager or supervisor, "Would you spend your personal money this way?"

Staffing issues and building a service orientation: Hiring IT staff with the necessary skills and service attitude is challenged by competition from private sector employers as well as from other school districts with competitive salaries. Talented staff may not stay very long in a K-12 environment. Additionally, IT staff applicants may be more inclined than some to seek remote work practices with their employer.

Another challenge for district staff occurs when scarce resources in training and preparing short-term employees who then move to more lucrative jobs in the private sector. Seek to make longer-term commitments and seek that from people being recommended for employment.

Stay abreast of changes and trends in the IT world to adapt as quickly as possible to employment opportunities and dynamics.

Districts often use consultants and contractors to implement and/or support systems. Creating an RFP to retain such a contractor requires the same care and definition of scope that we've outlined for other support service functions in this chapter. Make sure to clearly specify the commitment to deliverables and the length of time and costs associated with proposals of this nature.

Many aspects of information technology require technical leadership. It is challenging to find one person who can do it all. This limitation may require multiple positions. Examples of these diverse functions include Instructional Technology, Technology Infrastructure and Support, Information Systems and Data Analysis.

Cynthia Nelson, the recently retired technology supervisor in the Edmonds School District, stressed the importance of maintaining a service orientation across the IT staff. Because technology touches every aspect of the organization, collaborative skills are valuable and essential to match technical knowledge. Technology employees should avoid the temptation to tell other staff how to do their jobs. Instead, they should listen for what is needed, then show their colleagues ways technology applications can help achieve the desired goals.

Tips for superintendents

Shared vision: Too few superintendents provide direction for information technology concerns. Superintendents may lack experience with technology or under-estimate the anxiety created by rapidly changing technological tools and approaches.

To address the tension that rapid technological change brings to the school culture, a shared vision for the role of technology in the district's future would be useful. Work to build a shared vision will assist superintendents and provide IT leaders with the guidance to move forward.

Technology advisory committee: If the district doesn't already have a technology advisory committee, work to create it. Tap into a mixture of staff who have technology knowledge and those who are users. Add a mix of community members to enhance expertise and surface issues from parents and others. An advisory committee is one way to support developing and/or monitoring the technology plan. Such a committee will help develop and keep the district's technology approaches in line with student and staff requirements.

Fads versus innovation: Unfortunately, the fast pace of development and adoption of technology created solutions promoted as quick fixes to long standing issues. Some have been fads or schemes that were not practical or cost effective. These fads and "revolutions" have often failed to be successfully applied in primary, secondary, and post-secondary education.

Before plowing scarce resources and even more valuable staff time into the latest fad, carefully research the opportunities and options. Examine the district's plan and stick with it by being skeptical of quick-fix solutions.

Ask hard questions of the IT staff, vendors and potential consultants.

Seek to ideas and insight from others with expertise. Watters (2019) provides such insight into issues that will help identify the kind of concerns to know about and/or avoid.

Mintz (2021) describes various reasons that educational technology may fail to deliver on its promise. While noting the success of some technologies, he advises leaders to implement only technologies that help instructors do their job better, not displace them. Mintz (2021) further counsels using educational technology that will:

- Bring a wealth of instructional resources into the classroom.
- Monitor student engagement and learning; intervene promptly when necessary.
- Provide tools for analysis, visualization and project creation.
- Support active, collaborative and project-based learning.
- Ease grading and help instructors provide more constructive feedback.

E. Safety and Security

This section will help leaders learn to...
Know what needs to be understood about running a safe district.
Understand the key concepts that need to be considered if choosing to employ an armed security team.

Case Study

The district's high school had been the scene of a tragic shooter incident that resulted in the death of several students. Serious changes were indicated when the incident was evaluated to determine how to avoid a re-occurrence of the tragedy. A significant remodel of the school was initiated. When the school reopened four months after the shooting, in time for the start of a new school year, many safety alterations were evident in the physical setting.

Although the re-opening was marked with spirit, the safety features designed into the school were quickly bypassed by the staff because they didn't respond recognize the behavioral patterns required for them. Despite repeated appeals by the administration to adhere to the new requirements, the physical changes were rendered useless.

Why did the safety features fail? They were not intuitive and created and unreasonable burden on the staff. For example, exterior doors used a magnetic card reader to allow entry. If a staff member forgot to check themselves out, when next they attempted entry to the building, they were locked out.

Consequently, staff began logging themselves out right after they'd logged themselves in. Staff also the feared that a record showing the total number of hours staff were at the school would somehow be used against them.

If you were the superintendent…

How might staff have been directly involved in designing the system to be used in the school?

What actions might improve security yet work for the staff?

How do you ensure systems are in place and that they will work as planned?

When administration learned about the staff bypassing the security system, what should they have done?

What additional information will be needed and where might it be found?

Operating a Safe School District

Safety requires addressing questions with many aspects of the community and the school system. For example:

- Is the school safe from a child's perspective? To accomplish this simple task, many factors come into play. Does the child walk to school or ride a bus? This area of safety includes an updated analysis of the safe routes for walking and the bus safety and security plans detailed in Chapter 15—School District Operations, B. Pupil Transportation.
- Is the child safe at school or on the playground? Is the building kept clean and free of hazards? These areas of safety and security are detailed in Chapter 15—School District Operations, A. Maintenance and Custodial Services.
- Is the child eating a safe and healthy breakfast, snacks or lunch? These areas of safety and security are detailed in Chapter 15—School District Operations, C. Food Service.
- Is the child safe from online harassment? This area is touched by Chapter 15—School District Operations, D. Information Technology. What about a catastrophe or crises? These risks are addressed in Chapter 14—Enterprise Risk Management: What to Insure.
- Does each student feel like someone on the staff knows them and cares about their well-being? This focus requires hiring the right staff in

teaching positions, having the right administrators, and responding quickly to issues and problems.

Districts often create a school safety office led by a safety specialist who tracks these problems and makes recommendations to mitigate or prevent the issues from happening in the first place. When the district is not a large enough to afford a full-time staff member, enter into an agreement with neighboring districts to share someone with this expertise or work with the regional educational service district to provide such services. Also, seek community based resources through local and/or state agencies to support district safety efforts.

School districts increasingly tend to operate a school safety and security team. When choosing to operate such a security force security force members will be available to assist staff with school day security needs, after school and weekend programs, and with difficult or belligerent parents at board meetings or other district events.. Ensure that these district staff know and understand school board policies and adhere to them.

School security staff often have a military service or law enforcement background. Working with the local police department(s) to align procedures and develop agreed upon protocol for working with routine or unique school-based disruptions is essential. Often, shared planning and staff development opportunities can be designed to assist in this mutual understanding.

Increasingly, some states have begun to authorize faculty and staff members to carry personal concealed weapons at school or school sponsored events. Other states still require a "no firearms" policy for school property with the exception of uniformed law enforcement officers. These issues have become increasingly important discussions given the trend of high profile school-based shooting incidents.

Many school districts have arrangements with local law enforcement agencies to provide school resource officers (SRO) at its schools. The SRO may be supplemental to the school district's security team. Given the unfortunate, tragic school shootings at Columbine, Sandy Hook, Parkland,

Uvalde, and numerous others heighten the importance of a strong safety protocol. Whatever local conditions exist, it is essential that school superintendents and school leaders be thoroughly knowledgeable regarding school safety plans and ensure that these plans, procedures, state and local laws and regulations are implemented in full force and reviewed on a regular basis.

When the school district has school resource officers (SROs) or other law enforcement personnel assigned to schools, some important questions to ask are:

- Are only some schools covered? If only some, what is the risk at other schools or facilities?
- Are law enforcement personnel present on all school days?
- Do they take direction from the principal or work independently?
- How do law enforcement personnel work with your safety and security personnel?
- How are SROs funded?
- Will the SRO carry a service weapon and how will its presence be addressed within the school building?

Because the SRO is a uniformed police officer, she/he will likely carry a police-issued firearm. This issue is normal and appropriate to the presence of an officer of the law who is in uniform. Still, it may raise questions with the students, staff, and/or community.

Tips for superintendents

To operate a safe and secure school, consider all aspects of the field. Do not assume that everything is okay with safety and security. Add or review metrics that tell you how you are doing. These can include playgrounds, incidents at school, worker's compensation claims, injuries, bus driver complaints, etc.

F. Ancillary Services

This section will help leaders learn to...
Know what needs to be understood about operating a warehouse.
Know what needs to be understood about operating a print shop.
Address the need for some form of physical intra-district mail delivery.
Understand the key concepts that need to be considered in making decisions about these ancillary services.

Case Study

A warehouse supervisor had the autonomy to hire temporary warehouse employees. He also was allowed to determine how many hours these employees would be paid and could do so without the authorization or direct knowledge of anyone else. This supervisor used his authority to fraudulently verify that two individuals (his wife and a friend) worked the hours indicated on their respective timesheets, which included extensive amounts of overtime when he knew that they had not worked any of the hours.

After the supervisor's actions, it was discovered that nearly $300,000 in fraudulent salary payments had been made by the district. After significant adverse publicity and an arrest, the warehouse supervisor pled guilty to conspiracy charges and served time in prison.

If you were the superintendent...
What systems can you envision might prevent this type of fraud?
How do you ensure systems are in place and that they will work?
The supervisor's wife didn't use his last name. How would the proposed system catch this condition?
What additional information will be needed and where might it be found?

Operating a district warehouse

A warehouse program that may have initially met an important need, may become increasingly expensive to maintain. As "just in time delivery" options are provided by many suppliers, the need for districts to warehouse extensive supplies for future use may not be necessary and an expensive service may be eliminated for a more efficient option.

Many schools plan and order future supplies in the spring and use an inventory of supplies combined with a forecast of future needs to place an order for the upcoming year. Payments for such orders must be made before the future budget is charged for the purchases. The purchases need to be carried as an asset and then charged to the expense budget in the next fiscal year. But, because the district has limited storage, the supplies are held in the school for the next school year. This "solution" runs the risk of someone getting into the supplies and "harvesting" the new order for something they need now (or wish to obtain without anyone's knowledge).

Contrast this scenario with one where the district has developed an ordering system with vendors that provide just the needed access at the time of planned use. The warehousing of supplies is therefore shifted to the vendor and the complicating accounting and physical storage issues are avoided. When staff recognize they're using the last item (or last few items), the office manager is able to initiate a purchase order to cover the need to the end of the school year. A storage problem is avoided, and the district doesn't commit funds for supplies it won't use until next fiscal year.

Adopting new processes may be a difficult change for some staff, but schools are doing so in increasing numbers. New staff bring new skills that often help alter the old ways of doing things. Next day delivery is increasingly available everywhere, including remote locations. Staff work this way in their personal lives, so applying this approach at school isn't nearly so complicated.

Districts are increasingly using the purchasing power of cooperatives to extend their savings beyond what can be accomplished by a single school. Monitoring is still required, so that a district can put out purchases for bid if necessary. This results in a direct savings to schools and can be accomplished even when schools only purchase infrequently.

Factors to weigh when considering moving away from a district operated central warehouse include:

- Does a warehouse make sense for the district? For example, vendor-based solutions provide the needed supplies promptly without district having to buy and inventory everything first? What software do you need for this specialized purpose?
- What are the long-term costs of a warehouse function versus vendor-based or cooperative buying? Consider the cost of a warehouse facility, salary and benefits for drivers and warehouse staff, delivery vehicles, the cost of goods, training of employees and administrative supervision.
- What is the plan for the displaced workers?

Operating a district print shop

A district operated print shop may use an offset press and high-speed copy machines as the primary method of reproduction. The print shop is probably used for a specialized purpose, high-volume runs with complex sorting and collating needs, and more colors than are available to the typical copiers in your district. Duplication of original prints, booklet-making, and folding are the print shop's primary functions. Services may be limited to in-house equipment. Some types of binding or drilling may also be available.

This set of high volume or specialized printing needs is changing based on the evolution of increased technology and more efficient copying services available from vendors. Moving printing functions to a vendor to provide unique or specialized printing needs is growing as an option because new copier technology solves many school-based needs more effectively.

Additionally, schooling responses to the COVID-19 pandemic have increased the acceptance and use of remote learning or computer-based access to content even when students are at school. This trend may substantially reduce the need for paper copies.

Intra-district mail service

The physical movement of some documents, materials, and equipment among various school sites is an important form of internal support. Certainly, technology such as electronic mail, scanning documents, and shared district files reduces this need, but some things just need to physically travel between and among schools.

No one answer will apply universally among school districts, but one feature of ancillary services is how to integrate diverse functions into them. Consider integrating the level of such support into decisions about a warehouse or a print shop. Another approach may be to incorporate such duties into the daily schedule of a maintenance or custodial position.

Key points to be considered

Typically, Internal Service Funds are used to account for the financing of goods and services provided by one department to other departments of the district, on a cost-reimbursement basis. This fund accounts for the operation of the warehouse for which supplies and materials are purchased, but the ultimate charge is transferred to the department or budget area using the service.

Not all states use an Internal Service Fund so districts in those states typically use the General Fund to collect printing or other centralize service costs. These costs may be transferred via a debit/credit transfer to the appropriate department or function. This accounting function must be managed to assure reimbursement access for state and/or federal programs requiring such documentation.

Tips for superintendents

- Ensure that your fiscal team utilizes the proper reporting format.
- Ensure centralized services cost centers conduct an end-of-year inventory.
- Examine past audit reports to see if they have noted concerns or recommendations that should be followed up.

The Business Side of School Success

- Survey the business community to evaluate options for use of vendors to provide services more economically.
- Consider re-assigning existing staff to other services/functions in support of school operations

Chapter 16

Capital Projects and Bonds

This chapter will help leaders learn to...

Identify key factors for planning capital improvements or adding school facilities.

Identify key questions for working with investment bankers on bond issues.

Understand and apply key concepts in guiding the design and construction of school facilities.

Consult technical and professional expertise when undertaking a capital improvement program.

Case Study

Arlene was just entering her new assignment as superintendent for the Vastly Underfunded School District, a large, growing school system near a major metropolitan area of her state. The district had begun a capital improvement program to modernize schools, but the plan was nearing the end of its funding. Arlene consulted with her chief operating officer about the status of the projects in the pipeline and was surprised to learn that no further projects were planned. The intention with the last set of projects was that the district would pause for several years before going to the voters for another bond sale authorization for the next wave of school improvements.

The Business Side of School Success

Given that the district had over fifty schools plus other ancillary buildings housing the administration and support service functions, Arlene is well aware that a pause in funding plans and waiting to begin work on more projects would be costly and keep the district behind in its efforts to link quality learning environments with student improvement initiatives. She noted that, if schools needed to be upgraded and renovated every thirty to thirty-five years, the district should be conducting two or three school remodeling and updating projects every year.

This approach to facility management required a plan and a long-term approach to funding the plan. To accomplish that effort, Arlene intended to lay out an approach to the school board in the coming months, knowing that it would be spring before a concrete funding plan could be presented to the community.

If you were the superintendent...

What do you think Arlene needs to do to prepare for this school board presentation?

What information does Arlene need?

Who should she consult with about these issues?

What pitfalls might Arlene need to consider?

Developing an educational facilities improvement plan

Before an adequate or workable facility plan is created, a credible inventory of the current reality related to facilities issues must be developed. Such a plan must be built upon knowledge of the degree to which each facility supports the current educational programs of the district. The age, condition and challenges with the exterior envelope, the expected life of the roof, heating, ventilation and air conditioning (HVAC) systems, the plumbing, and other mechanical systems of each facility must be evaluated. This facility needs assessment becomes the foundation for a viable long-range plan.

A long-range facility plan is best devised in consultation with a well-established architectural team that uses people with the required expertise to make this assessment of the current condition of the school facilities. Each of the sub-systems should be evaluated and rated for its remaining expected longevity. This process should consult with the district's maintenance and operations staff and use input from the school instructional staff to assess program adequacy. A scoring system can be used to weight the impact of each element according to district needs and community standards.

When complete, the facility score for each school facility will reflect the cumulative condition of the building based on the sub-system analysis. The comparison of cumulative facility scores serves as an objective way to identify facilities with the greatest need and urgency for remodeling or, in some cases, replacement. Understand that what gets upgraded, remodeled or built new will use these scores as a guideline. The scores are not automatically used to stage the work since that issue is influenced by political and economic considerations.

The facility condition assessment must be paired with the current and expected enrollment capacity of each school. The district's enrollment growth pattern will identify where additional schools need to be located or whether existing schools can appropriately be expanded. How the plan addresses the district's enrollment forecast must be incorporated into the facility need assessment.

Prepare project cost estimates

A facility needs assessment will support a timely, uniform process for estimating project budgets. Developing a comprehensive cost for each facility identifies the district's need for school modernization or replacement over the next five to ten years. The assessment will need to be regularly re-evaluated using updated cost estimates. Completed facilities will be moved to the back of the line and those next in line for attention will be brought into focus.

Using a benchmark for targeting each facility for a major facility modernization and update approximately every thirty years. This benchmark will allow planning to identify the number of annual projects that can be managed and funded each year.

The Business Side of School Success

Once the baseline facility needs assessment and project budget work is complete, the key task is identifying a core set of projects and work that can be accomplished in a specific five-or-six-year period. The length of this planning window may change based on economic conditions, current debt service obligations and community expectations. Tax rates and overall project costs will need to be determined and compared to the scale of projects needed.

As the project costs are being pulled together, the district should be selecting an advisor to assist with helping the district design the financing plan. Bond issues allow funds to be raised through the sale of tax-free bonds that are typically repaid with annual property tax levies. As with a home mortgage, the long-term investment of thirty years allows the capital project to be funded now.

Using bond sales as a financing tool includes future users of the facility in paying a share of its construction cost each year until the bonds are paid off. This rationale is worth remembering to share with citizens who may not initially like the idea of the district incurring debt. It is useful for current voters to understand future users of the facility will be paying a portion of the current cost of the building.

Annual property tax levies dedicated for capital construction or lease income may provide other valuable and important sources of revenue to support capital improvements. Annual operating budget funds are typically not deployed for expensive capital improvements. Alternative financing options will be explored at the end of this section.

The bond sale advisor will work with the district CFO to forecast district assessed tax rates for debt service (payment of interest and principal on the bonds). Merging this knowledge with the project budgets will allow various projects to be evaluated over a defined period and will assist in the development of a recommended capital financing plan for voter consideration.

Citizen planning or oversight committee: A citizen-based planning committee can be developed, often through appointments by the school board, to review and recommend the specific set of projects to be undertaken. The committee should review the work of the technical evaluation and professional facilities review. A broad-based citizen group adds power to the plan, builds citizen knowledge and support, and aids in the ultimate presentation of the plan to the voters.

The mix of projects, the rationale for them and the tax rate and cost implications can be worked out with the citizen planning committee. Often, several options may be evaluated, and the school board can then act to approve the option that best meets the district's needs.

Ultimately, if a bond issue or capital improvement tax levy may be the preferred funding source. The school board must adopt a resolution for presentation of the funding mechanism to the voters. This resolution will provide the means for voters to authorize either the sale of general obligation bonds that create the debt instruments described above, or a property tax levy to fund the projects.

At this stage of the proposal development process, leadership acumen, judgment and consultation processes are vital to success. Providing an accurate assessment of the need takes thoughtful effort and time; don't rush either of these factors. Listen to citizens, staff and school board members so the history of the district's previous efforts can be addressed. Trade-off choices and decisions will likely reflect what is learned through this process.

For example, a well-designed plan might still generate contentious debates that sink the funding plan before it's off the ground. Additionally, adapting well-crafted plans that include a relatively early benefit to every school serving every student builds a measure of necessary voter support for the next phase of the process.

Conducting an authorizing election

Once a construction program is solidified and the funding plan determined, the funding package will be presented to the voters of the school district. Voter authorization of the funding mechanism is required for either a bond measure authorizing long-term debt repaid by annual principal and interest payments generated from a property tax levy or a multi-year levy that collects funds without the issuance of debt instruments (bonds).

The percentage of voter support varies with some states requiring a fifty percent plus one or a simple majority, while other states require voter approval of 60% or more when a bond financing approach is being used. A capital levy that doesn't involve debt may be approved by a simple majority of the voters, but this approach may not supply sufficient funds to undertake the desired school projects. Numerous variations of each approach may be designed into the plan by working with the financial advisory team. The determination of which approach is chosen usually reflects the scale and urgency of the facility improvement program.

People who work for public entities like school districts (including and especially the superintendent) are likely prohibited by law from advocating a specific "yes" vote on such measures. Districts are required to provide even-handed information. See Chapter 11—School and Community Partnerships: Maintaining the Public Trust for a discussion about information sharing strategies and ways to plan school events to provide information to the public.

Advocacy is the role of stakeholders who wish to see the projects undertaken for the benefit of the community's children. School board members, especially if elected, will have more freedom to urge a yes vote, but superintendents and all district staff can only take such positions outside their work role. Citizenship rights are not waived, but extreme care must be taken to assure that advocacy actions are separated from one's work duties. To this end, using vacation days or meeting off school district premises in evenings may be necessary.

During work time, the superintendent and other leaders may present the facts and describe the plan without taking a position or urging others to vote in favor of the plan. While most school leaders' position is obvious, avoiding concrete spoken or written words of voting advice is essential.

Citizen groups are often created to act in this political support role. They must be citizen led, register with the state and provide reporting to the proper authorities of the donations and the names of people donating funds to support the election advocacy. School personnel are typically not prohibited from donating to such efforts but given the variety of local and state laws associated with these matters, we strongly advise knowing the limits of your role.

After a successful vote: selling bonds

If no long-term relationship exists with an underwriting, use the time running up to the election to conduct a Request for Proposals (RFP) engagement process. It might be wise to wait to act upon the RFP submittals until after the election, so the district is not viewed as being overly presumptive about the voters' approval.

When soliciting proposals, identify the track-record of the firm. The RFP should address these questions:

- How many sales have been handled in your state? Where?
- How does the firm forecast interest rates?
- How does the firm handle changes and/or trends in the district's assessed valuation?
- How has the firm helped other districts reach their desired outcomes?
- What process does the firm employ to with the bond rating agencies?

As with other hiring decisions, interview the person or people who will work with your district. Importantly, check the firm's references to obtain the insight from other clients.

Alternatively, the district may already have a relationship with an investment banker from previous efforts to incur long-term debt. Building a professional relationship is a valuable asset for planning and evaluating the full range of options to structure the bond sale. When the underwriter has history with the district, the collaboration builds confidence in the counsel provided.

Many important questions must be addressed early in the bond sale process. An experienced investment banker recently advised that "there are no dumb questions" when it comes to working with bond advisers and legal counsel. Clarity in the purpose and needs of the district is necessary to address these questions. Among the important decision to be made are:

- What cash flow needs will drive the use of the bond funds?
- How important is the projected tax rate for debt service? Must it be constant, or will fluctuations be acceptable?
- What are the costs of borrowing? How will net proceeds be determined?
- How will the sale best be handled? Will a negotiated sale produce lower costs than a public auction?
- How will the maturity dates and repayment schedule be structured?
- Will the district market the bonds to its citizens for private purchases? How? When?
- Does the district want to retain the right to call the bonds early in order to re-finance them? What is the cost of such a decision?

Sharing this important role with several investment banker firms is not out of the question. Sometimes, the size of the bond issue results in a good rationale for it to be split between several firms. Either way, these professionals will assist the district's financial team in the development of a prospectus about the district's operations, property valuation and the economic conditions of the region.

The investment banker will help the district schedule a review by bond rating firms (e.g., Moody's Investor Service, Fitch, or Standard and Poor's). This review is a rigorous outline of the district's financial operations, it's creditworthiness, and capacity to re-pay the debt issued. Each of these credit rating companies vary from one another, so consult with the financing team to select the credit rating, or ratings, appropriate for the district's use.

Often, the superintendent, CFO, and school board president will visit the rating agency's headquarters for a bond rating review. Sometimes, this review is conducted with the rating analyst visiting the district. Either way, the bond sale requires a rating based on the rating agency's process to evaluate the financial strength of the school district. This rating is used by investors to help identify their risk appetite and interest rate.

Districts with sound processes and a successful financial management track-record will earn a higher bond rating and lower interest rates. Some states will provide the state's credit rating as a backstop to the district's rating to accomplish lower interest rates that allow lower tax rates for debt service. Additionally, bond insurance might be purchased to accomplish some of these savings. Purchasing bond insurance may result in an overall savings but this action must be based upon an analysis using presumed bond interest rates.

The district will also require a relationship with an attorney specializing in bond issues. This legal role is not generally something that can or should be handled by the district's general counsel, although the general counsel can be invaluable in helping to select the proper bond counsel.

The documents authorizing the sale contain covenants that may build requirements into the district's operational plans. Evaluating these covenants requires expert legal help in concert with the investment banker and the district's leadership team, especially the CFO. Be sure to clearly identify covenants publicly in a school board meeting prior to final approval of the bond issue.

One other professional role that is wise is the hiring of an independent financial adviser (FA) to review the results of the bond sale before it is accepted by the district's board of directors. This FA role is filled by someone with extensive bond investment experience. The FA will render an opinion on the viability of the sale, the proper level of interest, and the sequencing of the principal payments. The FA adds a measure of trust for the school board and the community that the sale is competitive and appropriate given the economic conditions in play at the time of the sale. We have seen an FA challenge the initial offers made by an investment banker which ultimately saved the district taxpayer dollars. The banker's team wasn't happy because their bond salesman had to work harder, but the savings indeed more than paid for the FA.

Most bond issues by school districts create attractive interest rates because the interest is exempt from Federal income taxes for the investor. In certain times, such as those existing in the 2019-2021 era, taxable bonds may be more appropriate than tax exempt bonds. While unlikely, it is conditions such as these that make the integration of a wise investment banker with solid legal counsel and an experienced financial advisor beneficial for the district and its taxpayers.

After notice to the investment community, a bond sale is handled by the banker. It's a bidding process where investors, often large insurance companies, retirement funds and the like, will buy tranches or segments of the bonds with specific maturity dates. Bonds are usually retired over twenty, twenty-five or thirty years, but some segments will be shorter in duration. Districts may also seek to allow local citizens to buy bonds although the investor usually purchases them in increments of $5,000. Bonds are also traded on the market and can be bought and sold by individuals or large-scale investors at either a discount or a mark-up, depending on market conditions.

Upon completion of the sale, bond proceeds are deposited in the school district's capital projects construction fund. This fund is separate from the General Fund so that construction costs don't interfere with the operating budget management and related metrics that are used for comparisons over time. Funds will probably not be spent immediately, so a thoughtful investment schedule should be aligned with the anticipated cash flow of the capital improvement program. Seek assistance as investment income from the proceeds of tax-exempt bonds is governed by Internal Revenue Service regulations to avoid enticing the district to profit from the management of bond proceeds. Seek the advice and counsel of the financial advisor and/or legal counsel with respect to this process.

Other financing options: As noted above, annual multi-year capital levies may be a tool to support the capital construction work in a capital projects fund. Additionally, some districts may own leased property and the annual revenue could support the sale of revenue bonds not supported by voter-approved property tax levies. Short term financing tools such as revenue anticipation notes may be used to match project funding needs with the revenue cash flow.

The use of these alternative financing methods may create complexity and some risk, but they may be beneficial for the schools and the community's taxpayers. Wise legal counsel and smart financial advice is invaluable, but none of these tools eliminate the need for understanding and thoughtfulness by the superintendent and her/his financial team.

Bond refunding considerations: Regular evaluation of existing debt is an important part of monitoring the district's financial health and options. Changing economic conditions, bond values, and interest rates must be monitored over the life of a bond issue. When conditions warrant, net taxpayer savings may result by incurring the cost of re-issuing the remaining outstanding bonds and retiring the initial debt. Obtaining a lower interest rate and potentially re-structuring the debt repayment schedule can lower costs and open future bond issue options for voter consideration.

The school board authority to re-finance the initial bonds must be incorporated into the initial bond sale documents for this option to be exercised. How to structure the re-financing issue will require engagement of the investment banker and legal counsel.

Exercise care in communicating with the voters about what is being done and why. Emphasize the debt service savings that will accrue from taking on the expense of a re-financing plan.

Acquiring property

Locating the site for school buildings can be problematic. Sometimes, wise predecessors led the district to acquire vacant land well ahead of the anticipated need for the school buildings. In other situations, emerging development could never have been funded or adequately anticipated. Regardless of the circumstance, the school siting issue must be addressed.

If possible, acquiring land at current prices may be necessary as a budget element in the funding proposal. In the absence of sufficient property for a school site or to grow the size of an existing school site, public school districts sometimes use eminent domain laws to acquire the necessary property. The use of this process can be fraught with political issues, but it is a channel of property acquisition that allows the school district to proceed.

Legal processes exist in most states to regulate how eminent domain is implemented and how the price will be determined for the property owner whose land is acquired. Exercise care and thoughtful communication and effort to site schools or acquire additional property. Use eminent domain only as a last recourse that involves consultation with the school board and experienced legal counsel.

Building the buildings

Once funding is secured for school remodeling or construction, another process must be in place to effectively and properly accomplish the goal set forth in the funding proposal. This complex process is not the purpose of this guidebook, but the wise superintendent will have already been thinking ahead to put proper construction management structures in place. This work includes validating the educational program objectives to be met within the new or remodeled facilities, handling the interaction between users and design architects, setting standards for all the systems and hardware that will be installed, managing the bidding and selection of contractors, construction meetings and building inspections and closeout as construction ends.

One key question to address is where responsibility for the capital construction should be assigned. Often, if the scale is sufficient, a capital projects office is created. This office may be located within the scope of the business office, the Facilities Management leadership team, or it may separately report to the superintendent or chief school support administrator. Some districts hire construction management firms to handle all the administrative and management functions associated with design, construction and inspections. This decision will reflect the skill, experience and breadth of knowledge available to your support services administrative leadership.

Superintendents and school boards will experience an increased set of issues to address, too. Assuring involvement among the internal school users of the school or other facility is one factor, but providing communication with patrons, parents of students and local governmental regulatory and approval agencies (usually at the city or county level) often takes senior leadership engagement and facilitation energy. Use the construction process as an avenue to build strong, effective relationships with those community-based entities that have such roles.

In our shared experiences, tapping into the architectural community will provide access to the knowledge and the people the school system can rely upon to effectively complete school construction work within budgets and on time. Find experts who have a proven they can accomplish this shared outcome and follow their guidance.

If new schools are included in the construction program, consider how to engage current educational staff in the design of the educational program, guidance that will be used by the school design team. Clarity about the educational program to be operated within the school is vital. Some districts will tap a planning principal to coordinate and lead this interface with the architectural team.

Once the design is completed and local building code and permitting agencies have reviewed the construction plans, present the design documents (prepared by the architectural firm) to the contractor community for bids. Follow the state's establish bidding processes. Explore alternative construction management processes such as General Contractor as Construction Manager (GCCM) approaches.

More detail about the structures and issues may be found in Benzel and Hoover's *The School Superintendent and the CFO: Building an Effective Team, 2nd Edition* (2021).

Summary of facilities planning steps

- Complete a facility needs assessment.
- Prepare long-range enrollment forecasts by level of students (and school).
- Develop a long-term-facilities plan that meets these projections and corrects the most egregious facility deficiencies.

The Business Side of School Success

- Prepare project cost estimates for potential projects.
- Focusing on what can be constructed in a five-to-six-year timeframe, select the facilities your community will support. This will require community engagement and a board resolution.
- Prepare estimated tax rates.
- Conduct an authorizing election. Be sure to run your campaign the correct way.
- When selling bonds:
  - Identify investment bankers through an RFP.
  - Seek a bond rating from a rating agency.
  - Analyze purchasing insurance (some states my lend their underlying credit rating).
  - Select bond issuance legal assistance and prepare resolution authorizing the sale of bonds.
  - Identify a financial advisor as your independent lens on selling bonds. They should review the results of the bond sale before it is accepted by the district's board of directors.
  - Bond sales will be deposited into your Capital Projects Construction Fund.
  - Develop an investment plan that aligns with the cash flow needs of the construction work.
- Hire or contract for construction management.
- Select architects (if you haven't already done this).
- Follow proscribed bidding procedures under the guidance of the design architect and legal counsel.
- Create clear communication and decision-making channels within your organization and with architects and construction managers. These processes should address how change orders are made and handled by each party.

Section III

Summarizing the Focus

Chapter 17: Strategic Issues

Chapter 18: So, What's Next?

Chapter 17

Strategic Issues

This chapter will help leaders learn to...
    Recognize when using data is meaningful and when it is not.
    Apply leadership skills to set the future agenda.

Case Study

Jamal has completed his second year as superintendent in a suburban district that exhibits much civic pride. He'd recently negotiated a three-year contract with his teaching staff and hired a couple of new principals.

Despite these accomplishments, he is at wits end. He's tried every tactic he can comprehend but his district's student achievement results slipped lower each year. His board is hounding him to show positive results.

In desperation, he's searched through all the data on test scores. Still, the best explanation he could show was that the district's students were maintaining achievement levels in some areas, while others continued to decline. This condition is not the improvements he's seeking.

If you were the superintendent...
    What questions should Jamal be asking? Of whom?

How do you improve if you're also responsible to keep the place going?
Can you think of interim steps that Jamal should be taking?
What additional information will be needed and where might it be found?
Given Jamal is investing in a more aligned curriculum, how long will it take to begin showing improvement?

As we reflect on our experiences, many elements of school leadership are fundamental and have remained consistent over time. Transparent decision-making and leadership integrity will never stop being fundamental to success. Funding levels are always a constraint, discerning public interests will always be challenging, demands on schools increase without more days being added to the school year, and requirements to test students persist. Political leaders repeat historic calls for higher student achievement by adding burdens to educators, usually without sufficient resources. Results are elusive.

The challenging goal of improving student achievement often defies finding appropriate ways to measure improvement. Keeping people focused on the data makes decisions hard to systematically accomplish because relying on data isn't a natural human behavior. After investing time, talent, and energy into a new program, be sure to examine whether improvements are shown in the data.

Even with sustained leadership, emerging issues sometimes override the desired focus. When leadership changes, many staff see initiatives quietly fall away without any examination of its effects or effort to learn from the effort. Developing a culture of learning requires a consistent leadership focus on examining results.

While many reasons exist for this loss of focus, one of the major challenges is distraction. Schools and their leaders are overwhelmed by external forces that often cannot be avoided or controlled. A new board member (or several) may arrive with an agenda, the need to find a long-term replacement for a trusted administrator out for emergency surgery, budget challenges, a controversial personnel issue, and contract negotiations are just some examples of distractions that must be managed.

The Business Side of School Success

Perhaps more significantly, as Jennings (2020) concludes, true efforts to improve student performance require "reorienting school reform so that advocates spend as much time and effort on social and economic reforms as they do on school improvement" (p.120). Underlying societal issues like racism, poverty, and changing demographics create additional stress that must be factored into school improvement strategies and fiscal allocations.

Keeping a laser focus on the educational actions that support student achievement efforts requires sustained leadership. The superintendent's obligation, despite the ebb and flow of distractions, is to leave the district better than it was upon arrival. That outcome is the ultimate measure of leadership success.

While this book is focused on the non-instructional aspects of district leadership, it might be appropriate to wonder why we are addressing educational reform at this point. We believe that strategies to improve instruction and the culture surrounding it emerge from motivated people looking at data to see trends. Digging through the data and benchmarking outcomes against the best data possible from neighboring or like-sized districts is a powerful tool to initiate student improvement efforts.

The key to success is building a culture that values these initiatives to improve, whether by a principal and a team of teachers, an enterprising program manager, or a parent or citizen group. Resist the initial urge to minimize or ignore improvement suggestions based upon its source. Rather, use the idea to figure out what to do. A collaborative effort is the most productive way to get positive results.

What can be done to get started? Engage the community through the school board and leadership team and work with individuals who can assist you in your efforts. Recommend that the school board appoint a citizen advisory committee to explore, dialogue, and give feedback on each step of the research process. Consider how to include principals, teachers and support staff in this engagement because they will provide invaluable input into the process while also learning new skills.

How does the district compare to other districts? Compare the district to those considered exemplars. Start with internal. Do not be distracted by canned measures of performance imposed by the state unless the community agrees that such measures are worthy of being emphasized.

Benchmarking: Collect data on school district performance. What is the district doing that is unique? Identify the drivers, beliefs, processes and culture that lead to the results in districts or other organizations and build upon them. Good data tell a story, so what do the data indicate? What does success look like?

Examine the data that are available. If existing, available data don't reveal much about the district's status or gaps are discovered, start to collect the necessary data. If possible, build a history of the data elements (five years may be sufficient) to find trends. Is the district declining, staying the same, or improving?

Trial balloons: From the data, select a few key elements that can be used to generate dialogue and create appropriate tension within the organization. Talk to the school board and to community groups, too. If the trends are positive, look for the reasons and celebrate this success. If the data aren't flattering, use them to start honest conversations with the district's leadership team to identify barriers or practices that are restricting or hindering the desired performance.

Monitoring: Be sure to continue to collect the data as it develops. One key concept, employees rarely engage with data that they have no chance of impacting. Search for ways people can influence the results.

Revise and restart: As the data emerge, results may be different than desired creating the need for revisions or a reversal of initial actions. Do not lose the momentum but continue to probe for actions that demonstrate effective, timely changes in behavior that produce desired results.

The Business Side of School Success

What to measure

Active, ongoing engagement with performance indicator data may reveal unexpected shifts in focus. Try to confine the focus on a limited number of issues rather than spreading efforts too broadly. With that precaution, this list of potential elements to measure provides some topics to consider, especially for teams with limited prior experience with basing its investigations on data:

- Successful readers by fourth grade: It is important that children learn to read. Reading is a necessary tool in all areas of learning. Identify a measurement tool that reveals the percentage of successful readers. Track progress over time.

- Successful transition to middle school: Find and utilize ways to measure success along multiple dimensions to monitor and measure whether students are making positive transitions to a more independent learning setting.

- Transition into high school, also known as the 9th grade success rate: How many credits does a high school student need to earn each grading period to stay on course to graduate? Measure this variable over time and look for intervention strategies that improve the trend.

- High school enrollment patterns:
    - Do the high schools retain students or take various actions to send them to other programs?
    - Are some sectors of the student population not being reached by an appropriate program or service?
    - Does the gender or ethnicity of the students correlate to inclusion or exclusion?
    - What is the monthly enrollment and/or attendance pattern each year?
    - Does it decline as the year progresses?
    - Declining enrollment or attendance rates may indicate a systemic practice is causing the decline and may be embedded in the school culture. Examine the cause or causes.

- Where do students leaving the school go? Develop programs to effectively track and engage these students.

- High school seniors earn various scholarships and grants to pursue post-secondary learning. Engage students in identifying the sources and amounts of these scholarships. Many offers do not get reported so expect some wild increases the first years this is encouraged. Find a way to celebrate success that is visible to all.

- Define and report on the various program options available to students. Connect these options to various characteristics of student interest and need.

- Track the percentage of students pursuing credits at the university or community college.
   - Does this effort generate simultaneous high school credit?
   - Does the district offer a college in the high school credit option
   - Monitor student activities and successes after high school.

- Where are students a year or two after leaving high school (e.g., post-secondary enrollment, working, military)?

- How many students are enrolled from neighboring districts? How many resident students seek out-of-district enrollment?

- Track the number of students eligible and receiving free or reduced-price school meals on a monthly basis as a proxy for the socio-economic condition of the community served by each school.

- Net promoter scores: A net promotor score measures the percentage of patrons or customers rating their likelihood to recommend a service, school, or district. This score reveals just how loyal and happy families and students are with their experiences. We suggested surveying your community with a modified version that asks, "have you recommended us?" Follow up with a free text question, "tell us more." Ask questions about performance of the schools and district. Track these results. These

The Business Side of School Success

can be useful for diverse school and district-level purposes including passing levies and bonds.

Chapter 18

So, What's Next?

Throughout this book, we've presented various finance and related issues that require leadership attention and superintendent knowledge. We recognize that no one person has all the expertise to fully guide and manage the details of every aspect of schooling. The superintendent is the only person in the organization, though, that is called upon to balance the best mix of skills and choices to accomplish the school system's vital educational mission.

To that end, this chapter seeks to help superintendents and their key operational executives be aware of the key issues and behaviors that should be in place to protect the district's mission and safely and effectively serve its students.

Create an effective culture

The organizational design may change from time-to-time, but the culture of the district will drive almost all actions. As superintendent, building a positive, learning culture is fundamental to serving your students well.

One of the most important aspects of a positive, learning culture is your own behavior when faced with challenges, decisions and choices. When district staff observe the superintendent as a listener, curious about alternative methods, and eager for honest feedback in order to assess the effectiveness of previous choices their trust and confidence will grow. A willingness for continuous learning and improvement will emerge.

Jamie Dimon, Chairman and Chief Executive Officer of JPMorgan Chase, in his 2021 shareholder letter, noted that:

> Facts, analysis, detail…facts, analysis, detail…repeat. You can never do enough, and it does not end. Complex activity requires hard work and no uneducated guesswork. Test, test, test, and learn, learn, learn. And accept failure as a "normal" recurring outcome. (p.21)

This wise counsel applies to school leadership much as it does in other business and organizational settings. Dimon (2021) uses that same letter to amplify the leader's duty with these five key expectations (p. 21-23):

- Enforce a good decision-making process…have all the right people in the room with all the information.
- Examine raw data and focus on real numbers…in essence, disaggregate key data sets to determine what is happening within them.
- Understand when analysis is necessary and when it impedes change…bureaucrats can torture people with analysis, stifling innovation, new products, testing and intuition.
- Before conducting an important analysis, assess all factors involved…lay out all the important variables to be sure all of them are evaluated.
- Always deal with reality…and deal with both certainty and uncertainty.

Effective superintendents set the "tone at the top" with respect to team interactions. Set clear expectations for how advice is given and received from the key executive support team. Meet regularly with those key advisers. Expect honest feedback and clear, concise information. Expect all parties to know about the whole system. For example, the CFO needs to know about educational program obligations and curriculum issues just as the chief academic officer needs to know about operational concerns and fiscal obligations.

We often used the phrase "tell me what I need to know, not what you think I want to hear" to communicate the importance of information sharing and analysis. To make this concept workable, though, the superintendent must exercise great care and responsibility toward those who say things that may be difficult to accept. Inappropriate responses will be viewed as "killing the messenger" and that message will spread like wildfire. One error of this kind will quickly alter the integrity needed for future feedback and diminish the effectiveness of superintendent leadership. Be careful.

Be curious

We suggest that regular sessions with the CFO be scheduled just prior to regular meetings of the executive team be used to identify the current fiscal status of the district and be alerted to any unique circumstances. Early notice will allow counsel to be given to the CFO with enough time to calibrate information sharing with the whole team.

We advise that standard information presentations be created to reflect the core fiscal drivers in the district and state. At a minimum, these factors might include:

- Enrollment status and student attendance rates (more important if revenue formulae are based on attendance versus enrollment).
- Monthly revenue by source (e.g., local, fees, state sources by category, federal).
- Property tax collection rates.
- Payroll cost by month separated by administrative, certificated and classified. Show benefits for each group separately as well.
- Accounts payable by month with a listing of largest payments to vendors.
- Budget spending variance analysis by program and key administrative areas.

Dig into these numbers with questions. Pay particular attention to timing and spending or revenue variance.

But also, be careful. Many times, an executive request or requirement to address some problem generates another issue of equal or even greater negative impact. This occurrence is the result of failing to see the issue in a larger, systemic context. Step back, examine the issue for its root cause and address that issue rather than the more superficial problem. This practice tests patience and requires courage, but it is worth the effort.

Reporting requirements

Reporting the district's fiscal status to state and federal funding authorities will be an important factor that most likely will be led by the CFO and perhaps key program administrators. General fiscal revenue streams from the state are based on a variety of factors from enrollment to tax levies or other "drivers." Large categorical programs like special education, technical education or pupil transportation will likely be driven by distinctive formulae that require additional reporting. Make sure to track these factors and that the CFO and her/his team are filing all appropriate state reports are in a timely manner.

Some Federal and state funding sources and other unique grants from philanthropic or community entities may be managed using a reimbursement or claims process that obligates the district to submit detailed evidence of payments (e.g., payroll and vendor payments). The granting entity will review these submittals to assure the expenses conform to grant guidelines or requirements. These claims will require detailed attention from the program manager; failure to make the right allocations could void the grant or result in non-reimbursement of expenses. Expect the program manager and the CFO team to collaborate to make sure this process doesn't undermine core funding.

Each of these reporting areas is worthy of careful review during routine meetings with the CFO and the leadership team.

Keep people informed

We've already noted that capable superintendents may get into trouble with operational or fiscal matters. Perhaps the best way to avoid such an outcome is maintaining an ongoing, effective information sharing protocol that begins with the CFO and extends to senior executive briefings, to all administrators, to the school board, and to the community. Make sure that fiscal commitments are monitored and tracked by the CFO and that the CFO is empowered to rectify mistakes that might lead to over-committing the budget.

Use regular budget and fiscal reporting to build knowledge of key variables, dynamic changes and expected outcomes. When unanticipated events occur, having identified these factors will support better exchanges of variance causes and impacts. Together, these efforts build trust based on competence and good intentions.

School board meetings are a prime venue for regular fiscal reporting. When things go as expected, know that it won't be newsworthy. Still, do not shirk this reporting requirement when circumstances aren't as positive as desired. Being consistently transparent builds trust and earns goodwill among all concerned. As noted, it is an important way to buffer the unexpected issues that will eventually enter the fiscal equation.

Conclusion

No one action is magical when complex systems of finance are involved. Some people will avoid learning or knowing about these factors but delay and avoidance is never a good way to resolve the challenges and choices required to live within the fiscal means of the school system. Teaching others about these factors and using finance and operations to reinforce the educational mission of service takes time, knowledge and judgment. Rely on the district leadership team to help accomplish this important duty to deliver successful educational promises for the community.

The Business Side of School Success

Appendix A
Sample Cash Flow Analysis
(dollars in thousands)

	July	Aug	Sept	Oct	Nov	Dec
Cash Balance Forward	2,560	10,782	6,269	12,444	18,646	14,131
Receipts						
Property Taxes	340	680	450	680	570	560
Payment in lieu of Taxes	--	--	--	8,200	1,200	1,200
State Aid	30	2,280	9,500	11,500	570	340
Regional District Aid	30	200	345	70	--	--
Interest	2	2	--	2	30	2
Other	170	500	670	690	800	900
Transfers: other funds	900	85	120	230	210	220
Tax Anticipation Notes	12,000	930	3,900	--	--	--
Medicaid	150	80	50	40	5	5
Total Receipts	13,622	4,757	15,035	21,412	3,385	3,227
Disbursements						
Payroll	3,580	3,530	4,790	4,850	4,920	4,900
Regional district payments	--	--	920	--	--	--
Benefits	900	880	1,200	1,210	1,230	1,230
Warrants (A/P)	770	850	1,000	850	900	1,000
Debt Service	--	--	--	300	--	150
Tax Anticipation Notes Payable	--	3,900	950	8,000	850	--
Transfers: other funds	150	110	--	--	--	--
Total Disbursements	5,400	9,270	8,860	15,210	7,900	7,280
Ending Fund Balance	10,782	6,269	12,444	18,646	14,131	10,078

The Business Side of School Success

	Jan	Feb	March	April	May	June
Cash Balance Forward	10,078	5,958	3,818	8,593	11,938	11,608
Receipts						
Property Taxes	1,920	1,950	2,450	2,700	1,700	1,500
Payment in lieu of Taxes	--	--	--	--	--	--
State Aid	1,350	1,650	9,640	9,870	6,740	1,140
Regional District Aid	5	1,290	55	50	50	1,160
Interest	3	3	3	20	25	5
Other	800	950	875	700	600	500
Tax Anticipation Notes	--	--	--	--	--	--
Transfers: other funds	--	--	--	--	--	--
Medicaid	2	2	2	5	5	5
Total Receipts	4,080	5,845	13,025	13,345	9,120	4,310
Disbursements						
Payroll	4,900	4,800	5,000	4,600	4,750	8,900
Regional district payments	900	1,000	1,000	1,000	1,000	1,000
Benefits	1,250	1,275	1,250	1,200	1,200	2,200
Warrants (A/P)	1,000	800	1,000	1,400	1,000	1,000
Debt Service	--	--	--	300	--	150
Tax Anticipation Notes Payable	--	--	--	1,500	1,500	130
Transfers: other funds	150	110	--	--	--	--
Total Disbursements	8,200	7,985	8,250	10,000	9,450	13,380
Ending Fund Balance	5,958	3,818	8,593	11,938	11,608	2,538

(See notes on following page.)

Notes related to the cash flow analysis

1. Prepare a cash flow analysis as part of the budget development process to make sure that sufficient cash will be available at each month to cover expected or budgeted disbursements.
2. As the fiscal year unfolds, compare the forecast to actual experience to examine variances. Investigate the nature of the variance and provide an explanation to the school board and others.
3. If significant variance emerges, use the warning to initiate a dialogue about whether actions to modify spending are warranted. Engage key stakeholders in this dialogue.

Appendix B
Key Ratios Based on Balance Sheet Items

RATIO	CALCULATION	INDICATOR
Operating Efficiency Ratio	Total Revenue divided by Total Assets	Indicates how well a school district is using its total assets to generate income. The higher the number, the more efficient the school district.
Liabilities/Fund Balance Ratio	Total Liabilities divided by Total Fund Balance	Indicates the number of times a school district can meet its obligations with net assets. A ratio of greater than 1:1 means that obligations cannot be met.
Current Ratio	Current assets divided by current liabilities	This is a measure of a district's ability to meet its current obligations. A standard indicator of fiscal health is a ratio of at least 2:1

| Fund Balance as a percentage of Adopted General Fund Budget | Fund balance divided by GF budget | Enables tracking of adequate fund balance. Depending on the reliability of revenue sources, this factor ranges from 3% on the low side to 10%. Local conditions and priorities will influence this percentage. |

Source: Everett, R.E., Lows, R.L., & Johnson, D.B., (1996).

The Business Side of School Success

Glossary of Key Terms

Accrual(s): A method of accounting that recognizes revenues when received whether earned or unearned and expenditures when incurred whether paid or unpaid.

Accounting: The department responsible for ensuring that funds are used as they are intended and are accurately recorded in the district accounting system. Also, a required activity in providing reliable fiscal information, guidance, and accountability in the use of district funds.

Accounting Period: See Fiscal Period.

Accounting System Access: Controlling access to different parts of an accounting system via passwords, lockouts and electronic access logs to keep unauthorized users out of the system while providing a way to audit the usage of the system to identify the source of errors or discrepancies.

Accounting System: The records and methods established to record and summarize financial information and produce financial statements and reports.

Accounts Payable (A/P): Accounts payable is money owed by a district to its suppliers; shown as a liability on the district's balance sheet.

Accounts Receivable (A/R): Accounts receivable are legally enforceable claims held by the district for payment of items ordered or services rendered but not paid for by the customers.

Action Plans: A detailed plan outlining actions needed to reach one or more strategic goals. Alternatively, it can be defined as a "sequence of steps that must be taken, or activities that must be performed well, for a strategy to succeed".

Adopted budget: The organization's official plan for revenues and expenditures for the current or upcoming fiscal period formally adopted by the governing board of directors. The budget is an estimate of resources to be applied to achieving the district's goals and objectives.

Adverse Audit Opinion: An opinion from the auditor indicating a deficiency in the organization's financial statements may result in the statements not fairly presenting the district's true financial position.

Advice (or Remittance Advice): A letter sent by the customer to the supplier when payment is made.

Allotment: The part of an appropriation that may be encumbered or expended during a given period. As used in this text an allotment is the result obtained when an annual budget is broken down into monthly amounts. This process can be applied to revenues or expenditures and is the first step in a mechanism used to track progress during the fiscal period. See also Variance Reports.

Ambiguity: Unclear or uncertain. Something ambiguous can be deceptive, either intentionally or unintentionally because the interpreter isn't able to figure out the actual meaning.

Ancillary position: A person working to support others, often with specialized training to provide students with unique services or support.

Anticipated expenditures: Estimated expenditures that are identified in the budget and labelled for a specific fiscal year.

Anticipated revenues: Estimated revenues that are identified in the budget for a future fiscal period.

Anticipated Per Pupil Expenditures: The total expenditures in the budget divided by the projected students.

Anticipated Per Pupil Revenues: The total revenues in the budget divided by the projected students.

Appropriation: An expenditure limitation adopted by the governing body (school board, city council or state legislature).

Approval authority requirements: Requiring specific managers to authorize certain types of transactions can add a layer of responsibility to accounting records by proving that transactions have been seen, analyzed and approved by appropriate authorities.

Architectural Team (Design Team): The architectural firm's representatives who are responsible for the project design.

Assessed valuation: The property valuation used by a school district to determine the tax levy when a tax rate is applied to it.

Assets: Anything owned by the organization that has monetary value. It is usual to define a threshold value that identifies assets worth tracking on the balance sheet versus those that are consumed or expensed annually.

Associated Study Body Fund: A fund on deposit (with each county treasurer or other allowable institution) for each school district to manage activities, athletics, music, clubs and other student events.

Assigned Fund Balance (see also Contingency Funds): A portion of the ending fund balance that has been set aside by the governing body to use for a particular purpose or purposes.

Attendance: An approach to counting students based on daily, physical attendance used by many states in their state funding formulas.

Audit: The examination of records and documents and the securing of other evidence to determine the propriety of completed transactions; ascertain whether all transactions have been recorded properly; and confirm whether the financial statements of the organization have been presented fairly and in accordance with defined accounting standards. The audit is conducted independently by a separate public agency of the state, or a private certified public accounting firm contracted specifically for an independent financial review.

Audit Cycle: Typically, audits are required for every fiscal year.

Auditor: Internal Auditor, External Auditor, Claims Auditor. Most districts have all three types of auditors. An auditor is a person authorized to review and verify the accuracy of financial records and ensure that companies comply with tax laws.

Audit Finding: A weakness in internal controls or an instance of noncompliance with applicable laws and regulations that is presented in the formal audit report to the governing board.

Audit Response: The district is provided an opportunity in the audit process to officially address the audit finding(s). A Corrective Action Plan is usually developed as part of the response.

Balanced Budget: A spending plan in which the total revenues are equal to or greater than the total expenditures.

Balance Sheet (also Statement of Financial Condition): A financial statement which discloses the assets, liabilities and equities of the organization.

Bank Statement: Provided by the County Treasurer or the institution that holds the consolidated district funds, these monthly reports must be regularly reconciled for both validate revenues and expenditures.

Bargaining Agreement: See Collective Bargaining Agreement (CBA).

Base (or base spending): A determination of the current level of spending with adjustments made for costs not likely to recur.

Before and After School Transportation: Getting students to school before the regular start time or taking students home after the regular stop time.

Benchmarking: Collecting data on the school district's performance and comparing it with exemplar districts.

Benefits: See Health Benefits.

Bid Alternate: Bid alternates are specific components of a construction project that are not included in the base price of a bid or proposal. Alternates are called out separately in the request for proposals or bid form, along with a request for pricing that adds to or deletes from the contractor's base bid.

Bid Award: Once all the bids have been reviewed, a bid tally lists all acceptable bids by vendor and by quoted price, from lowest to highest; an award is officially made by the school board to the vendor who submitted the lowest bid and who possesses the required qualifications for the contract.

Bid documents: A series of documents that is responsive to a Request for Proposals or Bids.

Bid or bidding process: The procurement procedure under which sealed bids are invited, received, opened, examined and evaluated for the purpose of awarding a contract. The bidding process is used to select a vendor for subcontracting a project or for purchasing products and services that are required for a project. The district officially advertises for bids and often sends the bid to a list of likely vendors for response. The vendors analyze the bid and calculate the cost at which they can complete the project.

Bloodborne Pathogens: Bloodborne pathogens are infectious microorganisms in human blood that can cause disease in humans.

Bond issuance insurance: A layer of financial support provided by an external source or company to lower risk to bondholders of district default and reduce the need to pay higher interest rates.

Bond rating: Issued by a rating agency and applicable to districts; the rating establishes the fiscal stability of the school district and affects the interest rate payable for the sale of bonds or other forms of debt. Note: This rating affects the bond sale, but subsequent ratings are important to bond holders.

Borrowing: Short-term borrowing, either from another fund, or from your financial system is a symptom of inadequate reserves.

Bow Wave (Tail): The future budget effects of actions taken part way through the current fiscal period. An example would be creating a new position and hiring a full-time teacher halfway through the school year. In the current fiscal period, the budgetary impact is only half of what it will be in the next fiscal period, but the full annual cost needs to be recognized in the upcoming budget.

Bribery: The offering, promising, giving, accepting or soliciting of an advantage as an inducement for an action which is illegal, unethical or a breach of trust.

Budget: A plan for revenues and expenditures for the current or future fiscal period. This term may also apply to the entire organization or various subsets of the organization's budget (see also Adopted Budget or Program Budget).

Budget allocation: A budgetary allocation is the amount of cash, or budget, you allocate to each item of expenditure in your financial plan.

Budget assumptions: A list of the key assumptions and decisions that were used in the process of creating the budget.

Budget Deficit: If revenues are overstated, or if expenditures are understated, the potential for a budget deficit exists. A budget deficit results in any year in which revenues do not cover expenses.

Budget Development Calendar: A multi-month schedule of the actions necessary to pass a budget. It should include the major events and major players.

Budget Development Process: The process in which the budget moves from development to finally approval by the school board (and or municipality). The process typically includes parameters which guide the budget as it is being developed.

Budget Decision-making Errors: The tendency to ignore adverse information until too late to react to it in a thoughtful manner.

Budget Efficacy Errors: Budget is inadequate to reach objectives or does not adequately address multiyear issues.

Budget Human Dynamic Errors: Errors caused by a breakdown in communication resulting in misinformation being used.

Budget Implementation Errors: An inadequate communication, training, or ability to adjust the resources needed to accomplish the objective.

Budget Production and Assembly Errors: Types of errors made in the process of developing the budget that make it inaccurate.

Budget Recommendation: The Superintendent's recommended budget sent and presented to the school board. The recommendation should address all the issues that can reasonably be anticipated, meet budget parameters adopted by the board, and include the Superintendent's plans for the future.

Budget Reserve or Contingency: An amount included in the overall budget that serves as a hedge against unforeseen financial emergencies. Sometimes must be established by a separate action of the governing body.

Budget Status Report: A report, typically monthly, prepared by the fiscal team and presented to the governing body after reconciliation with the monthly banking statements. The report summarizes the most current financial position of the district. This term may also be used at the program level to report the current financial position to the fiscal team or executive team.

Budget Suggestion: In budget preparation, suggestions are items presented from a variety of sources to be considered as the budget is prepared.

Budget Unintended Consequences: When implemented, results are not expected or require additional resources to resolve.

Budgeted Per Pupil Expenditures: See Anticipated Per Pupil Expenditures.

Budgeted Per Pupil Revenues: See Anticipated Per Pupil Revenue.

Bus Fleet: See Fleet.

Bus Safety Drills: Drills to practice safely unloading from a bus in an emergency.

Bus Safety Inspections: Inspections to ascertain whether a bus is safe to drive and if it has all required safety equipment.

Business Office: Encompassing term that usually denotes all the functions reporting to the Chief Financial Officer.

Capital Projects: A Capital Project is a project that helps maintain or improve a district's asset, often called infrastructure. It is a new construction, expansion, renovation, or replacement project for an existing facility or facilities.

Capital Projects Fund: In fund accounting this is the fund where expenditures supported by voter-approved bonds, transfers from the general fund, and capital improvement levies are recorded. These funds are used to account for the financial resources used to purchase facilities, construct new facilities or refurbish existing facilities but not operate the facilities.

Carryover (Carry Forward): The practice of allowing schools and certain programs to use unspent money from the prior fiscal period. Federal and state allocations often come with carryover limits. Districts often have carryover practices that are allowed for some budgets and not others. It is sometimes a strategy for districts to allow school-based budgets to be carried over into the subsequent school year to avoid the "use it or lose it" behaviors at the end of the fiscal year.

Cash: Currency, coins, checks, money orders, bankers' drafts and bank deposits.

Cash Availability: As of any date of determination, an amount equal to the cash held by the district, less, the district's then existing current liabilities and commitments. Liquid resources available at the district's financial institution to meet spending obligations.

Cash Flow: Spending is not constant each month of the fiscal period and revenue arrives at various times. Monitor the outflow and cash available to meet spending commitments. Cash on hand reflects the fund balance, plus revenues, minus expenditures to date must result in the remaining cash availability. Use a cash flow forecast to maintain fiscal viability.

Cash Management: The process by which cash is estimated, invested, and made available to cover expenses.

Change Orders: A formal process where the Contractor Team submits changes to the originally bid scope of work and cost to the Architectural Team and Owner Team for resolution. A Change Order may correct a design error or cover an upgrade or reduction in work or materials.

Chart of Accounts: A list of accounts systemically arranged to identify expenses and revenue by categories and sources.

Chemical Safety: Includes all those policies, procedures and practices designed to minimize the risk of exposure to potentially hazardous chemicals. This includes the risks of exposure to persons handling the chemicals, to the surrounding environment, and to the communities and ecosystems within that environment.

Chief Financial Officer (CFO): May be recognized by another term, such as Business Officer or Chief Business Officer (CBO). The individual oversees all work and functions of the district's finances and sometimes other support services.

Circuit Breakers: A form of property tax relief. It may apply to the elderly, disabled veterans, senior citizens, homestead exemptions, low-income, or other special populations.

Cohort projection: A student enrollment forecast that includes birth-rate assumptions, in- and out-migration, annual grade level advancement, and other factors to create a student enrollment forecast for a five-to-ten-year period.

Collective Bargaining: A process of negotiation often governed by state law between employers and a group of employees aimed at agreements to regulate working salaries, working conditions, benefits, and other aspects of workers' compensation and rights for workers.

Collective Bargaining Agreement (CBA): A written legal contract between an employer and a union representing the employees. The CBA is the result of an extensive negotiation process between the parties regarding topics such as wages, hours, and terms and conditions of employment. This document includes all the written agreements developed during negotiations or other regular labor-management consultations.

Community Design Charette: A short demonstration by Architects to show what they see as possible designs for a school construction program.

Consolidated Year-end Financial Statement: The general ledger accounts for each fund are updated and used to prepare this report as of the last day of the fiscal year.

Competitive Bidding Process: See Bid Process.

Conflict of Interest: Occurs when a person who holds a position of implicit trust and has a competing professional or personal interest that motivates their decisions.

Contingency Budget: Often typical in capital projects to cover the unforeseen or unknown costs encountered during construction.

Contract: See Collective Bargaining Agreement.

Contract Amendment: A formal addendum to the labor agreement adding procedures or clarifying an issue.

Contractor Team: Representatives of the contractor on a building project.

Contingency Funds (see also Assigned Fund Balance): Resources set aside by the governing body to deal with unforeseen fiscal emergencies.

Corrective Action Plan: A plan developed during the monitoring process conducted by an external agency. Also, the district's response to an Audit Finding.

Cost Containment: The practice of controlling expenses by reducing or limiting spending to stay within specific budgetary limits, allowing businesses to improve profitability without long-term damage to the district.

Cost estimate: A cost estimate is the approximation of the cost of a program, project, or operation. The cost estimate has a single total value and may have identifiable sub-component values. Cost estimation in project management is the process of forecasting the cost and other resources needed to complete a project within a defined scope. Cost estimation accounts for each element required for the project and calculates a total amount that determines a project's budget.

Crisis Management Team (CMT): The district incident response team, prepares the district to respond to potential emergencies. It also executes and coordinates the response in the event of an actual disaster.

Cross-training: A tool prepare multiple staff members with the knowledge to perform various fiscal function with the goal to reduce embezzlement in school district fiscal transactions.

Current Ratio: The ratio of assets to liabilities. An acceptable ratio is 2:1.

Curious behavior: Any anomaly that should be explored in a case or action by school district employees or vendors.

Custodial: A service in school district to keep the buildings clean and safe, including performing minor repairs.

Custodial Funds: Custodial funds are used to report fiduciary activities that are not required to be reported in pension (and other employee benefit) trust funds or private-purpose trust funds where the government's role is purely custodial, such as the receipt, temporary investment, and remittance of fiduciary resources to individuals, private organizations, or other governments. Custodial Funds differs from a Private Purpose Trust fund in that there is no formal trust agreement. The school district is acting in an agent capacity for some other organization, government, individual, or fund.

Customer Service: The degree to which district personnel meet the needs of those using district services or seeking appropriate information.

Debt limit: The debt limit of the school district (used in capital planning); likely established by state law.

Debt Service Fund: A separate fund used to collect revenue, typically from property taxes, to pay principal and interest on the school district's long-term debt.

Deferred Maintenance: Every district should have an assessment of its major building systems, when required maintenance was last performed, and listing what should be performed (the Deferred Maintenance list). Development of a comprehensive list of deferred maintenance should include a cost estimate and a presentation of the schedule for resolving the issue.

Deficit: The excess of liabilities and reserved equity of a fund over its assets.

Deposit: A sum of money placed or kept in a bank account, usually to gain interest. Also, a sum payable as a first installment on the purchase of something or as a pledge for a contract. To store or entrust with someone for safekeeping.

Direct Expenditures: Those expenditures specifically traceable to specific programs, activities or functions.

Disaster Recovery Plan: A formal document created by the district that contains detailed instructions on how to respond to unplanned incidents such as natural disasters, power outages, cyber-attacks and any other disruptive events.

District Mission: The specific task or set of tasks with which a district is charged to accomplish (e.g., educate children).

Diversity, Equity, Inclusion, Belonging (DEIB): The operational label for efforts focused about the behavior of district employees that defines a district culture honoring and respecting all its clients: students, parents, staff and leaders.

Door-to-Door Service: A Transportation service provided to students who require transportation, usually through an Individual Education Plan developed for students with special needs where the bus driver picks up and returns the child to the child's home.

Due Process: A course of formal proceedings (such as legal proceedings) carried out regularly and in accordance with established rules and principles.

Educational Outcomes: Outcomes that matter to the district and shed insight into the operations. One example is the graduation rate.
Efficient Business Practice: An effective service provided at the lowest reasonable cost.
Encumber: See Encumbrance.
Encumbrance: An accounting control devise that reserves portions of the budget as expenditures that will soon be incurred. A system for tracking outstanding obligations. For example, purchase orders submitted for curriculum materials are encumbered so managers know the budget has become obligated.
Enrollment: A system of counting students based on students enrolled in the district used by many states as the basis for the state funding formula.
Enrollment Forecast: Predictions of future enrollment levels commonly prepared by district personnel. These projections are often developed by comparing actual enrollments through time to identify trends and predict future enrollments.
Embezzlement: The theft or misappropriation of funds placed in one's trust or belonging to one's employer.
Equalization Ratios: A ratio used to adjust the assessed value of district's property comparing it to the actual market value of property in the municipality in order to equalize tax payments among entities. The ratio may be called by other names (e.g., an indicated ratio in Washington State) and used to equalize the assessment and tax payment processes for school districts.
Enterprise Risk Management (ERM): The natural, physical, legal, health, educational, social and political, risks facing the school district. ERM is a continuous process of risk identification, taking actions to mediate the risk and assessing the response before making further assessments and modifications.
Employee Benefits: See Benefits.
Expenditure: The action of spending funds. Also, an amount of money spent.
Expenditure Estimation: See Cost Estimate.

Extortion: Occurs when a district employee demands payment from a vendor, community member of donor to influence or decide in a beneficial way.

Extra-curricular funds: Money collected or paid to support co-curricular student activities that includes district approved, school-related activities that generally take place after school hours.

Facility Needs Assessment: A comprehensive assessment of the district's facilities conducted by architects and contractors.

Facility Planning Task Force: A committee established by the school district to make recommendations to the administration and school board about projects to be considered in a bond proposal.

Federal Aid Budget: In some states, federal funds are reported in a separate fund and thus not included in the General Fund.

Federal Budget Cycle: The federal budget year begins October 1 through the next September 30 and does not typically align with the district's budget cycle. District's must estimate what these resources.

Federal Payroll Taxes: The mandatory taxes paid in part by the district and also deducted from funds due employees. These taxes fund Medicare and Social Security programs.

Fiduciary Fund: A fund used to account for fiduciary activities in which the school district acts as a trustee; these funds are included in the district's financial statements. Examples of these funds include extra-classroom clubs, scholarship funds, and a labor union welfare trust.

Final acceptance: The act of the school district to ensure that all construction work is properly completed (typically identified on a punch list) so that retainage funds held in escrow can be released to the contractor.

Financial (or Fiscal) plan (or Spending Plan): See Budget.

Financial Balance Statement: This statement displays the district's assets and liabilities with an equity balance usually called the Fund Balance.

Financial Reporting: The financial results of an organization that are released to its stakeholders and the public. Financial statements include the income statement, balance sheet, and statement of cash flows.

Financial Reports: Written records that convey the district's business activities and the financial performance. Financial statements are audited by government agencies or independent accounting firms to ensure accuracy and for tax, financing, or investing purposes.

Financial Status Report: See Budget Status Report.

Financial System: The computer software used by the district personnel to maintain accurate records of the financial activities of the district. The district should limit access to the system and assure that it provides metadata to assure proper use or investigate inappropriate actions. The system may be comprehensive or consist of multiple add-on programs.

Fiscal (Budgetary & Internal) Controls: A system of checks and balances that includes procedures within the system designed to reduce error, fraud or abuse or to assist with keeping expenditures within authorized budgetary amounts. For example, two individuals should be required to count cash as deposits are made.

Fiscal Plan: The adopted budget represents the fiscal plan for the district.

Fiscal Year or Fiscal Period: The twelve-month calendar that covers the time for which the budget of the organization applies. For school districts, the fiscal year is often not the same as the calendar year and may begin anywhere between July 1 and September 1. Some entities may budget for periods of time longer than twelve months, but this practice is not typical for school districts.

Fleet: The buses, vans, trucks, and cars maintained by the district's Transportation Department. Also, the equipment used by the maintenance and grounds staff.

Flywheel Turning: The analogy of the flywheel applied to organizational momentum in the work of Jim Collins. Each revolution of the planning cycle is intended to accelerate the momentum and move toward the desired outcomes for students. Leadership focus is the key to sustaining this process.

Food Service: A department within the district that takes care of serving food to students following federal and state guidelines.

Food Management Company: A private contractor who works with the district. They file necessary reports and manage your staff. The contract must be bid periodically.

Food Service Fund: Some states require a separate fund to account for this program. Others include it as part of the General Fund.

Forecast: A prediction of future anticipated events. In this context it usually means estimates regarding revenues or expenditures.

Forecasting: The process of making predictions based on past and present data and most commonly by analysis of trends.

Forecast (or Forecasting) bias: Assumptions used in the forecasting process that are wrong because they are too conservative or too optimistic. In this context bias introduces inherent inaccuracies that are difficult to detect and potentially avoidable.

Formula-Based: State allocations that use enrollment, property wealth, geographic considerations, or school district (or school size) as factors.

Fraud: Deceit, trickery, or breach of confidence perpetrated for profit or to gain some unfair or dishonest advantage.

Fraud audit: An audit specifically looking for fraud. Also, an audit to prove fraud occurred and how much was taken.

Fraud Hotline: An anonymous tip line actively publicized to encourage staff or citizens to report suspected fraud.

Fraud prevention: Any concrete action taken to discourage or limit fraudulent actions.

Fraudulent behavior: The behaviors associated with fraud.

Free or reduced priced lunch eligibility: Following federally established family income criteria to qualify students with nutritionally balanced, low-cost or no-cost meals. May include breakfast, lunch or both meals. The number of students qualifying for this program is an indicator of the relative poverty level of the population served by the school or the district.

Fuel: Gas, diesel or an alternative used to power district equipment and the vehicle fleet. It is an inventory item that must be controlled to avoid unauthorized access.

Fund(s): The accounting records of the district are assembled into various funds based on the nature of the program. Each of the eleven categories into which all funds are classified in governmental accounting has special rules and allowable uses.

Fund Balance (Equity): The accumulation of revenues minus expenditures. Each fund maintained by the district has a fund balance. Fund balance can be used in future years for purposes determined by the school board. The excess of assets over liabilities. If liabilities exceed assets, the fund balance is negative (and this is a problem to be resolved).

Fund Equity: The difference between assets and liabilities. Fund equity includes reserved and unreserved fund balances.

Generally Accepted Accounting Principles (GAAP): A set of principles set by the General Accounting Standards Board (GASB). All districts are required to adhere to GAAP following their state guidelines.

General Fund: One of the funds used by governmental units. For school districts this is the fund in which the almost all routine educational operations of the district are recorded.

General Ledger: The ledger combines all components of the fiscal affairs of the district and provides a comprehensive view of all the school system's financial activity. Both revenue and expenditure accounts are separate ledgers within the General Ledger. They are derived from the school board adopted budget and form a management tool for monthly status reports and tracking both expenditures and revenue progress. States may call this vital tool by different names, but the key concept is that month-by-month management of the annual budget is essential to sustaining trust and understanding the fiscal condition of the school district in dynamic times.

General Obligation Bonds: A common type of municipal bond in the United States that is secured by a state or local government's pledge to use legally available resources, including tax revenues, to repay bondholders. The interest earned by these bonds may be taxable or not, depending on its design.

General Operating Budget: See General Fund.

Ghost Employee: An employee for the district has been terminated or a fake person created in the system. The fraudster changes the employee's address to their own or a different one and continues processing their payments.

Hacking and Ransomware: Occurs when someone uses technological tools to break into the entity's software system to modify or corrupt data, then demands payment (a ransom) to release uncorrupted data.

Hazardous Routes: Transportation routes must be reviewed periodically to ensure students are not walking to school through or along a dangerous route.

Health Benefits: Medical and dental insurance programs are often offered to eligible employees based on the employment agreement or contract.

Historical Financial Trends: The pattern of revenue or expenditures from previous fiscal periods. These may be used to improve forecasting of future events.

Human Resources (Personnel): The department charged with finding, screening, recruiting, and training job applicants, as well as administering employee-benefit programs. Also, the personnel of the district comprising the skills and talent necessary to accomplish this mission.

Human Resource (Personnel) Records: A clear, reliable software system of maintaining current and historical records for all district personnel is essential to protect the district from potential claims. People who have left the district may call upon the district at some future point to verify employment dates, seek resolution of a retirement question, or address other related issues. Because wages and benefits have taxable effects for individuals, having access to ex-employee records for at least seven years is essential.

Illegal Gratuities: When someone gives something of value to a public official because that public official does or fails to do some act.

Incident Command System: The Incident Command System (ICS) is a standardized hierarchical structure that allows for a cooperative response by multiple agencies, both within and outside of government, to organize and coordinate response activities without compromising the decision-making authority of local command.

Incident Command Protocols: The protocols used by the ICS to conduct its mission and communicate to other organizations.

Independent auditor: An auditor who is not employed by the district and complies with defined professional principles and standards.

Indicators: Ratios used to assess the fiscal health of the district.

Indirect Expenditures: Those expenditures incurred for organization-wide purposes. These expenditures are accumulated in a cost center and can be distributed to programs, activities or functions and added to Direct Expenditures to reveal a total cost of doing business (e.g., maintenance of buildings, utility expenses and business office functions).

Individuals with Disabilities Education Act (IDEA): This federal act provides funding for eligible children with disabilities to receive special education and related services.

Indoor Air Quality (IAQ): The air quality within and around buildings and structures. IAQ is known to affect the health, comfort, and well-being of building occupants. Poor indoor air quality has been linked to sick building syndrome, reduced productivity, and impaired learning in schools.

Information Technology (IT): The use of systems (especially computers and telecommunications) for storing, retrieving, and sending information.

Inherent Risk: In ERM inherent risk is current risk level given the existing set of controls and not the hypothetical notion of an absence of any controls.

Instructional Software: The programs supported by the district to aid teachers. This may include classroom management software, curriculum, learning objectives, and much more.

Insurance: Core Coverage, Umbrella Plans, Liability, and Errors and Omissions insurance is used to protect against losses of equipment, facilities or damages caused by the actions of district officials or personnel. A practice or arrangement by which a district provides a guarantee of compensation for specified loss, damage, illness, or death in return for payment of a premium.

Insurance Broker: A professional advisor who acts as an intermediary between a district and its employee representatives and an insurance company, helping the former find a policy that best suits their needs.

Intake Procedures: Refers to the process for reviewing requests and the plan for dealing with them.

Internal Control: A process designed to provide reasonable, reliable assurance regarding the achievement of business objectives.

Inventory: See Physical Audit of Assets. These are items required to be placed on your inventory of assets to ensure that they are protected and maintained.

Invoice: A list of goods or services provided with a statement of the sum due for these items. Invoices should contain all the information to appropriately pay the vendor.

Intangibles (Intangible Assets): In accounting this is the value according to the advantage or reputation a business has acquired (over and above its tangible assets).

Imprest Fund (Petty Cash): A management technique that provides access to cash for employees to make purchases. Typically, these transactions are limited in size and are reconciled against invoices to restore a limited dollar value to the account.

Interest: Income earned from investments of money until needed. Also, an expense paid when accounts are overdue or for bond or other forms of debt instruments issued by the district.

Internal controls: The controls a district uses to discourage or mitigate losses from fraud or embezzlement (e.g., one person records cash receipts, another person prepares the receipts for deposit with the banking entity).

Key Performance Indicators (KPI): A type of performance measurement. KPIs evaluate the success of an organization or of a particular activity (such as projects, programs, products and other initiatives) in which it engages.

Labor Relations: The relationship between the management of a district and its workforce in general and labor organizations in particular.

Liabilities: Debt or other legal obligations arising out of transactions in the past that are payable but not necessarily due. Encumbrances become liabilities until they are paid when the services or materials for which the encumbrance was established have been rendered or received.

Log-in: The procedure through which access to systems occurs and that is controlled (hopefully limited to authorized users) by the vendor or district.

Long-range facility planning: The district's ability to plan necessary for capital construction for a period of years.

Long-range financial plans: An investment plan or strategy that encompasses more than one year. A long-term financial plan involves more uncertainty than anything short-term because, typically, trends are more easily predictable in the short term.

Low-Risk Investments: Financial instruments, such as United States Treasury Bills or certificates of deposit from local financial institutions, with a high probability of repayment and generally lower levels of interest.

Lowest Responsible Bidder: The bidder who fully complied with all of the bid requirements and whose past performance, reputation, and financial capability is deemed acceptable, and who has offered the most advantageous pricing or cost benefit, based on the criteria stipulated in the bid documents.

Medicaid Reimbursement: Reimbursement of costs for certain health support services provided to Medicaid-eligible students.

Maintenance: The work needed to keep a building, vehicle or equipment in sound operating condition. This is often the name used to identify the department responsible for the maintenance of district facilities, fields, and property.

Management review: A study of current practices and operations typically done by an outside group to ascertain the present strengths and challenges facing a district.

Mandates: Actions required by one level of government upon another (e.g., a state law requiring a certain school district action).

McKinney-Vento: A federal law addressing the needs of homeless students and requiring out-of-district transportation for them in certain situations.

Memorandum of Understanding: A written document used to clarify the collective bargaining agreement.

Metadata: A tool that provides information like the author, file size, the date the document was created or other information about the aspects of data.

Micro-climates: Different weather conditions impacting your district that make communication of your transportation decisions more complex.

Mid-Day Runs: Typically used for the transportation of students who only attend in the morning or afternoon.

Millage Rate: One mill is equal to one-tenth of one percent. The rate per $1,000 of assessed valuation that is used to calculate total taxes due on property is called the millage rate.

Misfeasance: Simple errors which confound the accounting records for the district (e.g., charges made to the wrong account or in the wrong amount).

Monitoring: Also known as fiscal monitoring, program monitoring, budget status, budget review. A method of taking the expenditures and revenues, adjusting, and estimating the amount to be collected (revenue) and the amount to be spent (expenditures) to the end of the fiscal period. It will typically include estimating staff, staffing costs, temporary staffing needs, supplies, training, conferences, and any one-time expenditures. Current or actual data are compared to what is planned for the same period and any variations explained. Monitoring can be done on a department, program, or for the entire organization.

National School Lunch Program (NSLP): A federally assisted meal program operating operated by the U.S. Department of Agriculture. It provides nutritionally balanced, low-cost or no-cost lunches to children each school day.
Negotiations: See Collective Bargaining.
Non-bid purchases: Purchases below the threshold set by the state law or board policy that requires bids.
Notes to the Financial Statements: Disclosures required for a fair presentation of the financial statements of the organization.

Occupancy date: The date when a facility under construction is turned over to the district.
Operating Capital: Funds used for the day-to-day operations of the school district. The salary and benefits of most employees are paid from the operating capital, as well as overhead expenses such as electricity, materials and supplies for classrooms, and contracted services.
Operating Deficit: The result when expenditures exceed revenues for a given fiscal period.
Operating Efficiency Ratio: Total Revenue divided by Total Assets.
Over Customized: An action to modify purchased software to meet unique district needs that often results increased complexity and higher costs of support and ownership.
Owner Team: The school district team authorized to advise architects and contractors on a regular basis. They play a part in reviews and comments on proposed change orders.

Payment Schedule: Payment schedule is either parameterized or customized. A parameterized schedule is determined by market conventions, and usually includes payment frequency (annually, quarterly, monthly, weekly and so on); day of payment; start date and end date. A customized payment schedule is a series of fixed dates agreed by both parties as to when payments are made.

Pension contribution: Employer contributions to the pension plans of individual employees.

Performance Bond: A bond purchased by a contractor of the district from an insurance company replaces or requires a vendor to meet expectations according to a contract. In the event of default, the bond may be used to hire another contractor.

Performance Indicators: See Key Performance Indicators.

Periodic Reconciliation in Accounting Systems: Occasional accounting reconciliations can ensure that balances in your accounting system match up with balances in accounts held by other entities, including banks, suppliers and credit customers.

Personal Protective Equipment: For employees this can range from disinfectant wipes to COVID-19 masks. More broadly gloves, respiratory protection, or other equipment designed to keep workers safe when handling hazardous materials or operating equipment.

Personnel: See Human Resources.

Personnel Records: See Human Resource Records.

Physical Audits of Assets: Physical audits include hand-counting cash and any physical assets tracked in the accounting system, such as inventory, materials and tools. Physical counting can reveal well-hidden discrepancies in account balances by bypassing electronic records altogether.

Preliminary budget: A draft version of the budget during the development phase that has not been adopted by the school board or other governing group.

Print Shop: A centralized support program that does special printing for the administration or schools. A print shop performs specialized printing using colors, or binding.

Program Budget: A subset of the organization's budget that is organized by program or function of the organization, e.g., special education, pupil transportation, or vocational/technical education.

Progress payments: Payments to a contractor for the construction accomplished to date.

Project Alternatives: An option, or series of options, included in a bid document that are may be accepted (or rejected) by the owner at the time of bid award.

Projected Enrollment: Estimated student enrollment for a specified period of time, usually presented by grade level

Projected Expenditures: Estimated expenditures for a specified period of time such as the fiscal period.

Projected Revenues: Estimated revenues for a specified period of time such as the fiscal period.

Property Taxes: Taxes may be generated from three categories of property. One category is real property, land and permanent structures on the land. The second category is tangible or personal property. The third category is intangible, property that has value, but because of lack of substance, has no value in and of itself. The property is valued, and a tax rate is applied to the value to calculate the total tax due.

Property Wealth: Property that has a money value or an exchangeable value. The relative value of the assessed value of a district, often expressed per pupil in order to allow comparisons among districts.

Property Value: Refers to the worth of a piece of real estate based on the price that a buyer and seller agree upon. In other words, the value of a property at any given time is determined by what the market will bear. For the district this may also mean the sum of all aggregated properties within the district.

Punch list: A list of items that need to be fixed or mitigated so the project can be formally accepted.

Purchase Order: A purchase order is a commercial document and first official offer issued by a buyer to a seller indicating types, quantities, and agreed prices for products or services. It is used to control the purchasing of products and services from external suppliers.

Purchasing: The process a district uses to acquire goods or services to accomplish its goals. The department responsible for purchasing.

Ratio of Liabilities to Fund Balance: Total Liabilities divided by Total Fund Balance

Real (Constant) Dollars: The value of money after adjusting for inflation (vs. nominal or current value -- the price without adjusting for inflation).

Real Property Tax: A tax calculated against the value of land and permanent structures on the land, usually expressed as rate per $1,000 of valuation.

Receipt: A receipt is a document acknowledging that a person has received money or property in payment following a sale or other transfer of goods or provision of a service. The action of receiving something or the fact of its being received.

Recommended Bid: Effectively, the lowest price from several vendors that are willing to provide the good or service. The recommended bid is the lowest price that is also responsible to all the conditions set for in bid documents.

Remote learning: A concept that became more fully realized during the COVID-19 pandemic that provides teaching and student engagement via computer access to the Internet. Students and staff may not be at the school location.

Rental: School buildings or unused space in school buildings may be rented to other school districts, charter schools, public libraries, churches, private businesses, or other government agencies.

Reports: Documents that contain data to assist in analyzing a school district's financial health: budget appropriation status reports, financial statements, audit reports, monthly treasurer's reports, cash flow reports, state and federal aid reports, and other revenue reports.

Request for Proposal (RFP): An alert to contractors that the district is taking bids or proposals for a set of defined purposes. Specific bid requirements provide the basis for bids or proposals from contractors. A business document that announces a project, describes it, and solicits bids from qualified contractors to complete it.

Requisition: In procurement processes, it is a request for goods or services made by a school employee to the person or department in the district that is responsible for purchasing.

Reserved Fund Balance: Reserved fund balances are funds that are used for specific costs such as encumbrances and employee payouts for compensated absences. The board may establish reserves in a number of areas: repair reserve, retirement contribution reserve, worker's compensation reserve, unemployment insurance reserve, insurance reserve, tax reduction reserve, debt service reserve, liability reserve, tax certiorari reserve, insurance recoveries reserve, encumbrances reserve, inventories reserve, employee benefit accrued liability reserve, and capital reserve.

Residual Risk: ERM term used to cover risk that is not controlled by the organization.

Resource Allocation: The process of assigning and managing assets in a manner that supports an organization's strategic goals.

Retainage: Funds earned by the contractor but placed in escrow on behalf of the contractor until Final Acceptance is approved indicating the work is complete and no subcontractor liens have been filed against the project's contractor.

Response Mechanism: A response mechanism takes evaluations of the importance of potential actions and selects the most suitable.

Retirement Systems: A department, usually of state government or the employer, that accepts retirement payments from employers and eligible employees for the future retirement use by the employees.

Revenue per student: Total revenue divided by the total number of students.

Revenue(s): Money received by the organization net of refunds and other correcting transactions. Types of revenue include local taxes, local non-tax, state, and federal.

Revenue Accounts: Revenues are the assets earned by a district's operations and business activities. In other words, revenues include the cash or receivables received by a district for the sale of its goods or services. The revenue account is an equity account with a credit balance. This means that a credit in the revenue T-account increases the account balance.

Revenue Estimates: Revenue estimation involves calculating the amount of money your district is likely to earn. Revenue estimation is usually calculated over a fixed accounting period, such as monthly or over a financial year.

Revenue Shortfall: Revenues are less than anticipated.

Riders: The number of students transported by your Transportation Department.

Risk: A condition similar to uncertainty but where there is a predictable series of possible outcomes and some of the possibilities include loss. The chance of loss or the perils to the subject matter of an insurance contract also, the degree of probability of such loss.

Risk averse: Reluctant to operate with some level of possible loss.

Risk Management Plan: A well-defined document that narrates how to deal with specific risks and what management actions must be taken against those risks to mitigate or remove threats to the project tasks and outcomes.

Risk tolerance: The degree to which an individual or board of directors is comfortable with some chance of loss.

School Board: A set of district residents elected by the district's voters to set policy for the school district and guide the superintendent.

School Bus Acquisition Fund: The fund used to plan for and expend the cost of acquiring buses or vans owned or operated by a school district. These are regularly used to transport students to and from school or school-related activities. The acquisition fund is used exclusively for the purchase of this fleet.

School Treasurer: A school treasurer handles the financial activities of a school district or similar institution. This position may be a part of the school board with responsibility for maintaining financial and accounting records.

Separation of Duties: A form of internal control that ensures no one individual can both approve and pay a bill. Sharing responsibilities between two or more people or requiring critical tasks to be reviewed by co-workers may also suffice if the office is small.

Special Revenue Funds: These funds come from specific revenue sources, such as federal and state grants. The funds are required to be used for specific purposes, such as school lunch operations, federal grant programs such as Title 1.

Stakeholder: A citizen of the district or a member of the district staff with an interest in district operations.

Standardized Financial Documents: Standardizing documents used for financial transactions, such as invoices, internal materials requests, inventory receipts and travel expense reports, can help to maintain consistency in record keeping over time. Using standard document formats can make it easier to review past records when searching for the source of a discrepancy in the system.

Start and Stop Times: The schedule of the times students must report to schools. It is a determining factor in the size and efficiency of your bus fleet.

State Allocation: The share or allocation from state resources to a district in a given fiscal year.

State Budget Cycle: Not typically aligned with the district budget cycle. District's must use their best guess as to what these resources will be.

Stipend: A form of compensation for specific additional duties.

Strategic Plan: A document used to communicate the goals and the actions needed to achieve those goals and all the other critical elements developed during the planning exercise.

Student Information Systems: Software system that tracks student progress through the years they are attend school in your district.

Supplement not Supplant: Usually means that federal funds cannot be used to perform a service that would normally be paid for with state or local funds.

System life cycles: The average age (or cycle) when a system becomes obsolete. Systems refers to major components, electrical, plumbing, roofs, etc.

Systemic Risk: In finance, systemic risk is the risk of collapse of an entire financial system or entire market, as opposed to the risk associated with any one individual entity, group or component of a system, that can be contained therein without harming the entire system.

System of Accounts: See Chart of Accounts.

Target(s): Specific limits on spending imposed by the superintendent or fiscal team that are different than the amounts set forth in the adopted budget.

Tax Caps: In many states, a cap (limit on the increase) is placed on the increase in assessed valuation or a cap is on the year-to-year increase in the amount to be raised in taxes

Tax certiorari: In some states, certiorari is the process whereby an initial property tax assessment is appealed, reviewed, and adjudicated by a court.

Tax Deferral: Tax deferral refers to instances where a taxpayer can delay paying taxes to some future period. In theory, the net taxes paid should be the same.

Tax-exempt municipal bonds: An instrument of specific value that generates revenue from its sale for a school district construction program; interest on the bond is generally exempt from Federal income tax exempt to the individual bond holder.

Tax Rate: The tax rate is the rate at which assessed property is taxed by calendar year.

Tax Relief: Any government program or policy initiative that is designed to reduce the amount of taxes paid by individuals or businesses. It may be a universal tax cut or a targeted program that benefits a specific group of taxpayers or bolsters a particular goal of the government.

Title Grants: Title I, Part A, provides funds for services to schools with high percentages of children from low-income families. Titles II through VIII provide funding for a variety of specific services that include English Language Acquisition, Emergency Impact Aid, and more.

Transportation Cooperative: A cooperative of two or more school districts in the management of their Transportation Programs. This may have a centralized hub or satellite facilities.

Total Assets: See Assets.

Total Liabilities: See Liabilities.

Total Revenue: See Revenue.

Total Fund Balance: See Fund Balance.

Transportation: The department responsible for the transport of students to and from school and to and from the activities of the schools.

Transportation Complaint Logs: A list of all complaints received by a transportation department.

Treasurer: See School Treasurer.

Treasurer's Report: See Budget Status Report.

Trial Balance Report: See Budget Status Report. Using a double-entry accounting system adds reliability by ensuring that the books are always balanced. Even so, it is still possible for errors to bring a double-entry system out of balance at any given time. Calculating daily or weekly trial balances can provide regular insight into the state of the system, allowing you to discover and investigate discrepancies as early as possible.

Trust but confirm: A spin on trust-but-verify proposed by Whittle, 2013. When confirmation processes and information sharing are valued by leadership to increase accountability and avoid conditions that might entice fraudulent behavior.

Trust Funds: See Custodial Funds.

Tuition: A sum of money charged for teaching or instruction by a school district. Tuition is most often charged to non-resident students or students who attend special programs.

Uncertainty: The existence of more than one possible outcome

Unemployment Compensation Fund: These are operated at the state level (there are rules that apply to a self-insured district or cooperative of districts) and are funded by a tax paid through the payroll system.

Unreserved Fund Balance: Unreserved fund balances are either designated for subsequent year's expenditures, thereby reducing the amount to be raised in taxes, or undesignated for cash flow purposes. The amount of unreserved, undesignated fund balance may be limited by statute at different levels from state to state. If the unreserved, undesignated (different terminology may be used such as unreserved, unallocated) fund balance is close to zero, it is an indication that insufficient funds may exist to cover necessary expenses.

USDA food commodities: Allocations from surplus agricultural stocks managed by the U.S. Department of Agriculture.

Value Added: The ability of an initiative to increase the value of an objective.

Variance: This is the difference between what was projected to happen and what has happened and applies to either revenue or expenditures.

Variance reports (reporting or analysis): The procedure by which the gap between what was projected to happen and what happened is reviewed. This is typically performed for both revenues and expenditures at a level of detail that provides insights into the gap for the remainder of the fiscal period.

Vendor: A person, business, or corporation that provides goods or services to the district.

Warehouse: Any centralized place where materials or manufactured goods may be stored before their delivery to schools. This function requires special treatment in financial records.

Weather Delays: Snow days or other unexpected changes in your schools' schedules that impact the end of the school year.

Working Budget: Refers to the system used by managers to track their decisions and commitments and reconcile them with the official accounting system as a mechanism for obtaining an accurate understanding of their fiscal status and projecting this to the end of the fiscal period. Fiscal staff may also use aggregate information from the working budgets of managers to create a working budget for the entire organization.

Working Capital: Working capital is a financial metric which represents operating liquidity available to a district. Along with fixed assets such as plant and equipment, working capital is considered a part of operating capital.

Working Draft: In budgeting, a technique where revenue categories are reduced to simply the development of the budget.

Workplace Injuries: Injuries or illnesses that occur in relation to an employee's job. Most states narrow the definition of a workplace injury to one that "arises out of and in the course of employment" to prevent employees from pursuing compensation for injuries not directly caused by the job.

Zero-based budgeting (ZBB): A method of budgeting in which all expenses must be justified for each new period. The process of zero-based budgeting starts from a "zero base," and every function within an organization is analyzed for its needs and costs.

Acknowledgements

Many colleagues and mentors helped and shaped each of us throughout our careers. They are too numerous to name here, but we are indebted to each of them for their guidance, friendship, and support.

We received thoughtful review comments to improve our effort from the following colleagues:

Dr. Becky Berg, Superintendent, Eastmont (WA) School District

Gina Bullis, CEO, Go Beyond Consulting and former assistant superintendent for finance and administration in Washington State

Joseph Dragone, Deputy Superintendent for Finance (retired), Long Island, New York

Brenda Hunt, CFO, Monroe (WA) School District

Bret Miller, technology leader (retired), Jeffco (CO) Public Schools

Dr. Jack McKay, former superintendent (WA), Full Professor and Emeritus at the University of Nebraska-Omaha, and Executive Director, Horace Mann League

Stan W. McNaughton, CEO, PEMCO Mutual Insurance Company, Seattle

Cynthia Nelson, technology leader (retired), Edmonds (WA) School District

The Business Side of School Success

Steven Nielsen, CFO (retired), Seattle (WA) Public Schools

Dr. Larry Nyland, Superintendent (retired), Seattle (WA) Public Schools

Dr. Glenys Hill Rada, Director, Washington State University Superintendent Program and Associate Professor, former superintendent (WA)

Dr. Roger Rada, Superintendent (retired), Oregon and search consultant

Dr. James Rickabaugh, Superintendent (retired), White Fish Bay (WI) School District

John Rose, investment banker (retired)

Dr. Simone Sangster, CFO, Bellingham (WA) Public Schools

Dr. Alan Sebel, Associate Professor, Graduate School of Education School Leadership Program, Touro University, New York

Dr. Cindy Stevenson, Superintendent (retired), Colorado

References

Adams, B. K., Hill, Q. M., Lichtenberger, A. R., Perkins, J. A., & Shaw, P. S. (1967). Principles of Public School Accounting (State Educational Records and Reports Series: Handbook 11-B). Washington, DC: U.S. Government Printing Office.

Baker, B. D., Green, P., & Richards, C. E. (2008). Financing Education Systems. Pearson Prentice-Hall.

Beasley, M. (2020). "What is Enterprise Risk Management (ERM)?" North Carolina State University, Poole College of Management, Enterprise Risk Management Institute, July 20, 2020, 9 pp. Retrieved from: erm.ncsu.edu/library/article/what-is-enterprise-risk-management

Benzel, B. and Hoover, K. (2021). The Superintendent and the CFO: Building an Effective Team, 2nd edition, Rowman & Littlefield Publishing Group.

Board of Education v. Mergens, 496 U.S. 226, 236 (1990)

Born, C. (2020). Making Sense of School Finance, a Practical State-by-State Approach, Rowman & Littlefield Publishing Group.

Brimley, V., Jr., & Garfield, R. R. (2002). Financing Education in a Climate of Change (8th Ed.). Allyn & Bacon.

Burrows, D. (2017). Understanding Washington's Tax Structure. Bookmasters.

City of Kitchener, Ontario, Canada. How Property Assessment and Taxation Works. www.youtube.com/watch?=_pw2HJUMytY

Collins, J. (2001). Good to Great: Why Some Companies Make the Leep and Others Don't. HarperBusiness.

Collins, J. (2019). Turning the Flywheel: A Monograph to Accompany Good to Great. HarperCollins.

Cortner-Castor, C. (2009). Trimming the Budget: How to Make the Cuts. School Business Affairs, July/August 2009, p. 27-29. Association of School

Business Officials International, 44790 Maynard Square, Suite 200, Ashburn, VA.

Dimon, J. (April 7, 2021). JP Morgan Chase & Co., Chairman & CEO letter to shareholders. Annual Report 2020.

Epstein, J.L. & Associates. (2019). School, Family and Community Partnerships, Your Handbook for Action (4th edition). Corwin, A SAGE Company.

Everett, R. E., Lows, R. L., & Johnson, D. R. (1996). Financial and Managerial Accounting for School Administrators. Association of School Business Officials International.

Furin, T.L. (2022). Combating Hatred for the Soul of America: Watershed Moments for Transformational Educators. Rowman & Littlefield Publishing Group.

Fiscal Stress Monitoring System. (January 2022). Office of the New York StateComptroller.https://www.osc.state.ny.us/files/local-government/fiscal-monitoring/pdf/system-basics.pdf

Fischer, R., Ury, W. (1981, 1991). Getting to Yes: Negotiating Agreements Without Giving In. Penguin Group.

Hentschke, G. C. (1986). School Business Administration. Berkeley, CA: McCutchan.

Jennings, J. (2020). Fatigued by School Reform, Rowman & Littlefield Publishing Group.

Legal Guidelines Regarding the Equal Access Act and the Recognition of Student-led Noncurricular Groups. U.S. Department of Education. https://www2.ed.gov › guide › secletter › groupsguide

Levenson, N. (2022). Smarter Budgets, Smarter Schools: How to Survive and Thrive in Tight Times, 2nd edition. Harvard Education Press, Cambridge, MA.

Meador, D. (2020). Examining the Role of an Effective School Superintendent. ThoughtCo. Retrieved from: thoughtco.com/role-of-an-effective-school-superintendent-3194566.

Mintz, S. Inside Higher Ed, March 21, 2021. Retrieved from: https://insidehighered.com/blogs/steven-mintz.

National Center for Education Statistics. (2003). Financial Accounting for Local and State School Systems, Chapter 8: Activity Fund Guidelines, 2003 edition. Washington D.C.: U.S. Department of Education. Retrieved from: nces.gov/pubs2004/h2r2/ch_8.asp.

Parla, J. (2020). Shortchanged Proficiency in School Finance. School Administrator, 9(77). AASA, October 2020. 19-20.

Ray, J. R., Condoli, I. C., & Hack, W. G. (2005). School Business Administration: A Planning Approach. Pearson Education.

Thompson, D. C., & Wood, C. R. (2001). Money and Schools. Larchmont Eye on Education.

Walters, A. (2020). Hack Education: The 100 Worst Ed-Tech Debacles of the Decade. National Education Policy Center School of Education Boulder Co. Retrieved from: http://audreywatters.com/ .

Index

Accounting 13-14, 78-86
    Purpose of 79-83
    Types of funds 81
    Guidelines, co-curricular activity funds 117-121
Activity funds 115
Advocacy organization 143-144
Accounts payable 24
Accounts receivable 24-25
Achievement, student 3-6, 34, 41, 241-242, 245-247
Ancillary Services 221-225
    Intra-district mail services 224
    Print shop 223
    Warehouse 222-223
Assessed value determination 71-72
Attendance 59
Attorney client privilege 165
Audits 25, 84, 122-134
    Federal single audit 84
    Fraud and embezzlement 131-132
    Internal controls 129-131
    Management of 125-127
    Types of 128

Banking 25-27
Benchmarking 244
Benefits, see Employee Benefits
Bidding 21-23, 238
Bond sale, see Capital Projects and Bonds
Budget Development 13, 31-49
    Accomplishments 48

Budget Development (continued)
  Additions 41-45
  Advocacy 47
  Analysis of 36-37
  Budget preparation calendar 35
  Communicating about 47-48
  Community involvement in 45-46
  Decisions 46-47
  Errors and Challenges 37-41
  Responsibility for 32-33
  Reductions 41-45
  Start and finish 34-36
  Superintendent's role 37
  Why necessary 34
Business Office 8-30
  Analysis of the future 28
  District size 27
  Functions of 12-13
  Strength of staff 27-28
  Other considerations 27-28
  Role of 10-12
  Reporting relationship 28-30

Capital Projects and Bonds 226-239
  Acquiring property for 236-237
  Bonds for funding projects 232-235
  Construction of buildings 237-238
  Cost estimates 228-229
  Citizen advisory committee 229-230
  Educational facilities improvement plan 227-228
  Election process 230-232
  Facility condition assessment 227-228
  Opposition groups 145
  Other financing options 235
  Refunding bonds 236
  Selling bonds 232-236
  Summary of the process 238-239

Cash flow analysis 95-96, 103, 254-256
Categorical aid 54, 60
Chief Financial Officer (CFO)
    Accounting 13-14, 78-86
    Audit preparation 127
    Banking services 25-26
    Bond sales 233-234
    Budget development leadership 13, 31-49
    Cash management 25-26
    Enrollment reporting 59
    Expenditure management 15-16
    Financial indicators 108-110
    Forecasting status 111
    Fund balance management 96-100
    Insurance and risk management 25
    Knowledge of educational programs 249
    Payroll Office 17-21
    People informed 251-252
    Property tax issues 66-77
    Purchasing 21-23
    Reporting relationships 28-29
    Reporting requirements 251
    Revenue monitoring 65
    Role in leadership 10-11
    Supervisory duties 11-12
Co-curricular activities 113-121
Collective bargaining 155-160
    Bargaining team membership 158
    Parameters for 157-159
    Process 159
    School board role in 157
    Superintendent's role in 155-157, 160
Communication 47-48, 138-142, 144
Community partnership considerations 136-146
    Communicating with 138-142
    Family and community engagement 140
    Opposition groups 145

Community partnership considerations (continued)
    Superintendent's role 47-48
    Voting on finance measures 140-143
Crisis management team 172-173
Culture 132, 149, 248-250
Curiosity 250
Custodial services 185-189
    Environmental considerations 182, 190
    Staffing standards 188
    Training for 154, 190

Disaster recovery planning 173
Discipline and investigations 153-154
Diversity 152

Embezzlement prevention 131-132
Employee benefits 17-20
Enrollment 59, 107
Enterprise Risk Management 25, 168-177
    Conduct of 170-171
    Crisis management team 172
    Defined 169
    Disaster recovery planning 173
    Inherent risk 171
    Insurance to address risk 175-177
    Residual risk 1710-172
Expenditures 15-16

Federal Payroll Taxes 19
Financial advisor, bond sales 234
Financial health 101-112
    Assessment of 102-103
    Factors impacting 108-110
    Key ratios to use 110, 257
    Location of data for 110
    Questions to ask 103-108
Financial reporting 84

Fiscal Stress Analysis 85
Food Service 203-208
    Evaluation of 207
    Food commodities 205
    Meal pricing 206
    National School Lunch Program (NSLP) 205
    Superintendent's role 204
Forecasting 36, 111
Fraud prevention 18, 27, 117, 120, 126, 128, 131-133
Fund balance
    Estimating of 98
    Management of 96
    Reserve Fund categories 96-97

Generally Accepted Accounting Principles (GAAP) 13-14, 79-80, 84
Generally Accepted Standards Board (GASB) 13, 80, 84
General Ledger 14-16

Health Benefits 20, 151
Human Resources 17-18, 147-160
    Discipline and investigations 154
    Diversity, equity, inclusion, and belonging 152-153
    Duties of 149-155
    Employee assistance 153
    Employee benefits 17-21, 151-152
    Labor relations 155-160
        Bargaining team 159
        Parameters set 157
        Process 159
        School board's role 157
        Superintendent's role 156-157, 160
    Mandatory benefits 18-19, 152
    Position descriptions, titles and compensation 150
    Professional development 154
    Record maintenance 155
    Recruitment 153
    Retirement 19, 153

Human Resources (continued)
    Staffing 150-151

Information Technology 209-216
    Educational technology issues 211
    Emerging issues 213-214
    Technology advisory committee 216
    Security and privacy 213
    Shared vision for 215-216
    Staffing and service 214-215
    Superintendent's role 210-212, 215-216
    Virtual schooling 212
Insurance 25, 175-177
Internal controls 18, 27, 126, 128-129, 132, 180-181, 276
Intra-district mail service 224

Labor relations 155-160
Legal Counsel 161-167
    Attorney client privilege 165
    Client clarity 167
    Relationship 163-164
    Selection of 166
    Tension with 165
    When to use 163
Limited open forum 116

Maintenance and Operations 180-191
    Contracting for 185-188
    Custodial services 186-189
    Deferred maintenance 184-185
    Environmental issues 190
    Questions to ask 183-184
    Superintendent's role 181-184, 191
    Training 190
    Work order system 190
Mandatory benefits 19-20, 151-152
Measurement of progress 243-247

The Business Side of School Success

Media relationships 138-140

Non-curricular student groups 116-117

Operations 178-179
Opposition groups 145

Payroll Office 17-18
Print shop operations 223
Professional development 154
Program monitoring 87-95
    Example of 93-95
    Developing an approach 91
    Superintendent's role 90
Property taxes 66-77
    Assessed valuation 71-72
    Collection process 72-73
    Comparison among districts 75-76
    Tad caps/limits 73-74
    Tax levy defined 68-70
    Tax rate 70
Pupil Transportation 192-202
    Accidents 199
    Complaint management 194
    Contracting for 200-202
    Driver training 199
    Efficiency versus service levels 199-200
    Emergency operations 200
    Evaluation of 197-198
    Operational considerations 197
    Safety 199
    School schedules impact upon 195-196
    Special Education 195
    Special program considerations 196
    Student behavior and discipline 197
    Superintendent's role 170-172, 178
    Weather 200

Purchasing 22-24

Recruitment 152-153
Retirement systems 19, 152
Revenue 15, 50-65
    Bond issues and other referenda 57,
    Federal sources 48-49, 55-57
        Every Student Succeeds Act (ESSA) 61
        Individuals with Disabilities Education Act (IDEA) 62
        Other grants 63
        Other revenue sources 63-64
    Interest income 50
    Local sources 47, 49-51
        Miscellaneous 51
        Other districts and governments 51
        Payment in lieu of taxes 50
        Property taxes 49, 60-70
        Rental of property 56
        Sale of property 56
        Tuition 56
    Monitoring of 65
    State sources 47-48, 57-55
        Formula based aid 53
        State aid 53-54, 57-59
        Categorical aid 60-61
        Competitive grants 61
Risk Management 25, 168-177

School safety and security 217-220
Sick Leave 20, 151
Strategic issues 241-247
Stress Analysis (see Fiscal Stress Analysis)

Tax levy 68-70
Tax rate 70
Tips for superintendents
    Ancillary services 224-225

Tips for superintendents (continued)
    Human Resources 160
    Information technology 215-216
    Food Service 208
    Maintenance and Operations 191
    Pupil Transportation 202
    Safety and security 220

Voting
    Advocacy organization 143-144
    Bonds 57, 229, 231
    Communication 142-144
    On school finance measures 140-142
    Opposition groups 145
    Property taxes 55
    Strategies for 142-143

Warehouse operations 221-223
Work order system 190

About the Authors

Dr. Brian L. Benzel was superintendent in Mead, Edmonds and Spokane (Washington State) from 1984 to 2007 with a break for a few years to work in the private sector. He served as Chief Operating Officer in the Seattle Public Schools and later as Vice President and CFO for Whitworth University in Spokane, WA, retiring in 2013.

Prior to his school district and university service Dr. Benzel worked for the Washington State Legislature, the state's Office of the Superintendent of Public Instruction, and as the Business Manager for the Mead School District.

He served as chair of Washington State's Task Force on Schools for the 21st Century (1987-1992) and later as a member of the National Council on Education Standards and Testing (1992) and was a state commissioner to the Education Commission of the States (1990-1995). He also served as a member of the Washington State Commission on Student Learning (1993-1999). In 1993, he was selected as a finalist for National Superintendent of the Year.

Dr. Benzel earned his BA in Business from Washington State University, his Master of Public Administration from the University of Washington, and the Ph.D. in Educational Leadership from Gonzaga University.

Dr. Benzel lives in Redmond, WA, where he currently serves as a director for the PEMCO Mutual Insurance Company. He is married to Cynthia, a retired elementary school principal. They have two married children and four grandchildren.

The Business Side of School Success

Dr. Kenneth E. Hoover worked in state government, with a special assignment as the governor's budget analyst for the K-12 system before serving as the CFO in Edmonds, Washington, from 1990-1994 during the time when Brian Benzel was the superintendent in that district. He was assistant superintendent in Aberdeen, Washington, and the chief operating officer for Jefferson County, Colorado, before becoming superintendent. He served Monroe, Washington, in that capacity from 2006 to 2015.

Dr. Hoover was also a financial consultant for a number of districts (including Los Angeles and San Francisco) and organizations (primary among these was the New American Schools Development Corporation).

Dr. Hoover has served a number of community and state-level policy organizations and committees. He has published with the Center for the Study of the States, The American Research Association, and the Washington State Office of Financial Management. With Dr. Benzel, he is co-author of *The Superintendent and the CFO: Building an Effective Team, 2nd Edition*, (2021, Rowman & Littlefield Publishing Group, 4501 Forbes Boulevard, Suite 200, Lanham, Maryland 20706).

Dr. Hoover earned a BA (emphasis on business administration) and Master of Public Administration degrees from the Evergreen State College, Olympia, Washington. He also earned a Ph.D. in educational leadership and policy studies from the University of Washington, Seattle, Washington.

Dr. Hoover is retired, and lives with his wife on a catamaran in southeast Alaska. He has written five novels under the pen name K. E. Hoover.

Dr. James Parla served as a superintendent of schools in New York and New Jersey for more than seventeen years. He also served as an assistant superintendent for business, elementary school principal and classroom teacher. In addition to his experience as a public school administrator and teacher, Dr. Parla served as a member of his local board of education for fourteen years.

Dr. Parla received recognition for his service in public education. The majority of his career was in New York where he received the PTA Jenkins

Memorial Scholarship Award, New York State PTA honorary life membership, honorary membership in the Tri-M Music Honor Society and many proclamations from local and state legislators. In New Jersey, he was recognized as number 14 on Mercer County's list of the "25 Most Interesting People in 2013."

Dr. Parla was a frequent presenter and panelist for the New York State School Boards Association regarding a variety of topics in education including curriculum development, careers in education and school finance. He also participated as a guest speaker and panelist at Adelphi University, Hofstra University and Dowling College. He was a member of the Adelphi University School of Education Advisory Committee, Nassau Music Educators Advisory Board and the Board of Directors of SCOPE, a nonprofit organization supporting schools on Long Island. He is past president of the Nassau County Council of School Superintendents.

Prior to pursuing a career in public school administration, Dr. Parla served as Assistant Dean of the Hagan School of Business at Iona College and Director of Public Communications for NYNEX. He is currently an adjunct faculty member in the Urban Education Leaders Doctoral Program at Columbia University Teachers College and the Graduate Education Program at Touro College. He is also a member of the School Advisory Council, Treasure Coast Technical College, Florida.

Dr. Parla received a Bachelor of Science degree from the State University of New York at Oneonta, a Master of Arts from Adelphi University, a Master of Business Administration from Iona College and a Doctor of Education from Columbia University Teachers College.

Made in the USA
Monee, IL
30 July 2022